BLACK BOSS

John
Rozier

BLACK
BOSS

Political
Revolution in a
Georgia
County

The University of Georgia Press
Athens, Georgia

Copyright © 1982 by the University of Georgia Press
Athens, Georgia 30602

Set in Mergenthaler Times Roman type
Design by Sandra Strother
Printed in the United States of America

Library of Congress Cataloging in Publication Data

Rozier, John.
Black boss.

Bibliography: p.
Includes index.
1. Afro-Americans—Georgia—Hancock County—
Politics and suffrage.   2. McCown, John.   3. Hancock
County (Ga.)—Politics and government.   I. Title.
F292.H3R69   305.8'96073'0758623   81-1298
ISBN 0-8203-0568-5   AACR2

To
Dorothy

Contents

Preface

In the shouting and tumult of the 1960s, the headlines were made in Watts and Washington, in Birmingham and Selma. Without much notice, a revolution was going on in the old rural Black Belt, in counties like Hancock in Georgia and Greene in Alabama. John McCown, a young black man with a thirst for power, a glib tongue, and an active imagination, built a small kingdom in Hancock in the old plantation country of Middle Georgia. He made it the first county to be run by blacks since the Reconstruction era.

Hancock, a county of considerable importance in antebellum days, was dreaming away, peaceful and quiet, when McCown came. I had left there in 1935 to go off to college, but my family ties went back to the county's beginning not long after the American Revolution, so I read with keen interest stories about this new leader bringing change to an old plantation county.

First, the news stories told of jobs being created by a huge catfish farm, of housing projects and millions of dollars attracted to the poor rural county. Later, headlines reported demonstrations and arson and shootings and sporting clubs armed with M-1 rifles. Increasingly interested in the strange stories coming from the once peaceful county, I began to save every item that came my way from the *New York Times*, the Atlanta newspapers, and national magazines. The file grew thick, overflowing a file cabinet.

What kind of man was John McCown? Was he the Black Jesus the Hancock country folk revered or was he an opportunist enriching himself and building a power base? Why did the Nixon administration hand him millions of dollars when other poverty programs were being cut off? Why did the Ford Foundation entrust millions to a young man without business experience?

No easy way led to the story of John McCown. It could not be dug out of library files and family records in the usual academic way. It had to be put together patiently from hundreds of interviews—some brief telephone calls, some lengthy visits. Several of the longer interviews were recorded on tape. I started using this method in every case but

ix

quickly discovered that many people did not want their remarks recorded. I took notes for most of the interviews, using pencil and pad. In some cases I followed up the interview with telephoned questions. Most of the interviews were with Hancock County people, black and and white, of widely varying views. Many were with people in Atlanta and Washington and New York. I visited Mr. McCown's mother in South Carolina and his wife in Hancock County. Despite the suspicion engendered by a decade of bitterness and the federal trials, most people did talk, some guardedly, some openly and candidly. A few times, I met rebuffs and disappointments.

John McCown is still a very controversial figure. In my desire to thank the many people who helped me I need to make it very clear that none of them is responsible for the nature of these pages. Only I bear that responsibility. Most of those I talked with I found interesting, polite, delightful to know. A few of them I felt were rogues and they were perhaps the most entertaining of all.

I am indebted to the National Endowment for the Humanities for a grant that sustained me in my search and to Emory University for giving me leave to accept it. To Emory, I am further in debt for the assistance and encouragement of Dr. Fred Crawford, director of its Center for Research in Social Change, and for quick and skilled help from its reference staff at the Woodruff Library. The names of those who gave of their time for lengthy interviews appear in most cases with their remarks in the book unless they asked to remain unidentified. I am forever grateful to them and to all who were helpful to me, with special thanks to Richard Harwell, former director of Special Collections, University of Georgia Library, now retired, and to Reg Murphy, publisher of the *Baltimore Sun*, formerly editor of the *Atlanta Constitution*.

BLACK BOSS

1

Hancock County

"The trouble with these people
is that they aren't from any place."
—*Flannery O'Connor*
at a New York publisher's party

Hancock County, Georgia—sleepy, gentle, and Old South—
was not prepared for John McCown when he came driving
into Sparta, the county seat, in 1966 in a broken-down old
Chrysler. "They thought I was just a kid," he later told a reporter. "I
hated white people. I had two .38's just for white people." [1] When he
arrived in Sparta he was thirty-one years old, black, muscular, and
handsome. He was also very broke.

Within five years he won complete control of the county and owned
hundreds of acres of land. He had taken over the Georgia Council on
Human Relations and had talked the Ford Foundation and the United
States Office of Economic Opportunity (OEO) into commitments of
millions of dollars. In that short time he had made Hancock County the
first black-controlled county in the United States since Reconstruction
days. [2]

Paternalistic and apparently relaxed in its race relations, Hancock
County still maintained segregated water fountains in its antique court-
house and segregated schools twelve years after the 1954 Supreme
Court decision outlawing them. Before the Civil War, Hancock was
Georgia's leading farming county in the heart of the Middle Georgia
Black Belt. In 1840 it produced nearly twice as much cotton as Mor-
gan, its nearest competitor. [3] David Dickson (1809–1885), called the
"prince of farmers," attracted planters from across the South to his
Hancock plantation to learn the latest farming methods.

With the coming of McCown, Hancock soon had a new kind of plantation master, an updated mirror image of the old. He built no columned

1

mansion but began to erect a large modern home on the Ogeechee River. He raised no cotton and saw to it that few others did. He ordered T-shirts with the word "Slave" printed across the front. For a British television company from London, he put on his slave shirt, mounted his white mare, and rode through a crowd of blacks assembled for the filming in a pecan grove. The blacks were dressed as if for a scene from *Gone with the Wind*, their heads in bandannas. The cameraman asked for a retake. The pecan gatherers dumped their bags of pecans and began to pick them up again. McCown rode through the bowed backs in the field as the cameras ground away.

At McCown's famous fish fries in Mayfield, prominent guests gathered on the rambling Victorian porch of the old Birdsong house, looking out on the crowd of lesser folk in the front yard. "It was like a plantation scene," said one observer. "The only difference was that the bigwigs on the porch were mostly black, but they were big blacks from foundations and the federal government." There were other touches: a private plane, Cadillacs and Lincolns, a landing strip. David Dickson never imagined such luxuries. Georgia had seen nothing like it since black radical Tunis Campbell ruled over the coast around Darien in Reconstruction days.

McCown took control of Hancock's elegant Victorian courthouse in 1968. It faces a small park and from its high spot on Sparta's Broad Street looks north along the highway going to Greensboro. The courthouse emphasizes that Hancock is a county of great contrasts. Three-fourths of the county's population are black. The town of Sparta is a white enclave, its government controlled by whites. In the 1970 census, Hancock had 9,019 inhabitants, of whom 2,172 lived in Sparta.

Nowadays the courthouse is black territory and whites are rarely seen there. It is a center for the county's blacks, alive with visitors. Built in 1881–83, the distinguished courthouse made a bold statement from the county gentry that the Civil War and Reconstruction had not crushed local spirits. In a recent book, a professor of architecture described it as "a masterpiece of Victorian architecture magnificently rising from the hill upon which the town is located."[4] Old-time Spartans have a particular feeling about the courthouse and its clock that booms out the hours. "Driving back to Sparta I feel good when I see that tower. I know I'm back in Hancock County and it's the best place in the world," said one.

Major Charles Abercrombie, a Revolutionary soldier from North Carolina, laid out the town and its courthouse square in 1795, naming it Sparta for the bravery of its inhabitants in their struggles with the Indians. (No light matter; eight years earlier Indians had burned every house in the neighboring town of Greensboro and murdered many citizens.)

The courthouse and the Drummer's Home Hotel across from it dominate Sparta's tiny business district. The Drummer's Home was built in 1840 to replace the Eagle Tavern, a 1790s structure where notables such as LaFayette had been entertained. Sparta lay on the stagecoach route from Augusta to Milledgeville (the antebellum capital), which continued through Creek Indian country west of the Chattahoochee River and on to Natchez.

The Artillery Company of Hancock celebrated July 4, 1810, at the Eagle Tavern with Parson Mason Locke Weems as the speaker. (Weems's active imagination created the story of George Washington and the cherry tree.) Dinner guests drank sixteen toasts, including one to Thomas Jefferson, "the brightest satellite that ever revolved round a political globe."[5] Everybody was not so well entertained as Parson Weems. When Tyrone Power, the Irish actor, made a journey through Middle Georgia in 1834, he spoke of the impassable route and described his good fortune in being rescued from a sojourn at Sparta that he could not contemplate "without a shudder."[6]

James Silk Buckingham, a professional world traveler, was even less enthusiastic when he visited in 1839, finding the road through a dense pine forest the worst he had ever traveled. Three coach lines, the Mail Line, the Telegraph Line, and the People's Line, served Sparta and their passengers arrived at the same time. Buckingham found the public table "revolting" and turned away in disgust to dine on hard biscuits in the coach. "The ancient Spartans themselves, with their black broth and coarse fare, could not have been farther removed from luxury than these Spartans of modern days," he wrote.[7]

Across Broad Street from the venerable Drummer's Home Hotel is the *Sparta Ishmaelite*, a weekly newspaper which celebrated its hundredth birthday in 1978. A remarkable iconoclast, Sidney Lewis, established the paper and gave it a flavor as unique as its name. The biblical Ishmael was noted for his independence. G. Burnett Moore published the paper in its centennial year, a task he had performed for most of his eighty-four years. The *Ishmaelite*, more like a letter from

3

home than a newspaper, goes to former residents scattered across the United States. Editor Moore addresses the readers as old friends in his front-page column and makes note of those in far places who have renewed their subscriptions. A front-page story gives something of the flavor of the paper and the community in the late 1970s.

> Willie I. Warren, one of the Ishmaelite's older Negro subscribers, died a few days ago after living in Hancock County all his life. He was a good citizen and had many friends, white and black, especially in Western Hancock County.
>
> He told us recently he had been a subscriber 48 years and never missed but two copies in the mail. That is a good record and he paid for it promptly each year.
>
> We extend sympathy to his family.

West of the courthouse square, Broad Street narrows. When the state highway department paved the street in the 1930s, they widened it throughout the town, cutting down ancient elms and oaks. At the west end they encountered a polite but firm woman who came with her rifle and threatened to shoot when the first tree was felled. The trees still stand.

The old trees saved by a rifle shade some handsome homes, including the oldest house in Sparta, the Rossiter-Little House, which began as a log cabin in the 1790s and was thought to have been used by the early settlers as a place of defense against the Indians. The columned home across the street built in the 1830s by Wilson Bird, son of a Revolutionary soldier, later served as a summer home for a Savannah family in the days when yellow fever and malaria were perils of the low country. Sparta sits at an elevation of 560 feet on a ridge at the fall line that marks the shore of an ancient sea. Some Middle Georgians still call the fall line the gnat line. In the lower country to the south, gnats flourish and the inhabitants are adept at blowing gnats out of their eyes while continuing to talk. Malaria was a hazard south of the fall line until World War II.[8]

The first Hancock settlers were Virginians and North Carolinians who came seeking land grants after the Revolution. They raised tobacco and grain and their own food. They came to a lovely, unspoiled land with fish in the clear rivers and wild game in the woods—deer and rabbits and possums, wild turkeys and birds of every description.

4

The back country still shows how it was. In the east end of the county, the road from Jewell, a little village that sits astride the Ogeechee River, runs north to Mayfield past the federal plantation house at Rock Mill. The hills have been stripped of their timber by clear-cutting, opening a vista which sweeps away over the hilltops, blue and hazy in the distance.

William Shivers built his Rock Mill plantation house on the banks of the Ogeechee in 1820. It stands four stories high, with seventeen rooms and two enormous chimneys to serve its twelve fireplaces. Dr. Olin Shivers, an Atlanta physician and relative of the builder, bought the house in 1967 and restored it handsomely. Georgia author Vinnie Williams described its grounds. "The roots of old-time roses are everywhere. So are flowering bulbs, scuppernong vines, crape myrtles, sweet shrubs. Elms and oaks fringed with resurrection fern shade the roof and squirrels scamper among the seedling pecan trees." Stables, carriage houses, blacksmith shops, barns fanned out from the house. There were rows of cabins for several dozen slaves. Shivers's factory at Jewell manufactured cotton goods, wool yarn, and carded wool. The forty hands who worked there each got $7.75 monthly wages.[9]

Near Mayfield, the meadows around the Ogeechee are deep green and full of cows. The land is lush and rich like the Kentucky Bluegrass country. The Ogeechee River Mill, painted a fresh barn red, has been grinding corn since 1872. Beside a big solid dam of concrete and stones, a tree leans out over the dark green mill pond, a treehouse in its branches fitted out with a carpet. A child's swing made from a tire arcs out over the mill pond.

The road past Mayfield on to Powelton leads to Hancock's oldest settlements. Horeb Baptist Church is a simple white frame structure, but something about its location gives it a stern dignity. Set well back from the road, it is approached by a wide gravel driveway lined with great oaks and pines. Horeb Church records date back to 1792, two years after the Indians formally ceded the land. Parris, "a man of color," was admitted to membership in 1796. After the Civil War, the church assisted black members in building their own meeting house, but it was not until 1890 that "Clack, the last colored brother, had his name taken from the church record."[10]

Powelton, in the northeast section of the county, lies near Wilkes County, the earliest settled part of upland Georgia. At one time, it was

5

a village of some importance and the home of some of Georgia's early leaders in religion, politics, and education. Jesse Mercer (1769–1841), leader of Georgia Baptists in the early nineteenth century, preached at Powelton Baptist Church for twenty-eight years. The Baptist State Convention was formed there in 1822. William Rabun (1771–1819), a governor of Georgia, served as a clerk and chorister of the church. Only a few houses remain at Powelton today. It is a poor and deserted-looking place, though the surrounding countryside is beautiful. Richard Malcolm Johnston (1822–1898), Georgia author, educator, and lawyer, grew up at Powelton on his family plantation, Oak Grove. His *Dukesborough Tales* about life there is a homespun and plain work, like Joel Chandler Harris's stories of Middle Georgia plantation life.

In the Springfield community a few miles from Powelton once flourished one of America's most remarkable black families, the Huberts. Dr. Lester F. Russell, a member of the family by marriage, has collected the stories handed down from early slave days in his book *Profile of a Black Heritage.*[11] Before the Civil War the Huberts worked as slaves on the Hubert plantation across the county line in Warren County. When the war ended and they were set free, their former master helped them rent a farm and gave them a bale of cotton.

The black Huberts did so well with their rented farm that in 1869 Zach Hubert struck out on his own and rented a place eight miles away at Powelton. There he joined the white Baptist church. In 1871 he bought a farm, becoming the first black in the area to own land.[12] Later, his brother Moses bought a farm also and the Hubert family gathered in the Springfield area of Hancock County. Zach married Camilla Hillman and they had twelve children, all of whom they sent through college. The Huberts organized a church at Springfield, and later a school.

Zach Hubert was respected by both the black and white communities. He helped maintain rapport between the races that kept the county free of lynchings. Considered unusual among the counties of the South, Hancock was noted for good race relations until the troubles of the 1960s.

When Zach Hubert died in 1926, the *Sparta Ishmaelite* called him "the most remarkable Negro in this section of the state." Although born in slavery, the newspaper said, Hubert "had amassed a fortune since the war and his estate is estimated to be worth at least $100,000."

The story went on to say that all of his sons and daughters held responsible positions at Negro colleges over the country. Two of his sons became college presidents, one a minister, one a college professor, another a high school principal, and still another executive secretary of the New York Urban League. All of his daughters were educators.

The Hubert family decided to honor their remarkable parents by making Springfield a center for black life. Benjamin organized the Association for Advancement of Negro Country Life to promote the work at Springfield and recruited such members as George Foster Peabody, Dr. William H. Kilpatrick, and Eleanor Roosevelt. By 1934 they had built a community center, a store, a canning factory, health center, home for teachers, dairy farm, boys' camp, cafeteria, farm shop building, and swimming pool. Until World War II, Springfield remained a thriving utopia, but its best young farmers left during the war and did not return.

Stanley High, a CBS commentator in New York, said over the air on January 4, 1938,

> I visited the "Log Cabin" community last fall. At night some of the neighbors gathered with Ben Hubert. Half of those who came were white; half were Negroes. They pulled up their chairs in a large semi-circle in front of a roaring fire and talked about farming and politics; about such things as the potato crop and Gene Talmadge; about the family down the road that had typhoid fever, and the bridge on the west branch that the rain had washed away, exactly as neighbors anywhere else talk about such things. . . . Most of the important history that is being made in America right now isn't in the headlines and never will be. Hancock County so far as I know has never made any big news, but like the rest of America I'm talking about it's making its share of history. They don't go in for lynchings in Hancock County. They go in for scientific farming, and education, and getting acquainted. That's why it's called a "lynch-proof" county.[13]

Ben Hubert (1887–1959) tried to revive the excitement at Springfield after the war. In October 1948 he called teachers, ministers, and farmers together at the Log Cabin Community House. He told them,

> All of us are living on the land here in Middle Georgia, or we are serving men and women who earn their living and their life from the soil. . . . We have here a little heaven if we only knew it and took advantage

7

of what we have in land, in trees, in farm possibilities. The soil is the base of every good thing in life. . . . Some people cry about the lack of opportunity. I have not found anyone stopping me from making my land, my cows, my chickens, trees and farm crops better than other men around me, regardless of their color. I have found on the other hand that when I have proved what I can do with the land white men and black men come to me, happy to know that I have found the way![14]

Much of Springfield is now in decay. The Log Cabin center still serves the community as a meeting house and even as a place to vote. The Huberts own land still but they have become city folk.

Hancock names ripple off the tongue—the rivers Ogeechee and Oconee; the creeks, Beaverdam, Big Buffalo, Little Island, Sandy Run, Shoulderbone, Whiteoak, Green Spring. Homes and plantations bear names like Pomegranate Hall, Glen Mary, Sunshine, Brightside, Covey Rise, Old Dominion, the Hollies, Pleasant Valley, Cornucopia. Place names are lyrical: Mayfield, Jewell, Shoals, Springfield, Pride, Mount Zion, Linton, Devereux, Granite Hill. The people worship at country churches with names like Hickory Grove, Shady Run, Darien, Nebo, Zebulon, Bethel, Balerma, Island Creek, Beulah, Galilee, and Fairmount.

The variety of scenery in the county's 478 square miles is astonishing. South of Sparta the land falls away to sandy plains, some of it scrub oak and piney woods country. To the north around Powelton and Mount Zion, the terrain rises into the red clay hills of the Piedmont. This is what the early settlers called the oak lands, which they prized as healthier and more fertile. Early tax books distinguished between oak lands and pine lands.

Hancock County lay on the frontier when it was created in 1793 and settlers had frequent troubles with the Indians. The Oconee River, the county's western boundary, marked the dividing line for Indian territory, and not until 1802 did treaties extend the line west of the river. When the second United States Census was taken in 1800, Hancock had the largest population of any Georgia county, 14,456 (half again as much as it would have 170 years later), exceeding that of Chatham (Savannah), oldest county in the state. The rich lands across the Oconee were soon opened and the restless farmers moved into the virgin lands of Middle Georgia and on into Alabama and Mississippi.

The myths of the cavalier and the grand plantation have obscured reality. Early Middle Georgia settlers generally were "rough, poor, but honest people, with little or no fortunes, and who were quite as limited in education as in fortune," wrote W. H. Sparks (1800–1882), a notable lawyer who grew up in Middle Georgia in its frontier days. Settlers, industrious and frugal, lived in rude cabins built of poles and gathered around stockade forts for security against "the prowling and merciless Creeks and Cherokees."

The settlers were Virginians and North Carolinians. Sparks thought the Virginians "generally more cultivated." The mix of tough yeoman farmers and the better educated sons of the Virginia gentry produced a unique society in Middle Georgia, which Sparks claimed furnished all of Georgia's distinguished sons before the Civil War with few exceptions and gave Georgia leadership over her Southern sisters.[15]

Sparks attended the only law school in the United States in 1820, the famous school in Litchfield, Connecticut, taught by Tapping Reeve and James Gould. His fellow students included the father of a notable Middle Georgian, Lucius Quintus Cincinnatus Lamar (John Kennedy selected him for his *Profiles in Courage*). Among his classmates were Hancock men T. G. Holt and Hopkins Holsey, who were later elected United States congressmen. Other friends were Charles J. McDonald, one of four governors provided Georgia by the small white community of the county, and Walter T. Colquitt, one of a series of United States senators and congressmen who came from there.

Hancock and the cotton gin grew up together. Eli Whitney patented the machine one year after the county was established, changing farming dramatically as cotton became a major crop in the South. By 1826 Georgia was the greatest cotton-producing region in the world. As early as 1820 the prospering Hancock planters were replacing the early crude cabins with large and comfortable houses and even grand mansions; with their growing number of slaves, they forced out most of the yeoman farmers. Hancock County's white population fell as the slave population increased. Never after the 1810 census did the county have more white inhabitants than black.[16] When the Civil War broke out, six planters owned more than one hundred slaves each; David Dickson had more than two hundred and fifty. The county contained 430 slaveholders and 8,137 slaves.[17]

9

As the planters grew rich, they quickly created academies for their children at Powelton, Mount Zion, and Sparta. Mount Zion, on the road from Sparta to Greensboro, has almost disappeared except for the old Presbyterian Church restored by the Hancock County Society for Historical Preservation, but in the early days it flourished as a center for education. Wealthy planters in Georgia and neighboring states as well sent their sons to the academy built in Mount Zion in 1811. Nathan Beman (1785–1871) and his younger brother Carlisle (1797–1875), graduates of Vermont's Middlebury College, made the school famous. Nathan Beman eventually moved back to the North to become a leader in the antislavery movement. In his household at Mount Zion lived a stepson, William Lowndes Yancey, who later was to be a leading spokesman for secession.

All of Georgia's early colleges had close ties to Hancock County. Methodist Bishop George Foster Pierce (1811–1884) of Sparta was the first president of Wesleyan College (female and Methodist) in Macon, and an early president of Emory College (Methodist) at Oxford. Nathan Beman accepted the presidency of the University of Georgia at Athens but never served because of his wife's illness. Carlisle Beman became the first president of Oglethorpe (Presbyterian) at Milledgeville. Mercer (Baptist) at Penfield in Greene County was named for Jesse Mercer. All of the colleges were then based in Middle Georgia and represented the state's leading religious denominations. The section dominated the state culturally and economically until the Civil War.

Not far from Mount Zion on the highway south to Sparta is the site of Pleasant Valley, the plantation of Dimos Ponce, who, along with a small number of other Hancock County planters, reformed farming and restored life to the washed-out hills of the cotton belt. A remarkable group of men, disturbed by the deep depression of 1837 and by the sight of gullied hills and abandoned lands, formed the Hancock Planters Club, which became famous throughout the South. Dr. William Terrell (1786–1855), its first president, endowed an agricultural chair at the University of Georgia, one of the first in the United States. Dimos Ponce proposed plans for crop controls almost a century before Franklin Roosevelt's New Deal. James Thomas experimented with techniques for managing slave labor, giving his slaves a five-minute rest period after each thirty minutes of labor, for example. Edmund M. Pendleton (1815–1884), a Sparta physician, wrote one of the first college texts in agriculture in the country. He was interested in the health of the black population, studying the diseases to which they seemed susceptible. Richard Hardwick's techniques to control soil erosion were widely published.[18]

Hancock, now one of the nation's poorest counties, was once a leader in the antebellum South. Farmers from all over the region came to the community to see the progressive methods of farming practiced there. Visitors commented in agricultural journals on "its white mansions, gardens and orchards, with all the unmistakable signs of taste, comfort and plenty in evidence."

Of many handsome monuments that stand in Sparta's ancient cemetery, one of the tallest marks the grave of David Dickson. The inscription simply says, "David Dickson, July 6, 1809–February 18, 1885, model farmer, true friend." An elderly woman recalled walking in the cemetery with her father when she was a child. When he came to Dickson's monument, he always said, "He ought to be over there at Ebenezer." Ebenezer was a black church. Dickson, called "the Prince of Farmers," never belonged to the Hancock Planters Club, although he was the outstanding pioneer in improving cotton production. As a young man he fell in love with Amanda, a slave girl in his father's household. He later inherited Amanda, lived openly with her, had children by her, and when he died, left them his vast estate.[19]

Dickson helped give the county its reputation for being a white man's playground, the home of a large population of mixed bloods whom old-time blacks called "no nations." United States census figures for 1860 refute the charge. In Hancock, mulattoes made up 2.6 percent of the Negro population compared with 8 percent for Georgia and 13.2 percent for the nation.

Even as a boy, Dickson began to question the Southern farming system and to devise a scientific system of rotation using cover crops, grasses, livestock, and commercial fertilizers. He was reportedly the first person to use Peruvian guano on cotton and within a few years he developed his own fertilizer, the famous Dickson compound. By 1860 he owned 13,000 acres of land and 250 slaves and estimated his wealth at half a million dollars.[20]

11

A remarkable teacher, Dickson trained all who came near him and he wrote extensively. Years after his death, as late as 1910, his advice on farming was still being published. "Never let it be said by posterity that it is harder for them to live because you lived before them. Leave your land better than you found it." [21] A few years after the Civil War, despite destruction by Sherman and the loss of more than $300,000 in slaves, he owned 30,000 acres of land, railroad stock, plantation stock, and farming implements. Dickson lived well, entertained in style, and received visitors from all over the United States who came to marvel at his farm. The nucleus of his Hancock plantation was still in operation in 1980.

Another prominent planter was Georgia's major religious leader, Methodist Bishop George F. Pierce. Bishop Pierce's plantation, called Sunshine and located four miles east of Sparta, adjoined Rockby, the plantation of author and educator Richard Malcolm Johnston. In his autobiography Johnston recalled that Hancock County was noted for its skillful, successful planters and that, as a rule, they treated their slaves well. Word of mistreatment might bring forth such a strong reprimand from Pierce at the Sparta Methodist Church that the guilty one would feel like "hastening to undo or repair any wrong." [22]

Pierce, like many of Hancock's planters, was a Union man and an old Whig. He had no use for abolitionists but he dreaded the results of secession. Though "as kind a master as ever lived," he believed "freedom to the Negroes to do as they pleased, would be freedom to go to the bad. . . . These were his views, never concealed, never apologized for. He held them to the end." [23] The bishop addressed the General Assembly of Georgia in 1863, attacking a state law that forbade teaching Negroes to read. "Our Heavenly Father certainly never intended any human mind to be kept in darkness and ignorance. . . . Let them learn from the Scripture that their relation is ordained of God— that He prescribes their duties and makes fidelity to their earthly masters a part of the service due to Him." [24]

In August 1864 Yankee raiders caused great excitement in the county. "Such commotion, running, hiding you never saw. The raiders came nearer than the river. They visited Henry Fraley's plantation, took all his mules, drank his brandy, ate his preserves and left, going toward Greensboro," the bishop wrote to his son in the army in Virginia. He inquired about his son's bodyservant Isham with the message, "Tell him to keep right side up."[25]

After the war the bishop did not sit around mourning his losses. He was soon off to raise the banner of the Methodist Episcopal Church, South, in the border states, where it had been forced out during the war, across the west and on to California. He set about raising funds for Emory College, stricken by the war and the loss of its endowment. He even raised funds to buy land for a Southern Methodist school in China.

When Bishop Pierce died in 1884, services had to be held in Hancock's new courthouse, so great was the crowd. Sectional feelings had eased. When funds were raised to erect a monument to him in the Sparta cemetery, a major contributor was George I. Seney, New York banker and philanthropist. Tributes poured in. "Of all the great Georgians I consider him the first," said L. Q. C. Lamar. "He was the most symmetrical man I ever knew," declared Robert Toombs, "the handsomest in person, the most gifted, the purest in life."

Where the Greensboro highway enters Sparta, to the right on a high hill stand two tall forlorn brick chimneys. They are all that remain of the antebellum Clinch house. The highway continues past the ruins down a steep hill and up another to the courthouse, which faces it across a small park with a severely plain Confederate monument in its center. Perhaps the most distinguished person ever to live in the Clinch house was a black who came there as a slave. He later became a bishop, helping found a church that grew to half a million members.

"I was born in Georgia, near Columbus in 1842, and at that time was the slave of James Holsey who was also my father," wrote Bishop Lucius H. Holsey (1842–1920) in his autobiography.

> He was a gentleman of classical education: dignified in appearance and manner of life, and represented that old antebellum class of Southern aristocracy who did not know enough of manual labor to black their own shoes or saddle their own horse. Like many others of his day and time he never married, but mingled, to some extent, with those females of the African race that were his slaves—his personal property. My mother was named Louisa and was of pure African descent. She was of fascinating appearance and comely parts.
>
> Her father was named Alex, and he was an African of the Africans.

13

He was short, thickset and of a stubborn and massive build. He lived to be nearly a hundred years of age.[26]

Before Holsey's master died, he allowed Holsey to choose a new master. The boy chose Richard Malcolm Johnston. In Johnston's household he taught himself to read. The white children and an old black man taught him the alphabet and he bought two Webster blueback spellers. "Day by day I took a leaf from one of the spelling books, and so folded it that one or two of the lessons were on the outside as if printed on a card," he wrote. "This I put in the pocket of my vest or coat, and when I was sitting on the carriage, walking the yard or streets, or using hoe or spade, or in the dining room, I would take out my spelling leaf, catch a word and commit it to memory. . . . When night came I went to my little room, and with chips of fat pine, and pine roots that were grubbed up from the woods nearby, I would kindle a little blaze in the fireplace and turn my head toward it while lying flat on my back so as to get the most of the light on the leaves of my book. . . . by these means I learned to read and write a little in six months."[27]

In 1862 Holsey married Harriett Turner, then fifteen, who had been raised by Bishop Pierce and given to his daughter as a maid. The marriage took place in the spacious hall of the Pierce residence, where the bishop's wife and daughters set tables down the hall spread with turkey, ham, cake, and many other dishes. The ladies of the house dressed the bride in "the gayest and most artistic style with red flowers and scarlet sashes predominating in the brilliant trail."[28]

Holsey became a minister after the war and helped organize the Colored Methodist Episcopal Church in America. He became a bishop at age thirty and later established Paine College for blacks at Augusta. Some blacks criticized him for working with Southern white Methodists, calling him and his followers "Democrats," "bootlicks," and "white folks' niggers." He wrote the church's hymn book and manual of discipline, living on until 1920 as its principal force. In 1975 the church, which had changed its name to Christian Methodist Episcopal in 1954, had 466,718 members.

Hancock County's leaders, Whigs and Unionists, mostly opposed secession but favored slavery. They could not conceive of their slaves as citizens. They followed Alexander Stephens, later vice-president of the Confederacy, who lived at nearby Crawfordville. As late as 1860 Stephens made a notable pro-Union speech, although he had resigned his seat in Congress the year before, saying, "I saw there was bound to be a smash-up on the road, and resolved to jump off at the first station."

Stephens's brother Linton Stephens (1823–1872) lived in Sparta on Maiden Lane, named in honor of a female academy that flourished there in the early 1800s. His home stood at the end of the street until it burned in 1937. Linton Stephens served briefly on the state supreme court, where his decision in favor of a slave caused considerable dissension. At the secessionist convention in Milledgeville, he strongly opposed leaving the Union. Nonetheless, when war came he raised a Confederate company and saw service in Virginia.

Hancock County voted strongly in 1860 for John Bell and the Constitutional Union party, thereby joining border states like Kentucky instead of the lower South, which went for the Southern Democrat Breckinridge. The county had always voted Whig and after the Civil War always voted Democratic in presidential elections, even in Reconstruction days, despite its large black population.[29]

Hancock County suffered relatively little physical destruction from the war but the labor system on which its economy rested was in a shambles. Even so skilled a planter as David Dickson was in trouble. Northern troops had stripped his plantation of stock and had burned his cotton. Dickson's slaves once produced ten to fifteen bales of cotton per hand plus eight hundred to twelve hundred pounds of pork. His hired freedmen were producing only three to five bales of cotton and almost no meat. The first year after the war, he lost $10,000 in hogs, sheep, and cattle killed by careless freedmen, who had developed a mania for hunting.[30]

Hancock County people scattered to many places and for many reasons. Sometimes people can withstand major crises better than minor annoyances. The latter prompted Richard Malcolm Johnston's decision to move to Baltimore, Maryland. Baltimore and Washington, D.C., were favorite havens for those who wanted to escape Reconstruction but still keep a toehold in the South.

Life on the plantation in a neighborhood where blacks outnumbered whites became far less agreeable after the war, Johnston wrote in his

15

autobiography. Blacks would no longer close his plantation gate, exposing his fields to inroads from cattle and other beasts. They tore off padlocks he put on the gate "to evince their consciousness of freedom" and insisted on walking through his yard.[31] Upset by the restless blacks and by the death of a favorite daughter, he and his wife and family moved to Baltimore.

It is difficult to judge people of one era by the standards of a later one. Bishop Holsey had chosen Johnston as his master and wrote of his kindness, even remaining with him a year after freedom came. Holsey, the red-headed son of a Georgia planter and his slave woman, wrote down his thoughts about slavery.

> I felt that I could not afford to be false even to those who appeared to be my enslavers and oppressors, and I have never regretted this course in after years. The training that I received in the narrow house of slavery has been a minister of correction and mercy to me in all these years of trouble, trial, labor and anxiety. I have no complaint against American slavery. It was a blessing in disguise to me and to many. It has made the Negro race what it could not have been in its native land. Slavery was but a circumstance or a link in the transitions of humanity, and must have its greatest bearing upon the future.[32]

Johnston, a sensitive and kind man, confided in his autobiography that while he had not considered it wrong to hold slaves, he began "to feel embarrassed and oppressed by the thoughts of the future of both races, especially in view of the fact that the inferior was increasing with great rapidity." He bore the responsibility for their care "with great seriousness" and after emancipation he felt "a sense of relief from very great responsibility—never before quite comprehended— though my estate was thereby reduced to nothing from fifty thousand dollars."[33]

Working out a new relationship with the freed slaves was the burning problem of the time. Alexander Stephens worried about it more and more, and he told Johnston that he used to have great confidence in the good sense of the people, but he "had begun to fear that they are not competent to cope with the great difficulties before them. The white people of the South are slow in being brought to see the necessity of doing justice to the Negro. The education of the latter is now absolutely necessary in order to make him useful to the white man."[34]

16

Hancock County, being reconstructed, elected blacks to represent it in the Georgia legislature. When W. W. Harrison and Eli Barnes were elected, the blacks held a military celebration at Dixie, a Negro settlement on the edge of Sparta. Their drilling and beating of drums could be heard distinctly, and rumors spread that they were preparing to take possession of the town. Scouts went from the local Ku Klux Klan to reconnoiter and returned to report the blacks were just having a big barbecue to celebrate the election.

Blacks moved tenuously into freedom. The old system, developed on the plantation, had to be adapted to the freedmen. No longer slaves, they became sharecroppers or tenants, often working the same lands they worked before. Dependent on plantation owners to finance their crops, for generations to come they, like their white sharecropper brothers, found or expected little more than subsistence.

Fifteen years after the war, Hancock County was producing more cotton than it had in 1860.[35] The new style of farming paid less attention to growing all needs at home and more to cotton alone; its emphasis on commercial fertilizer brought growth to the railroads and merchants and banks; Sparta started to grow. The 1879 directory listed eleven lawyers, most from old planter families. The town had three black shoemakers and one white one, a white cabinetmaker, a white baker, a white carriage maker, and a black blacksmith. Another black ran a meat market. There were seven physicians, a watchmaker, a surveyor, druggists, a confectioner, a banker and insurance agent who also had a general store and was justice of the peace, a contractor who ran a grist and planing mill, a fertilizer dealer, a photographer, a barber, an express and railroad agent, a dentist, an undertaker, and an insurance agent. Sparta had two saloons, a livery stable, a hotel, two newspapers, eleven general stores, and two grocery stores. Four women were listed in the directory: one was employed as the Western Union agent, one was a telegraph operator, another a grocer, and a fourth a milliner.[36]

During the entire period following the Civil War, the county showed a much higher percentage of its blacks as landowners than surrounding counties. Because blacks could buy land, the county became steadily blacker in its population makeup, reversing the trend in most of the South.

For poor black and white laborers, conditions in the old Middle Georgia plantation belt were generally bad for many years after the Civil

War. When the federal government surveyed cotton-growing areas in 1880, a special study was made of farm labor across the South. Parts of Georgia received optimistic reports, but the worst came from the Middle Georgia area that led the state twenty years earlier. "They are sometimes without bread for their families," read a survey of laborers in Greene County. "They are in destitute condition," said the report on Jasper County. "The condition of laborers is generally bad," said the report from Hancock.[37]

By the turn of the century, conditions had improved and both population and cotton production in Hancock reached new highs by 1910. World War I provided jobs in northern cities for the county's blacks for the first time on a large scale; hundreds of them left for such big eastern cities as Philadelphia and New York.

Sparta was rich and prosperous following World War I, with high wartime prices for cotton and a crop that overflowed the warehouses. Then came the boll weevils, which simply ate up the cotton crop. The economy collapsed. One banker shot himself; another, a major figure in the state, disappeared, to be discovered several years later in Hawaii. A merchant, once made rich by his farm customers, left bundles of their notes and mortgages to be dumped into a well in his garden. Hancock County fell into despair. Its agriculture never recovered from the collapse of the 1920s and nearly a third of its people left during the decade. When the national depression came in 1930, it brought ruin to the town's remaining bank and disaster to many citizens.

Some fine plantations survived in Hancock until after World War I. A particularly beautiful one called the Treadwell Place was bought for the cheap land in the 1930s. The new owners allowed the plantation house, one of the most splendid in the county, to fall into decay. In the 1930s property values fell so low that one large antebellum mansion sold for a few hundred dollars. The buyer, a sawmill man, cut more timber from the grounds than the place cost. Tax values in the county did not reach the levels of 1860 until 1967, when reevaluation and inflation pushed the values higher.[38]

Into the 1960s one large cotton farm continued to operate much as it had in early days, its white owner eating in a large communal dining hall with the many black workers on his place. By this time, most Hancock plantations had long since been bought up by timber and pulpwood companies.

The county's economy is strange. One knowledgeable businessman claims there are several millionaires today in the dirt-poor community. Farmers who collected land at depression prices are now wealthy on paper, yet the county's per capita income ranks with the lowest in the nation. Among Georgia's 159 counties, it was often in the bottom seven during the 1970s. In 1978 its per capita income was $4,212, which was 54 percent of the United States average.[39] Nowadays, Hancock County is financed largely by welfare. The biggest payrolls include welfare checks, social security checks, and the school system, which is heavily dependent on state funds. The only significant payrolls in the county other than government ones come from pulpwood, a large sawmill, a garment plant, and a small furniture plant. There is almost no farming. Hundreds of residents drive to jobs in other counties, most of them to neighboring Milledgeville.

Through all the changes, Hancock Countians and Middle Georgians retained a special feeling, a regional sense of place and belonging. Joel Chandler Harris, the creator of Uncle Remus, learned his craft across the Oconee River on the plantation of Joseph Addison Turner, where he worked as a young apprentice on Turner's newspaper. Harris believed that Middle Georgia "was and is the center of the most unique—the most individual civilization the Republic has produced."[40]

In contemporary times, Flannery O'Connor wrote Gothic tales at Andalusia, her mother's farm outside Milledgeville, in neighboring Baldwin County. When asked why Southern authors wrote about freaks, she replied that they were able to recognize one because they still had some conception of the whole man. The essence of the Middle Georgia spirit is to be found in her observation about guests at a New York publisher's party: "The trouble with these people is that they aren't from any place."[41]

It was to this Middle Georgia setting John McCown came in 1966. Unfortunately, neither he nor the government agencies nor the foundations that worked with him ever understood the spirit of the place.

2

John McCown

"All of us in our family were aggressive.
We had to be to live.
But if they pushed we pushed back."
—*McCown's uncle*

John McCown came from the Peedee section of South Carolina in Horry County, which includes Myrtle Beach and its gold coast. The Reverend William Malet, a British clergyman and writer visiting there during the Civil War, described the country near Conway, the county seat, as "a land of sand, of woods, of branches, of creeks and swamps—the hollow bark of the crocodile; the bellowing of the bullfrog all night long—the note of summer just as the cuckoo's is in England; also breaking the silence of the night, the mournful cry of the 'whip-poor-will.' " He spoke of the closeness of whites and blacks on the farms and plantations. "They grew up together and retain that friendliness into adulthood." [1]

McCown spent his childhood in Loris, a little town and a center of tobacco farming, near the North Carolina line, where he was born on Sunday, November 18, 1934. In Horry County, unlike Hancock, blacks were in a definite minority. The county, now prosperous, had a reputation in the 1930s for being poor white and mean. McCown was three years old when his father died driving a pulpwood truck which overturned and killed him. McCown often told reporters and friends that his father died when he was denied admission to the hospital because he was black. Such a tragedy could easily have happened in that time and place, but it did not. McCown's mother said her husband died instantly.

His mother, a bright, pleasant, and attractive woman, had to leave him and his sister with her mother in South Carolina while she went to New York City to work as a domestic. Her mother had a large family of her own to raise and times were hard. Sometimes the grandmother would divide an egg three ways to feed the children. Although poor and fatherless, McCown was born to no ordinary black family. Its members were unusually tough, aggressive, and intelligent. An uncle, not much older than he, talked about him and the family in the fall of 1978 at his comfortable middle-class home in Conway. McCown's mother, who had recently returned to Conway from New York, was present.

"Our grandfather was a minister," the uncle said. "One relative was dean of the School of Religion at Morehouse College in Atlanta, Dr. Martin Luther King, Jr.'s alma mater. Three of my brothers were ministers. The pattern with them was the same as with me, perhaps deeper. Basically aggressive, because anybody surviving that ordeal had to be."

The uncle, Covell Moore, talked about growing up in a typical black house in Loris in those days. "We could see the stars through the roof and the chickens under the house through the cracks in the floor. We used to take the food and feed the chickens—drop it through the cracks. I was in high school when John was in elementary school. Around the house he was about average like the rest of us, getting into all kinds of devilment, normal things that kids will do.

"I imagine every kid who comes up without a mother and father he can identify with is a very different kid. We came up without a father and with a mother who had a large number of children to deal with. My mother became John's mother while his was away supplying clothing and money. In the South in those days if you got ten dollars a week that was good money. People went up North to finish paying off their farms, to finish paying off their houses—whites as well as blacks. It is kind of interesting now that New York has gotten into a lot of trouble and some people say let her go, but they forget it has been a saving ground for many people in the South.

"My mother had to work," said the uncle. "Quite often we wore clothes our parents got from people they worked for. The older ones wore them, then the next one and the next. It was a scar on all of us to have to accept things from other people.

"Loris was a typically Southern town where I got in jail two or three times for just defending myself. You know, in Loris there were white street gangs and we were dirty children walking the streets. The whites wanted to push you off the street. All of us in our family were aggressive. We had to be to live. But if they pushed we pushed back. Many times I went to jail because I did defend somebody else. I'll never forget we were in the packing house working and this white boy wanted to make this black boy leave to go to his house and work for him. The black boy said, 'I can't, I got to work.' The white boy said, 'You lied to me,' and slapped him. I said, 'You let that boy slap you?' The white boy said, 'Hell, I'll slap *you*.' A big black fellow grabbed me and pulled me off him. The white fellow went home and got his shotgun and when I looked around there was the shotgun and as soon as he held the shotgun up a siren went off because the police patrol and his mother had followed him. We were into it, tussling with that gun. They dusted that boy off and carried him home and carried me to jail.

"Another time I was on the street shining shoes and that gang came picking at me and I grabbed the leader and we were fighting. We stopped traffic. I found myself flying through the air and in the back seat of a police car going to jail. The white boys went back home. A white lady saw this and followed me to the jailhouse. She said, 'If you close the door on him I'll sue the town.' She took me away from there.

"That was during my time. After my time, then my brother and then John. It was an awful thing for them coming up in that environment. It was tough. Whites ruled; whites dominated the town. You had no rights. These kids were determined to make things better. They grew up with that complex. They grew up seeing the Klans ride through town. As I look back on it, I'm sure that these things were a part of us all, especially John."

The law required separate schools for blacks in South Carolina in those days. John McCown attended Loris Training School, where he was president of his high school class, an active Boy Scout, and member of the basketball team. He once told a reporter he got into trouble for stealing chickens to help feed a visiting ball team.

"By this time," his uncle concluded, "John was growing up, getting to be a big boy, and my mother was getting old. It was time for him to find his mother."

"When he came to New York City he stayed out of school a few days," said his mother, taking up the story. "When I went down to school they told me. He said the class was too hard for him. He had not had the same studies in Loris and it made it difficult for him. He told me not to worry; he would make it up. He was in the tenth or eleventh grade." McCown, used to being on top in Loris, was humiliated to find he was far behind his New York classmates.

His mother lived in a tough part of Harlem. She even kept a lock on her telephone and once she was mugged on the street, robbed, and left with a broken leg. A woman member of the Georgia Council on Human Relations recalled a midnight visit she and others made with McCown to his mother's home. No taxi driver would take them to the address from a Manhattan hotel, so they finally went by subway. McCown told them he once robbed pay phone booths to pay off street gangs and lived in a section of the city full of drug pushers and prostitutes.

His mother is small and strong—a strong personality. She has been a domestic, a practical nurse, a seamstress, a milliner. Despite the crime and troubles, she liked New York and would still enjoy living there, but the pollution affected her health. In 1978, she was working for a black funeral home in Conway, living in a neat brick house, with her Plymouth Duster parked in the driveway. Her living room was full of thriving plants, lush and green. Her furniture was neatly encased in heavy plastic slipcovers, carefully fitted, and the same heavy plastic covered the carpets. Many pictures of her son hung on the wall.

John McCown met his wife, Annie Mae, in New York. A year older than he, born in Beaufort County, South Carolina, in 1933, she grew up in New York City, where they were married when she was nineteen. Shortly afterward, her husband joined the Air Force. The young couple first lived in Bangor, Maine, and then he was sent off to Thule Air Force Base in Greenland. Annie Mae McCown liked Bangor. "During this time I liked any place where he was. I would have liked hell itself, with him," she said.

When McCown wrote letters to her from Thule, his young wife would circle the misspelled words and return them to him, all neatly corrected. "He was gifted and a fast learner. Soon he got smarter than me. He went to schools near his post when he could."

His wife accompanied him to his next assignment with the Air Force unit at the Air Force Academy at Colorado Springs. Annie Mae McCown enjoyed Colorado Springs. "Our back door overlooked Pike's Peak and that was beautiful," she recalled years later.

Serving in this post, McCown first became active in the civil rights movement that was breaking across the country. Very early in his life he had shown ambition and a willingness to fight for first place. He was tough and fearless, once returning to his old home in Harlem to settle scores with a street gang that had wronged him. He claimed he never got promoted past sergeant in the Air Force because he rode his superiors too hard and pushed too hard.

"There were two Cadillacs at the Air Force Academy," said his wife, "his and the commanding general's. They thought he was in some kind of racket but he just kept up the payments. We've always had a nice car. Everybody thought he had money because in the military we would give parties but they didn't know everybody had donated. He really protected us." The couple had four children by the time they lived in Colorado Springs. "I didn't talk to anybody about him. I didn't want them to know as much about him as I did. He could take nothing and make something of it. I can remember when he went to the Salvation Army and paid six dollars for a suit. He looked great."

McCown was always reluctant to speak of his years in Colorado Springs. He enjoyed talking about himself and his plans, but he would quickly change the subject when probing questions were asked about Colorado Springs.

Annie Mae McCown felt secure in the military. "Secure" was a favorite word of this sweet-faced, sad-eyed woman, who used it at least a dozen times in an interview. "He didn't like to take orders. He signed for four years, got an honorable discharge, and then signed for six more. He didn't want to reenlist but his mother and I talked him into it. He got active in the civil rights movement. They gave him a general discharge after he served nine years and ten months."

McCown claimed his difficulties with the Air Force came about because of his civil rights activities. He was named "military advisor" to Edward Bradford, president of the Colorado Springs chapter of the National Association for the Advancement of Colored People (NAACP) in June 1962. The June 6, 1962 announcement in the *Colorado Springs Gazette Telegraph* said Airman first class John L. McCown had been at the Air Force Academy for three years and that New York was his home. Bradford praised McCown's "honesty and courage to speak the truth and to elaborate on his opinions." McCown would receive the support of the local NAACP chapters in his efforts to aid Representative Charles C. Diggs of Michigan in abolishing military bias, Bradford said.

"Military prejudice is a most detestable offense, hard to prove, yet even harder for the individual who must defend against it," McCown commented at the time. "The policy of equal treatment for all members of the armed forces, without regard to race, color, or religion is firmly established within the Department of Defense. The remaining problem is to avoid such broad terms as Defense and in simple language establish such a policy for its most widely used ambassadors, mainly the Air Force, Army, Navy and Marines."

McCown afterward told friends that what really launched him into the civil rights movement was the bombing of the black church in Birmingham, Alabama, in 1963 in which four children were killed. The Colorado Springs chapter of the NAACP created considerable controversy over a memorial march to the city hall that it sponsored Sunday, September 29, 1963. The city manager refused permission for the assembly at city hall, saying he had no authority to grant it, but he eventually backed down when the sponsors said they would hold the service anyhow. John McCown's name did not appear in the lengthy accounts of the program.[2]

Annie Mae McCown once said she never had peace of mind after 1961. "We just didn't have that togetherness after that." Charges for assault appeared against McCown on the Colorado Springs police blotter on July 20, 1961; for trespassing on private property, June 14, 1962; for disorderly conduct, noise and riotous conduct November 16, 1962; and for disorderly conduct and breach of peace, November 16, 1963. An Elks Club he operated had its license suspended.

Some charges against him could not be explained purely by civil rights activities; among these were numerous speeding arrests. The Colorado Springs newspaper reported three appearances in traffic court in a four-month period. In August 1963 he was fined fifty dollars for speeding (fifteen dollars suspended). On November 27, 1963 he was fined twenty-five dollars plus the previous fifteen dollars suspended and had his driving rights suspended for twenty days for speeding. On December 11, 1963 he was fined fifteen dollars for taking the right of way.

In addition to a bad credit record[3] and a long list of minor police charges, numerous items of gossip about McCown floated around Colorado Springs. An investigator later hired by suspicious Sparta whites reported that McCown had boasted of robbing banks, that he funneled money from the Elks Club into his own pocket and did not pay help or food bills, that he "shacked up" with a German girl and "took her for about $9,000." The report added that he owed many promissory notes to blacks in the Colorado Springs area who had tried to help him financially, that he held marijuana parties for black youths at the Elks Club, and that when he left Colorado Springs for San Diego he moved with the German girl, who was the mother of a racially mixed child.[4] He departed owing literally dozens of bills that were never paid and went to San Diego, where he worked for a time as a bread salesman and attended California Western University.

By 1965 McCown was back in New York, but he did not stay long. He held several jobs there, and his mother recalled, "He would go and work a while and then say, 'I can't work at that, seeing my people going through all that they are going through and buying all that no-good stuff.' He said, 'I can't stand it, Mama, just to see what they are buying.' They tried to make him supervisor of Jones Department Store. He worked there for about a week and he gave it up. He said to have a big sale and to see those people rushing in there buying that cheap stuff that wasn't no more than tissue paper, 'They couldn't make me manager of nothing like that.' He said, 'Mother, you've got to give me some money so I can go somewhere. In New York I can't find a job and I don't want to be here.' I was so upset that he wasn't satisfied. So I gave him money and I left for work. He was standing on the porch with his suitcase. You don't know how I cried. Then he went on to Martin Luther King."

When John McCown turned his face to the South, racial controversies were reaching a peak. Bull Connor and his Birmingham policemen had given the country a civil rights bill in reaction to events in Birmingham in 1963, and black leaders were determined that Selma and Sheriff Jim Clark would give the country a voting rights bill in 1965. McCown went to Selma. His wife was to say later that although his life was threatened in Hancock County, Selma was the most dangerous place he worked. He was associated at times with Dr. Martin Luther King, Jr.'s group; McCown's wife reflected that Dr. King had been a major influence on him.

26

"Nobody was killed here," she said of Hancock County. "They don't know what trouble is. I think Dr. King taught my husband a lot—patience, if nothing else. I don't understand the patience he showed in Hancock County because he wasn't that kind of person. There could have been bloodshed here and he could have led them. Dr. King was responsible for my husband."

An activist who would become a friend of John McCown was also at work in Alabama, and this associate was not an apostle of Dr. King's nonviolence. His name was Stokely Carmichael, and where Dr. King spoke of peace, Carmichael spoke of war. The conflicts between the two forces were conflicts in McCown's personality as well. By temperament, he was no Martin Luther King. Stokely Carmichael and he were to cross paths again, in Atlanta and Hancock County and in ways and times that damaged the cause of peaceful integration.

McCown plunged enthusiastically into civil rights activities, and in the 1960s he popped up everywhere across the troubled Southern racial scene. In 1965 and early 1966 he worked in Savannah. He had a way of creating friends and enemies with equal intensity and he lasted only four months as an Equal Opportunity Authority (EOA) employee in Savannah. The local EOA board found him "energetic but undependable." A black woman there accused him of wanting to run a "one-man" show. "No one person is going to provide a solution to all of these problems of poverty," she said. "He was temperamentally better suited to be a civil rights activist than an EOA employee."[5]

McCown was accused of making rash promises to poor people that could not be kept. One supervisor said he had difficulty in making McCown understand he was part of a team. "He objected strenuously to having supervision of any kind." Some Savannah black leaders, including the head of the local NAACP chapter, protested McCown's dismissal, however.

McCown also got into difficulty in nearby Hilton Head. Atlanta OEO officials complained of McCown's working as president of a Hilton Head black community organization and of his threats to demonstrate against an island motel. McCown clearly felt certain ties to the island. Dr. Martin Luther King, Jr., retreated to nearby Penn Center for spells of peace and rest during the black revolution. McCown's wife, Annie Mae Bligen, was born there. She spoke of it later, using a word that she savored. Blacks were very "secure" on Hilton Head, she remembered. These blacks kept mostly to themselves on the island and did not suffer from the slights and blight of daily discrimination by whites.

The struggles with school integration moved into the small towns of Middle Georgia in the fall of 1965. At Warrenton, a few miles across the Ogeechee River from Hancock, blacks sought to enter the schools and protested that they were beaten at the high school. At Crawfordville in Taliaferro County, adjoining Hancock to the north, blacks held marches and protests around the fading courthouse square and within a stone's throw of Alexander Stephens's old home, Liberty Hall.[6] Hancock County remained quiet.

But not Georgia's capital. For a time, Atlanta had escaped the riots that plagued other cities. Mayor Ivan Allen won high praise for his efforts to improve conditions for the black community and many national publications held the city up as a model. But in September 1966 Atlanta's riots erupted. They were barely riots by national standards, small and pale compared to Watts and Detroit, but very frightening at the time, accompanied as they were by destruction of property and danger to lives.

An incident with the police drew a crowd to Summerhill, a black slum in the shadow of Atlanta's new stadium. Mayor Allen climbed on top of a police car to speak and the crowd began to rock the car. Eugene Patterson, then editor of the *Atlanta Constitution*, wrote in his September 7 column, "Allen got on a police car and tried to talk to them. Demagogues knew what to do about that. They rocked the car violently until he was shaken off it." A news account spoke of a Negro who pushed the mayor off, climbed up shouting "Black Power!" and got the riot underway. John McCown bragged that he was the man who pushed the mayor off the car. Atlanta police records simply say John L. McCown was arrested the day of the Summerhill riots and charged with disorderly conduct. His friend Stokely Carmichael was a principal figure in the turbulence of that day.

President Lyndon Johnson's War on Poverty moved ahead at full speed during the mid-sixties. Sargent Shriver led the battle waged by the OEO. In a rush of idealism, poverty fighters embraced the principle of involving the poor in planning their own programs at the grassroots level, bringing to this work a predictable flood of people of different

28

motivations: a need for jobs, a genuine desire to help the poor and helpless, ambition, greed, thirst for power.

What motivated John McCown? When he left the Air Force and went to college, he joined the debate team. His research for debates led him to specialize in government antipoverty programs, whether they could work or not. He learned about government grants and developed excellent contacts in various regional agencies as well as with Washington officials, who were willing and anxious to help him. Was he an opportunist, a demagogue, or a devoted missionary to the poor? Perhaps he was a little of all of these. When he was young, working at a low level in black civil rights efforts in Colorado Springs, his enemies described him as crooked and power-hungry, yet his uncle said McCown cried as he showed him homes of the black poor in Hancock County. In any case, jobs in poverty programs were opening up for bright young people, and McCown soon landed one that led him directly to Hancock County.

As a community organizer with the Southern Rural Action Project, McCown could move about and pick the places he wanted to work. The recent death of L. D. "Duke" Kennedy, Hancock's black county agricultural agent, left a tempting vacancy at the top of the county's black power structure. In those days in rural Georgia the black county agent was often the most highly paid black around, and he usually operated as the unofficial community organizer. Community organizers did everything from helping get voters registered to seeking help for blacks who had been defrauded in land and credit dealings. Hancock County blacks had already conducted a voter registration drive, led by Marvin Lewis, principal of the segregated black high school and later county superintendent of schools.

Hancock County whites often asked during the traumatic McCown decade, "Why did he pick on us?" McCown frequently engaged in rhetoric. He loved word games and did not hesitate to give answers that sometimes conflicted and confused. To one reporter, he said he came there because a look in the almanac showed Hancock had the highest percentage of blacks in the state. To another, he declared that the real reason was blacks owned 60 percent of the land in the county. John Glustrom of the Georgia Council on Human Relations, which later sponsored John McCown there, said McCown chose Hancock

County because Dr. Philip Weltner, former chancellor of the University System of Georgia, had recently made an exhaustive study of the county that highlighted the need for specific changes. Still another answer seems likely. Hancock's divided blacks were ready for a new leader; their old one had died.

For a time after leaving Savannah, McCown seemed to have bases in Sparta, Atlanta, and Athens all at the same time. He established one base in Sparta, keeping a toehold in Hancock County while working as a consultant for the ACTION agency in Athens, which was set up as the antipoverty agency for several northeast Georgia counties. In addition, he was working informally with the Georgia Council, based in Atlanta.

Controversy, which accompanied McCown wherever he went, followed him to Athens. During his time there, McCown became involved with a nurse from Iowa, slim and blonde, who, with the aid of her congressman, eventually brought on an investigation of the ACTION agency by the OEO. Among other accusations, the woman charged that she was raped by McCown on Saturday night, September 9, 1967, while attending a weekend seminar at Madison, Georgia, which McCown had helped arrange. The nurse did not report the alleged rape to legal authorities until September 14, although she later wrote she had reported it to an ACTION official the following evening and had been advised not to press charges. A highly respected white woman from the Georgia Council on Human Relations attending the meeting ate breakfast with the nurse Sunday morning after the alleged Saturday night rape and said in a later interview that she seemed cheerful and undisturbed. That afternoon, at a session with a largely black audience, the discussion turned to color.

"I'll never forget it," the woman said. "They began talking about color and the light blacks were against the black blacks there. . . . It didn't have anything to do with the meeting but they got off on it. It was good for me because it was the first time I realized the deep feeling blacks have for each other because the light blacks have so many more advantages than the black blacks have. (Well, I did know that at one time at Atlanta University you had to send your picture to get in. If you were black black you didn't get in. . . .) Then they got kind of rough. I don't mean real rough, but they began on the subject of sex and I stopped it. I thought this little conversation had gone far enough. At one point John McCown turned to this white nurse and asked, 'Why don't you speak up and say who you know you would rather sleep with, a black man or a white man?' "

The nurse, accompanied by her mother and her boyfriend, went to Milledgeville for a conference with the district attorney of the judicial district that included Madison and with the Morgan County sheriff, but no legal charges were brought against McCown.

The newspapers delicately omitted the rape charges but carried the nurse's other charges in detail. She claimed McCown joined the ACTION agency and in effect took it over, changing its focus from black and white to black only, infusing it with his ideas and dominating it. She charged that the seminar, supposedly on political education and awareness, was in effect a "hate whitey" session. The nurse said that at the Madison seminar, emphasis was placed upon something referred to only as "the movement" and how to advance it through mass voter registration of blacks and control of the black vote. Her charges, made in a widely publicized letter to Congressman Neal Smith of her home state of Iowa, resulted in an investigation of ACTION by OEO at the request of Georgia's Senator Richard Russell and Congressman Robert G. Stephens, Jr., of Athens. Two counties in North Georgia thereupon voted to withdraw from the agency. McCown resigned and the director of the agency, Charles David Hughes, left ACTION.[7]

An OEO official who had to handle that and other crises caused by McCown described him as "a charming rascal, one of the best salesmen I have ever known. He was utterly ruthless and had the morals of an alley cat. I had a very vivid picture of the man as being swaggering, not just self-confident but extremely cocky. He had a lot of ideas and if he could do them legitimately okay; if not, he would do them anyway. He could have succeeded in any number of fields. He enjoyed spending money as much as he enjoyed stealing it. He was as fast and loose with every skirt that came around as with every dollar.

"He was a product of the times as well as of his own cunning," the OEO man continued. "He took advantage of the prevailing mood and milked it for everything. He was not unique; there were lots of others. He kept his name in the papers and enjoyed that, and he even enjoyed the negative publicity. The Atlanta newspaper reporters at first swallowed his line hook, line, and sinker. He may have served a useful purpose in that he gave courage to some others who were more honest and conservative."

A well-known Georgia politician, like most Georgia politicians when asked about McCown, refused to elaborate on his experiences with the man, either on or off the record. "That revolving son-of-a-bitch caused me more trouble than the rest of the state of Georgia," he shouted. A former state OEO official said simply, "John thought black was beautiful all of the time."

Hancock County learned fast about McCown. No matter where he went, the county he had chosen stayed very much on his mind. When he joined ACTION in Athens, he wanted to take Hancock County along with him. County groups had to belong to some antipoverty organization to receive the flow of federal funds. For Hancock, the main line had been the Oconee Area Planning and Development Commission (Oconee APDC) and the little local tap was the Hancock County Community Action Committee (CAC).

McCown fell out with the Oconee group, headquartered in nearby Milledgeville. He gathered the black members of Hancock's CAC together, told them Hancock had not gotten anything from the Oconee group, and urged them to go to ACTION instead. He even brought Director Hughes down from Athens to persuade them. As a result, the Hancock CAC voted to join ACTION, a move that was later questioned because there had not been a quorum at the meeting. Hancock finally stayed with the Oconee group.

The fall of 1967 found Hancock County badly split on the subject of John McCown. Hancock CAC members described him to Sharon Bailey, then a reporter with the *Athens Daily News*, as "well-educated, intelligent, dedicated, sincere, a man with good ideas, aggressive." But the same people also spoke of intimidation and threats. "From time to time there have been comments relative to possible boycotts and demonstrations if demands were not met," one citizen said. "He's caused more trouble in our county than anyone I know of. He's got a lot of good ideas, but tries to collect power."

Another charge was to be repeated many times during the next decade. One CAC member defined it when he said McCown's fight to get Hancock County into ACTION, Inc., had amounted to "a power struggle, not something so much in the interest of the poor." Months before his adventure with the nurse caused a shakeup at ACTION, McCown threatened Hancock County with a "long hot summer" if it did not go along and join that agency.[8]

"McCown was one hell of an impressive fellow," said a senior writer with a national news magazine. "Sharp and tough as hell and he had a lot of fun in him. He was like Charles Evers, only Evers got away with it and did it right. McCown realized he was smarter than most people. He decided to find a place where he could be king, and Hancock was perfect with its old dehydrated white power structure. McCown was a strong leader but also a bully."

John McCown had found his plantation. He would cultivate it for ten years with tax dollars and tax-sheltered grants from foundations. It was run as ruthlessly as any plantation of old but with a major difference: it never produced a crop and it never made a dollar.

3

The Georgia Council

*"The South wasn't going to pay
any money for civil rights anyhow."*
—Frances Pauley

I t is impossible to separate the story of John McCown and Hancock
County from the Georgia Council on Human Relations. Events put
McCown and the Georgia Council together at a crucial time for
both. That organization grew out of the Georgia Commission on Interracial Cooperation (CIC), founded in 1919 with the goal of correcting
injustices and improving attitudes of blacks and whites toward each
other. In 1956 the commission changed its name to the Georgia Council on Human Relations. While angering some conservatives by its
very nature, it nevertheless had a high reputation over the years and
attracted respectable leaders from both races. In the late 1960s the
board included such prominent blacks as Vernon Jordan, Julian Bond,
and L. D. Milton, and whites such as Mrs. DeJongh Franklin and Mrs.
J. Brittain Pendergrast of Atlanta and philosopher Richard Hocking of
Emory University.

The council had already selected McCown to be its executive director when the storm broke in the fall of 1967 over the charges made
about ACTION in Athens. Some board members felt that the offer to
McCown should be withdrawn. Father Austin Ford, a white Episcopal
priest who had won wide recognition for his work among poor blacks
at Emmaus House in Atlanta, was vice-president of the council at that
time. He and a majority of the board decided that they could not retract
McCown's appointment unless he was proven guilty.

"The Georgia Council board was up against it," Father Ford said.
"The last thing we could do was to further a character assassination
campaign. A lot of members got their backs up because they thought
people were trying to destroy him [McCown]." Another white leader

34

in the council who, like so many people involved in the affairs of McCown, asked not to be identified, said he was very much opposed to the appointment. Several black members had warned him against McCown, saying his image smacked of the huckster.

Frances Pauley, retiring executive director, put new life into the council during her six and one-half years there. Pauley brought toughness and determination, spiced with humor, to efforts to promote racial understanding in Georgia. She really preferred defending the rights of an illiterate black mother at the welfare office to attending genteel discussion meetings. Since the white-haired, blue-eyed Pauley looked and talked like any proper white Southerner's mother or grandmother, she was hard for good old boys in county courthouses to deal with. She did not act the way she looked, and she had been in the human rights business a long time, since back in the Roosevelt days.

Council members generally credited Pauley's enthusiasm for McCown with his being placed in her old job, but she remembered having some reservations. "Some people on my board had met John and had seen how efficient he was. They thought he would be good as my successor. I saw some things in John that I just a little bit distrusted, but I didn't really have any basis for it. I actually suggested a couple of other people I thought might be better directors for the Council but the board decided on John. . . . He [McCown] wasn't so sure whether he was going to take it or not. Then all of a sudden he said, 'Yes, I am going to take it.'" It was after that the charges of rape and "hate whitey" sessions came up. "Of course some members of the Council then decided they had better not hire him," Pauley said, "but they had already hired him. He had not been tried. I stood up with the majority of the board members, saying it wasn't right to fire him until he was tried and if he was not guilty, then not to fire him. They never made a case against him; there wasn't a case."

Members' dues (membership neared two thousand at its peak) and grants from foundations financed the council. Pauley was accustomed to making the rounds of foundations in New York City twice a year, because she had found "you could raise money a lot quicker in large sums. The South wasn't going to pay any money for civil rights anyhow."

Her work for the council ended with a final trip to New York in the fall of 1967 with the new director, John McCown, and with the vice-president, Father Ford. The hotel desk clerk had no record of reservations for three single rooms when they showed up, a white-haired grandmotherly woman, a white Episcopal priest in clerical collar, and a young black man. "He looked at us and said he didn't have any such reservations. He had only one large room." Having often out-maneuvered Southern sheriffs, Pauley was not to be undone by a New York hotel clerk. "With a perfectly straight face I turned and looked at them and said, 'Well, sons, shall we take the one room?' Austin and John were about to pop. Austin said, 'No, Mother, I've had my own room since I was twelve and I want my own room now.' By this time the man was so flabbergasted that he easily found us three rooms."

Pauley took McCown around, introducing him to officers and staff members of the foundations. "He got ten times the money out of those foundations that I ever did," she said. "He was a con artist, and he got money from the Urban League that I had never gotten and he also got money from the government. Now I never wanted money from the government. I would try to get a little group to take the government project. That way they had training in leadership, it was handled locally, and the money didn't come through the Council. I still think this was the best way to do it. John McCown didn't agree with me. He took all of the government money into the Council."

Pauley had spent her time prodding and pushing Georgians into accepting changes in race relations. In the mid-1960s, freedom of choice was a common way of meeting school desegregation brought on by the U.S. Supreme Court decision of 1954. She and fellow council members branded that plan a failure.

"Because of threats and harassment, lack of cooperation on the part of many school officials, and innumerable barriers to parents who consider transferring their children to white schools, the freedom of choice method had proved totally unworkable," the council reported. Pauley wrote in 1965 to John W. Gardner, then secretary of the Department of Health, Education, and Welfare, describing the situation in Hancock County.

> The Georgia Council on Human Relations has been working with school desegregation in Georgia for the last several years with great frustration. . . . The Freedom of Choice plans have very little choice or freedom for the Georgia Negro.

Recently we have been particularly concerned about the sad lives of the lonely children who are the only ones in an entire school system. A tenth grader named Sanford Edwards is attending the white high school in Sparta, Hancock County. This boy has been harassed and beaten by his classmates since the opening of school. He is determined not to quit. Last week he was again hit in the mouth while in the restroom. His father, Mr. Robert Edwards who teaches in the Negro school, asked the principal if some arrangements could be made for his son's protection in the restrooms. He was told "no." . . . In spite of the unpleasantness, he made three A's and two B's on his last report card.[1]

Hancock County's school problems would soon give McCown the lever he needed to organize the black community, and while he immediately jumped into the work as executive director of the council, he continued the organizing work in Hancock County he had begun in 1966.

When McCown came to the Georgia council, he brought with him a woman who was to work at his side the rest of his life. She was Marion Fraleigh, attractive twenty-four-year-old Cornell University graduate and native New Yorker, nine years younger than he. A dean's list student at Cornell's College of Home Economics, she received a B.S. degree in 1965 with majors in home economics education, textiles, and clothing. She came from Ithaca, New York, to Athens, where her husband was a graduate student at the University of Georgia. Her first year in Athens was spent as supervisor of student employees at the university cafeteria system and later she managed McConnell's Cloth Shop. Fraleigh first met John McCown in 1967 while working for ACTION in Athens. She had planned to teach home economics, but the ACTION agency employed her to travel in northeast Georgia counties teaching poor people to use surplus commodities and educating them in nutrition. McCown hired her at the Georgia council as a program coordinator. Later, when she moved to Hancock County, she bore him twin sons and kept their photographs on her office walls at the agency he organized, the East Central Committee for Opportunity.[2]

McCown had little formal education; he acquired his education in bits and pieces. Marion Fraleigh was not only very well educated, she was intelligent. Al Horn, Atlanta attorney and civil rights activist who worked with McCown and admired him, expressed high admiration for her, describing her as "a great person, thoroughly dedicated to the civil rights movement and working for the people. McCown had confidence in her loyalty and integrity. She did do all the implementing and he relied on her very heavily."

Another friend and supporter who soon appeared at executive committee meetings was Edith Ingram, a young black schoolteacher from Hancock County who was being groomed to run for ordinary (county probate judge).

Well before McCown drove into Hancock County in his old Chrysler, the black community was becoming restive. Its discontent centered on the schools. The white-controlled Hancock County school system began to adjust to the Civil Rights Act of 1964 the very next year with a freedom-of-choice plan effective July 1, 1965. Students would select the school they wished to attend and in the event of overcrowding, assignments would be made on the basis of proximity. System-wide faculty meetings were to be desegregated.

Few Black Belt counties across the South faced school problems as difficult as Hancock's. The entire county had only four hundred white students by the mid-1960s, less than one-seventh of the school population. In no part of the country had whites willingly put their children in schools with such a ratio of black to white. Typically, in large cities such a problem is met by shifts in housing patterns; whenever, in any section of the United States, blacks are overwhelmingly in the majority in a school, the whites who can do so simply move out. In the rural South, the most successful integration finally occurred during the 1960s in places where blacks formed a minority in the schools or where they did not constitute much more than half of the student body.

Like most rural Southern counties, Hancock had traditionally short-changed its black schools. Until World War II, black students were for the most part housed in pitiful shacks. Black teachers, usually poorly prepared, got considerably less pay than white teachers. Whites generally took the attitude that because they paid the taxes, public funds, meager at best, should be spent on whites. A perceptive white woman who had moved away from the county reminisced about her experiences as one of two women members of the Hancock school board in the 1920s. "We rode around looking at the county schools," she recalled. "Some of the black schools were in terrible condition and we reported that to the county school superintendent. He told me that if my father were still alive he could tell me who paid the taxes. The schools were supposed at that time to be separate but equal. If they had been more equal then things might be better now. After we made our report seeking help for the Negro schools they didn't put any more women on the school board."

During Herman Talmadge's governorship after World War II, Georgia began to improve its black schools. Talmadge had won his office by appealing to the most racist elements in the state but, spurred by rumblings from the courts, Georgia started to build some excellent new facilities for blacks and whites. In an effort to delay desegregation, the state equalized salaries for black and white teachers and black students began to ride in school buses. They rode in their own separate buses but at least they rode, in most counties for the first time.

In the 1950s, Hancock County built a large new central public high school for blacks in the Hunt's Hill section of Sparta, a community that contained most of the town's prosperous blacks. The new structure cost more than all previous schools in the county's history put together. At the time it was constructed, the white public school plant included an aging yellow brick elementary school dating back to the 1890s, a shabby four-classroom red brick building, and the high school, which had been financed by the Public Works Administration (PWA) of the New Deal in 1935. Now, twenty-five years later, black students were considerably better housed than whites.

The Reverend R. E. Edwards's son was among a dozen blacks who asked to attend the white Sparta High School in the fall of 1965; the rest dropped out before enrollment time. Widely conflicting reports circulated about young Edwards's treatment there, some of which were the basis for Pauley's letter from the Georgia Council to John Gardner. The Hancock school board minutes of January 4, 1966, still referred to black teachers without titles; whites were called Mr. or Mrs. in the minutes, blacks were not. These practices had been followed since the county's founding and were no different from those in most of the South, even at that late date. The minutes referred to an FBI investigation of charges that Sanford Edwards "may have been intimidated by one or more students at Sparta School." The black minister said the coach and a few teachers were nice to his son, but the coach told the minister, "When you see me in town, don't speak to me. The citizens of this town are about to drive me crazy about your son."

"The white Baptist minister told me he couldn't speak to me," Edwards said. "He would be flooded with calls asking him what he and that nigger were talking about. My son came home every afternoon as bloody as a hog. They had caught him in the bathroom and beat him up. These experiences did not make me bitter. Little souls, little ideals, little concepts."

"Reverend Edwards's son did it alone," said a black schoolteacher. "Other blacks would have sent their kids with him if he had asked. The boy had to do his chemistry lab work after the other kids had gone because officials feared the students would throw chemicals on him. They were very rude to him and no effort was made to protect him."

"Edward's son was a trouble-maker," declared a white school official. "He caused fights by bragging to white students that his parents paid more sales tax on his clothes than the whites paid altogether for theirs. Edwards himself was a thorn in my side before McCown came. He was the local NAACP leader and was always causing a problem about something."

On March 9, 1966 Superintendent W. M. "Red" Andrews told the board of education that guidelines for implementation of the 1964 Civil Rights Act "had been toughened to an exaggerated degree," and it was doubtful Hancock citizens could accept them.[3] Local whites set about planning for a private school, one of the first of many in Middle Georgia. The county newspaper, the *Ishmaelite*, reported June 23, 1966 that the school board was advertising the old Sparta grammar school for sale. Another story in the same issue said that a private school had been chartered by Sam Hollis, George Darden, and George Rives. Hollis was president of the Bank of Hancock County, Darden was a leading farmer, and Rives a wealthy landowner and cotton warehouseman. If Hancock County could be said to have an establishment in 1966, they were all in it.

Two weeks after the announcement of the proposed sale of the grammar school, the *Sparta Ishmaelite* wrote that it had been sold to the new private school for $8,100. The old yellow brick building, long outdated, was the pride of Sparta when it was built in the 1890s. It boasted steam heat, a large auditorium, electric lights, and indoor toilets. Several generations of white students had left their initials carved in the old wooden desks and children could trace the work of parents and grandparents. All could recall the splintery wood floors, freshly oiled—a hazard to bare feet—and the steam pipes that circled each room, crackling and hissing as the janitor piled big logs into the furnace.

Until World War II public schools in much of the rural South resembled private academies, and Sparta white schools had all the earmarks of the academies from which they derived. Into the 1930s students paid some tuition, bought their own textbooks, and took part in Protestant religious exercises. They attended chapel exercises at least once a week, and the prayers and rituals of the Protestant faith were firmly embedded in the practices and curriculum of the school. Students recited the pledge of allegiance to the American flag in chapel after marching into the auditorium to stirring Civil War tunes played on the Victrola by Bishop Pierce's granddaughter. A favorite was "The Bonnie Blue Flag." ("Hurrah, hurrah, for Southern Rights, hurrah! Hurrah for the Bonnie Blue Flag that bears a single star.") The limited curriculum aimed at preparing for admission to college. Social promotions were unknown and those who could not do the work dropped out. Bright students entered college well prepared. Discipline was strict and punishment was frequently corporal. Students, boys and girls, lined up in military formation to be dismissed at the end of the day. The school battles to come were played out against this historical background.

Revolution in the county focused on the schools, but the ballot box was the principal weapon. For a brief time in Reconstruction days, blacks had held office and had represented the county in the legislature. From that unwelcome experience grew the strong conviction of whites that they must never lose control of government again, and for a century they used every device available to them to assure their control. Their methods ranged from economic pressure to overt intimidation. A key weapon was the white Democratic primary, which was not struck down by the courts until after World War II. Blacks were not allowed to vote in the Democratic primary, since the party was held to be a private club. Since elections in the virtually one-party state were decided in the primary, blacks in Georgia were effectively barred from the voting process. A few leading blacks in Hancock County voted the Republican ticket, but most simply did not vote.

41

Following the Voting Rights Act of 1965, hundreds of Hancock blacks rushed to register to vote. In the elections of 1966 they named two blacks, James Smith to the county commission and Robert Ingram to the school board. McCown's role in the 1966 elections was limited, as he had only recently come to the community after losing his job in Savannah.

After their victory in the summer Democratic primary, the blacks were challenged again in the November general election by white write-in candidates whom they defeated by a vote of 1,500 to 1,100. Hancock was the first county in Georgia to have federal poll watchers under the new act. The *Sparta Ishmaelite* complained on its front page November 17, 1966 that poll watchers were unnecessary, "as Hancock County elections have always been fair to all races and such a procedure was unwarranted."

Justice Department officials in Washington said the election of at least nine blacks to county offices in the Deep South on November 8 marked a milestone in ending discrimination. John Doar, assistant U.S. attorney general for civil rights, said the department had sent 571 poll watchers to twenty-seven Deep South counties, including twenty-five ordered to Hancock, which listed 2,300 blacks registered and 1,611 whites. More than 1.5 million blacks were now registered across the South, compared with 687,000 before passage of the Voting Rights Act. The Justice officials reported no incidents in Hancock, although poll watchers were unable to convince local officials to use blacks as election clerks. "Nevertheless," said a Justice Department spokesman, "we received excellent cooperation from everybody involved. There was no tension, no animosity."[4]

The Hancock school board immediately threw up legal road blocks upon receiving its first black member, Robert L. Ingram, at the meeting of January 3, 1967. Ingram was the father of Edith Ingram, McCown's friend and ally. Ingram and his wife were also friends of McCown's from his first days in Hancock County. When McCown moved to Sparta and wanted to buy furniture for his home, the Ingrams accompanied him to a local furniture store and guaranteed the bill for the newcomer. McCown did not make his payments regularly and the merchant had to call on the Ingrams to encourage him to pay. The Ingrams were also hosts to Frances Pauley of the Georgia Council, who stayed in their home when she came to Sparta.

When Ingram presented himself at the school board's first meeting, the chairman brought up the matter of his conviction by a Hancock Superior Court jury for liquor law violations in 1945.[5] The board asked for a ruling on Ingram's eligibility to serve, and a month later Georgia Attorney General Arthur Bolton ruled that the conviction for "the crime of having liquor" did not disqualify a person from holding office.

Pressures on school board members, already in a tense and unrewarding spot, began to build. The white community was torn between those who wanted to give the schools a chance and those who wished to push the entire white group into a private school. Blacks accelerated their demands, and during 1967 two whites resigned from the board. The private white school flourished, attracting more and more students.

"John McCown caused the blacks to wake up and realize their political power," said a black schoolteacher. "He didn't have any fear and he would say what was going on. A very brilliant young man, he did an excellent job of waking us up. Since the 1954 decision of the United States Supreme Court had not come to Hancock County, he helped bring it."

The Hancock County power structure disliked public fights. "The old aristocracy, what was left of it, wasn't able to cope with a McCown," said a former president of the Georgia Council on Human Relations. "They liked pleasant agreements arrived at behind the scenes." That was not McCown's style, as the history of his activities in Colorado Springs, Savannah, and Atlanta shows. It was highly unlikely that Hancock County whites would accept his leadership. If there was one quality they valued in anybody, white or black, it was politeness, a quality many contemporary blacks would call servility.

Before McCown arrived, Hancock County's white community had started making some improvements based on Dr. Philip Weltner's 1965 study of the town and county published by the Regional Economic Development and Business Service Center of Atlanta University. But portions of Dr. Weltner's recommendations were too advanced for them to accept. "Seventy-five percent of the population of the county is Negro," he wrote. "You may look on this circumstance as a burden. Why not turn it into a distinct asset? Suppose they all moved away! How much wiser to make Negroes feel they belonged, that they were part of the community as workers, customers, and citizens. . . . Why not an all-out effort to get everyone eligible to register and vote? What news that would make! The tidings would reach across America to all parts of the world." A note of prophecy went unheeded: "If the twenty-five percent does not make the seventy-five percent feel they belong, outside leadership will see that they do. Leadership from that source will spell civic disaster."[6]

Dr. Weltner's social recommendations were ignored, but Spartans understood and acted on his call for more jobs and various physical improvements. The need to create jobs was desperate. In two decades following World War II, Hancock's farms had decreased from 1,600 to 600. The Hancock County Redevelopment Corporation was formed and created an industrial park with a major water source. The county's tax digest was quadrupled by a reevaluation program. The county's first hospital was built. A historical foundation created in 1966 set about restoring places of note, and its tours of Hancock's handsome old homes brought visitors and favorable publicity.

Meanwhile, the white community was adjusting easily to the presence of a black man on the board of commissioners. James Smith was the son of a farmer who had been highly respected. A moderate, he managed to get along well with both blacks and whites. He and Dr. George F. Green, a popular Sparta physician, and J. T. Stanton, Jr., a white farmer and lumberman, ran the county commission during the 1966–68 term, when McCown was establishing his power base among Hancock blacks. Dr. Green functioned not only as a county commissioner but also as mayor of Sparta. During the 1966–68 period, local governments made efforts to accommodate the black community, even in Sparta where no blacks held elective office. Paving was extended into black neighborhoods (whites had gotten their paving twenty years earlier, right after World War II). Gas mains and water mains, fire hydrants and street lighting were expanded throughout the town.

Gestures such as these did not appease McCown, whose ambitions fed on animosity and tension; without these he felt blacks would not make progress. The long somnolent county began to build new stresses and hatreds. Al Horn, a white Alabamian who became a racial liberal and as an American Civil Liberties Union lawyer aided McCown, had his own ideas about that. "When people start to make the change, that's when the hate comes out," he said. "When you are sitting in the catbird seat things look pleasant, but when the cat comes up to get the catbird, why, things change around.

"They had such things in Hancock County as putting people into jail for debt—for black people owing white people," he said. "It was still a semi-feudal system and while the harshness of the real ugly, hating parts of the South wasn't there, basically if a black person stepped out of line there was no question what was going to happen." Feelings later became so strong, Horn said, that he never got in and started his car in Hancock County without looking under the hood first.

"John was a lot more able to understand the white person's problems and dilemma than they were able to understand what he was trying to do. He had little patience with the white folks' notion of trying to maintain the status quo but he understood it," said Horn. "John did deal with a number of whites because he made an alliance with the sheriff. He had good relations with the old lady he bought the ECCO property from; he got along very well with her. She wasn't bound down with the Old South notion of blacks being kept in their place."

In January 1968, a few months after McCown became executive director of the Council on Human Relations, it adopted Hancock County "as a target area of major thrust." Edith Ingram headed a newly formed Hancock chapter of the council, which quickly enrolled ninety-seven members. McCown reported forming a welfare rights group of thirty members, a federal watch-dog committee "to bird-dog all governmental agencies operating within the county," and a political action committee to work on voter registration and voter education. Busy in political efforts in Hancock County, he noted at the March 1968 council meeting that he had received a grant from the Voter Education Project for his work. John Glustrom, white Atlanta businessman with a record of support for civil rights and other liberal causes, was treasurer of the council and a staunch friend of McCown's. At the March meeting, he persuaded the council to raise McCown's salary retroactively from $12,000 to $13,500.[7]

Although concentrating on Hancock, McCown found time to involve himself and the council in several dramatic confrontations in other areas that pointed up injustices to blacks. Portions of Lake Lanier, a federal lake and park, lie in Forsyth County, some thirty miles north of Atlanta. Following racial trouble there in 1912, blacks were driven from the county and none was allowed to spend the night there. Members of an integrated religious group testing the ban were physically removed from the county in May 1968. McCown notified the FBI, sheriff's department, and State Patrol that the council planned an integrated weekend trip to Lake Lanier in June. Hecklers met the group shouting, "Just wait until night comes!" But with the aid of state police who forcibly restrained the mob, the council and McCown brought blacks to sleep overnight in Forsyth County for the first time in fifty-six years.[8]

McCown decided to run for the Hancock County commission himself in the 1968 elections, opposing J. T. Stanton, Jr., white commission chairman who had displeased him by his lack of interest in increasing welfare programs. Stanton later privately described a McCown visit to him to talk about food stamps. Stanton felt there were jobs for those who wanted to work. "Some think no more of a job than a rattlesnake. They work for a few days and quit, always swapping jobs." He described McCown as arrogant. "He made it a point to upset anybody white."

Since Reconstruction days, nomination in the Democratic primary in Hancock County had been "tantamount to election," as politicians said. McCown prepared for the September 11 Democratic primary, pointing out that he had been selected by the Hancock Democratic Club, a black group formed to decide what the black slate would be. In his political advertisements, he argued that citizens of the county were not getting their share of federal programs or jobs. Acting as if controversy and hardened racial feelings had not always marked his every public move, he promised "to work faithfully and honestly to bring increased unity among all citizens of Hancock County." Stanton said the vast majority of Hancock County people "have cast away their fear of racism and molded friendships based on respect and civil equality." He charged his "New York reared" opponent with preaching hatred against whites and planning the removal of all whites from any positions of community leadership.[9]

McCown defeated Stanton by a vote of 1,919 to 1,514 in the primary. James A. Smith, the moderate black elected to the commission two years earlier, led the ticket with a vote that indicated many whites supported him. He overwhelmed his white opponent, Guy Clarke, 2,085 votes to 1,203. In the senatorial race, the Atlanta black leader Maynard Jackson ran ahead of Georgia's Senator Herman Talmadge in Hancock, with 1,796 votes to Talmadge's 1,412. Edith Ingram won over Helen Miller, the incumbent ordinary, by a vote of 1,870 to 1,603.[10]

"The obvious tension which exists in most Black Belt counties is noticeably softer in Hancock," wrote David Nordan, the *Atlanta Journal*'s political reporter, who visited there after the primary. "The white population seems to be resigned to being governed by Negroes. The fears they have are centered on the personality of the educated and articulate Mr. McCown, who they describe as an outside agitator." Nordan noted that having blacks in office was nothing new to Hancock Countians. James Smith, the first black commissioner, had been in office two years and "appears to have served without angering either whites or blacks—a fact demonstrated by the very large vote he received in the primaries." [11]

Whites, though resigned, remained suspicious. County Democratic Chairman Cliff Hill explained to the Sparta Lions Club how the primary elections would be handled "two years from now," but he questioned whether "any of us will have anything left to do with it." Dr. Green told Nordan, "We'll work the best we can with it. That's what we've always done." Hill said, "We've worked and lived with them all of these years . . . there's no reason why we can't now."

"The eyes of the world are now focused on us," McCown said in an advertisement in the *Sparta Ishmaelite* of September 26, 1968, following his victory in the primary. "Much will be written and much will be said about Hancock County. Historical progress is sometimes painful, but if we are to survive, not only as a county but as a nation, we must never fool ourselves into the thought that we should return to the good old days that never were."

In a letter to Dr. Philip Weltner written October 29, 1968, now in the author's files, Dr. Green talked about McCown without naming him.

As for the person you refer to as the new chairman of our county board, you will find him to be a person who by innuendo will try to give you a favorable opinion initially, then threaten you later. He came here with a "desire to render service to the community," and in the past month has threatened to "burn the town" in the presence of witnesses on three separate occasions. He has tried to break the coalition between the white and the Negro so that they are now at extreme odds, and then he states he wants biracial cooperation. When he presented himself to you as the new chairman of the board, he was following his usual method of implying what he is not. In the first place, he has not been elected since he

47

has opposition on November 5, and secondly the chairman of the board is elected by members of the board after having been sworn in the first Tuesday in January, following the general election.

The general election in November confirmed McCown's victory, despite a write-in campaign by whites. McCown defeated Stanton again, by a vote of 1,897 to 1,496. Edith Ingram once more defeated Helen Miller 1,934 to 1,532, becoming the first black to win the post of ordinary (probate judge) in American history.[12] These votes seemed to follow very closely the relative voting strength of blacks and whites in the county at the time. For the first time since Reconstruction, blacks had taken political control of a United States county.

Edith Ingram was increasingly important to McCown as her work, like his, expanded into many areas. Now the county ordinary, she also served as secretary to the Georgia Council and later worked in McCown's business enterprises. Ingram grew up in Sparta and attended school at Fort Valley State College, still a predominantly black institution. Returning to Sparta to teach, she was recruited to run for office. "In 1966 blacks were promised they would have some blacks working in the election as poll officers," she said. "When blacks arrived at the courthouse on election day the white ordinary told them she could not allow them to work as some people in the courthouse did not want blacks to work. The blacks decided that the white ordinary's politicking days were over. They kept urging me to run against her in the next election. I refused many times but one night I decided I would because it was so important, and I got elected."

The new black officeholders got a mixed reception. When Ingram took up her duties as ordinary, some employees at the courthouse were kind to her, she said. "The other people just didn't have anything whatsoever to do with me. I had a few threatening calls from people telling me when I came to work as I walked up the steps they were going to shoot me. I got a few ugly letters. If whites in town wanted a certified copy of something they would call up and ask for it and then they would stop at the door. They wouldn't have a seat. Pretty soon people found out that we would give courteous and efficient service and it sort of faded away."

Peter Range, a free-lance writer, met McCown and Ingram when he stopped in Sparta one day. He liked and admired the two, spending the afternoon in a dive drinking beer with them. In an article for *Esquire*, he noted that Ingram ruled over "gun-toter's permits" and deputized the sheriff's men. "She is kind of a political red-hot mama to the black community, McCown's chief whip in the county's legal system." [13]

The probate judge holds court in ground floor offices in the Victorian courthouse. The big, high-ceilinged old rooms are painted a pinkish purple and an antique fireplace mantel vivid yellow. Bright red bindings of county record books going back to 1793 add another note of color. Ingram, usually modishly dressed, is light-skinned with red hair. She lapses now and then into Hancock County black talk but maintains a stylish rhythm of speech. Her language, sometimes earthy, is calculated to set the teeth of Hancock gentry on edge.

The probate judge has a lively sense of humor and a collection of stories that show up some interesting aspects of human nature, particularly white human nature. One of her tales describes her first trip to a convention of Georgia probate judges. "Everybody was looking at me," she recalled. "A few said welcome but at lunch there were empty seats around me. A few younger people were friendlier. Nobody would eat or talk with me but in the middle of the night a few of the guys would call and ask if they could bring me a drink. At one of the meetings the president of the organization began to tell a story about 'an old nigger preacher.' When I complained, he said it would be all right for me to tell a story about an old white preacher. A patrolman told a joke about a white woman and her black poodle who was on welfare. He was on welfare because he was unemployed and black and didn't know who his mama and daddy were. After that a lot of people came and apologized. Since that time attitudes are better. They don't skip chairs anymore and they invite me to lunch."

She likes to tell about the little old lady from Texas who came in leaning on a walker. She was researching wills. Ingram was dusting around the office and asked the visitor if she could help her. The Texas lady replied, "No, honey, you just go on and finish your work and I'll wait until the ordinary comes." Finally convinced that a black woman was the ordinary, the Texan went about her work and was happy to find that some of her people were Revolutionary soldiers. She was happy until she ran across some Cherokee Indian ancestors, Ingram recounts.

"Then she said angrily, 'I might have known when you niggers got in here you were going to mess up the records.' That lady got up and walked out of here as straight as anybody and left her walker."

When she first took office, Ingram said she asked the whites who had helped with elections in the past to continue to do so. According to her, some of them declined, stating health and other reasons. A few, she said, wrote what might be called "hell, no" letters. Only one or two continued to help with the voting. "The others will just sit and find fault and that's all they want to do," she told a reporter. "All this old bullshit about writing the letters and requesting their return and running it in the papers, I don't do that anymore." [14]

News media outside Georgia paid little attention to the election of the nation's first black ordinary and the first complete black political control of a county since Reconstruction days. Some Georgia newsmen interviewed Ingram and McCown, but no one put together all the pieces of the story. McCown had not only been the first black in modern times to win command of a county, he had also taken on several contradictory roles. By virtue of his job with the Georgia Council, he became a de facto employee of the Ford Foundation and the federal government as they began to pour funds into his many activities. These nonpartisan and tax-exempt organizations were thus, through McCown, intimately involved in the political affairs of the county.

Now that McCown was a county commissioner as well as executive director of the Georgia Council and Hancock's new ordinary Edith Ingram was council secretary, minutes of the Atlanta meetings sometimes resembled those of a Hancock County commission session. For example, the February 6, 1969 minutes incongruously detailed McCown's proposals to do away with the county's prison system. Originally designed to foster better race relations across the state, the Georgia Council on Human Relations had very nearly become the governing body of Hancock County. A situation unique in American political history developed, as McCown built a small empire atop a growing base of government and foundation funds channeled through the council.

4

A Time to March

"Until McCown came I considered myself a moderate
in race relations. That's a hard spot.
The blacks call you a redneck
and the whites say you are a nigger lover."
—A Sparta businessman

Now the challenge from this point," wrote McCown in his annual report as executive director of the Georgia Council, "will be to exhibit this county as a model to the nation as to what can truly happen when people of all faiths work for economic progress without regard to race, creed or color." [1]

The key to economic progress was soon found. McCown revealed his plans for an elaborate complex calculated to transform pastoral Mayfield. Its chief ornament was to be a huge catfish farm—330 acres of land under water—funded by the OEO.

A cement-block plant was planned, as well as a village of three hundred homes to be built under Federal Housing Administration (FHA) programs. A proposed housing project three stories high included a shopping center on the ground floor; a movie theater, a service station, and grocery stores would follow.

The council published a brochure saying, "One illustration of Georgia Council's statewide program is what happened in rural Hancock County, in central Georgia, in 1966. Hancock is the beginning of Georgia's black belt. In this county, a 78 percent black population was ruled by a white minority. Here Georgia Council's goal, as defined by its executive Director John McCown, was 'to shape an area where blacks and whites could work together, creating an economically viable, socially harmonious model county.'"

The brochure went on,

51

Before the Council came, Hancock was economically dead and festering with racial hatred. The schools were segregated. There was no link between the county governnent and the majority of people who lived and worked there.

Now, through the work of the Georgia Council on Human Relations, blacks and whites work together in Hancock County to create economic progress for both races.

Now Hancock has blacks in important county positions for the first time. Whites are democratically represented, even though blacks could have removed them from every office in the county. Georgia Council wanted biracial cooperation.

The brochure's appeal was: "We need your gift to keep rural people from rushing into the cities, and festering in the ghettos there."[2]

The pamphlet quoted an unidentified black man who "murmured bitterly, 'There are still a lot of whites who would rather die and go to hell than feel they were pulled into prosperity by a black man.'" Varying versions of this colorful plaint, attributed to different people, were fed to reporters covering Hancock County during the next few years, and it appeared in many publications, including the *New York Times*, and in a British television production. One Georgia newspaper had to print a retraction after it reported that the wife of a prominent and conservative Hancock County man quoted her husband as saying, "I'd rather suffer in hell with a broken back than be dragged to paradise by a nigger." The reporter had mixed up his notes from the TV tapes.

McCown led a delegation from Hancock to Washington, D.C., to get some of his ambitious proposals approved. The group included two whites: Ernest Lowe, supervisor of federal projects in Hancock County schools, and Marvin E. Moate, state representative. Lowe, member of an old and respected Hancock County family, had retired to his family's farm near Devereux after a teaching career in the state's university system. He came from retirement to help save Hancock's public schools. Moate, a businessman and political leader, had served for many years in the state legislature, where he had acquired considerable influence and was elected speaker of the house. Moate later said the trip with McCown cost him several hundred white votes. The rest of the delegation included George Lott, president of the Hancock County Democratic Club, and Edith Ingram. They met with people at the National Urban League, with an aide to President Nixon, and with representatives of the OEO, the Farmers Home Administration (FmHA), Housing and Urban Development (HUD), and the FHA. OEO said it could not fund the entire catfish project at once but would give $225,000. The Economic Development Agency (EDA) wired $68,000 in response to one proposal.[3]

Initially, McCown was able to get some local white support. Sparta merchants agreed to accept an integrated office in the Broad Street business district, which was set up jointly by the council and the Urban League. White leaders such as Lowe and Moate worked with him, and a small group of whites served on biracial committees. But from the beginning, most whites were adamantly opposed to McCown. The national mood at the time was divisive. Americans everywhere were bitterly divided over many issues, the war in Vietnam being but one of them. In Hancock County, racial fears were easily aroused in a white community so greatly outnumbered.

The most controversial issue in 1969 was the public schools. Sensing their new-found political power and encouraged by McCown's leadership, blacks became more and more demanding about the schools. George Lott, a popular Hancock black who had been active in the Urban League, led a delegation from the Hancock Democratic Club before the school board, asking it to conduct the schools in such a way "as to continue federal funds." The delegation complained of crowded conditions at Hancock Central, the black high school built in the early 1950s. It also raised a key question: what plans did the board have to eliminate the dual school system?[4]

McCown, Lott, and Nathaniel Dickson, a well-known black farmer, came back to the August 1969 meeting protesting the board's failure to supplement salaries of certain teachers and urging the dismissal of a teacher who had aroused their ire. They warned that they would protest a planned millage increase in the courts and that they were keeping an eye on the board's efforts.

Handbills headlined "Emergency Meeting" and addressed to "Dear Parent" invited black parents to a public meeting at the black high school in early September. The message bore no names but listed as sponsors the Hancock County PTA, the local NAACP, the Hancock County Democratic Club, and the Hancock County Youth Group. The

handbill carried the McCown imprint, calling the school superintendent "Red." McCown chose to strip away titles and courtesies; "Red"
was the school superintendent's nickname and its use was sufficient
identification for a McCown announcement.

"For years and years now, we have been asking the superintendent
of Hancock County School system to do something about the over-
crowded conditions that exist at Hancock Central School. Yet to this
date he ('Red Andrews') has failed to become concerned with what he
thinks is just a Negro problem." The handbill failed to mention that
Hancock Central was a new school built in the previous decade at a
cost greater than that of all schools built in the county's history and in a
county whose population was steadily falling.

The publication went on to say, "It is time now that we face the following facts: 1. Our children are not receiving half the education needed to compete for any decent job, due to the over-crowded conditions.
2. Bus drivers hauling Negro children are working twice as hard and
twice as long—with no change in pay. 3. 'Red' is deliberately chasing
away qualified Negro teachers, by refusing to pay them what they are
worth. We will not stand by another day and allow this to happen to our
children, our bus drivers nor our teachers!" [5]

If every white school child in the county had remained in the public
schools and had been evenly scattered through the system, there would
have been three whites in each class of twenty-five. Nearly half of the
whites had already left the public schools and not enough remained to
integrate Hancock's black classrooms. It became obvious that the struggle was not a fight to bring about integration of the schools; the population makeup of the county made this impossible. The struggle was over
control of the school system and its payroll.

The remaining 250 or so whites in public schools were concentrated
in the old Sparta high school. In addition, a sizable number of black
students constituted about 20 percent of the enrollment there. Three
days after schools opened for the fall term in 1969, John McCown,
Edith Ingram, and George Lott went to the Hancock Central campus,
where they organized two hundred school children and marched them
to the auditorium of the predominantly white Sparta School Center. [6]
McCown spoke to the assembly, telling them they had come to the
Sparta Center to be enrolled, to which the school superintendent re-

sponded that such a drastic change was impossible. He temporarily recessed the schools and called a meeting of the school board. The board asked Robert Ingram, Sr., to get the opinions of other blacks and Ingram returned with the news that blacks were demanding total integration of school operations.[7]

Young blacks formed the real staff of McCown's revolution. He organized them early with parties and films. Black students began a boycott of the schools September 10, 1969 that was almost totally effective, costing the system $5,000 a day.[8] In Georgia the public schools in poor rural areas are largely financed by state funds based on average daily attendance. The largest payroll in Hancock County is the state-financed school budget, which provides practically all the white collar jobs available in the county.

Hancock's early school troubles were not widely reported in daily newspapers throughout the state, but Charles Pounders wrote about them in *The People's Voice*, published by the Georgia Council on Human Relations September 30, 1969.[9] Pounders devoted the entire front page to the story and to a photograph of a Ku Klux Klan rally that appeared in the *Macon Telegraph* on September 9. The *Telegraph* said the rally took place in Hancock County and was attended by about two hundred people. Pounders reported that law enforcement authorities in Hancock said no Klan rally occurred. Some sources insisted the photograph was made in an adjoining county.

Pounders wrote that the boycott climaxed days of tension which saw residents, both black and white, arming themselves as if preparing for a siege. He quoted one resident as saying, shortly after the Negro demonstration led county officials to shut down Sparta schools, "I've never seen so many people carrying firearms in all my life." According to Pounders's account, McCown was arrested by Sparta police and charged with parading without a permit. Officials would not allow a property bond to be posted to get McCown out of jail, Pounders wrote, despite the fact that he resided in Hancock and was a member of the county commission. McCown was finally released after posting a cash bond.

Tension reached such a fever pitch that for a time a showdown in the streets seemed a real possibility. School board member Robert Ingram, at that time the only black on the board, said a white man charged into one of the board's meetings and said in a highly emotional tone, "I've had enough. I'm ready to die over this thing and I'm speaking for two hundred more just like me." McCown was quoted as saying he had received several anonymous threats on his life in a period of only a few days.

On the first day of the boycott the school board had begun negotiations with a group of blacks: John McCown, George Lott, Jack Ingram, the Reverend R. E. Edwards, the Reverend Elijah Johnson, and John Kendrick. The next day, Andrews submitted a proposal to accept sixty more blacks from Hancock Central at the Sparta School Center.[10] The blacks rejected this and made a counterproposal that all 184 students be accepted and that black teachers be transferred to the Center.[11] The black negotiators also asked for personnel changes, naming specific persons to specific jobs. They suggested blacks to replace the curriculum director, the visiting teacher, and the lunchroom supervisor. They also demanded that black students not be penalized for their absence from school since it was for a just cause. They were particularly sensitive about segregated school bus routes, demanding that all buses pick up children until loaded to capacity, that no bus duplicate another's route, and that "under no circumstances will a bus driver transfer an old bus to another driver and he receive a new bus."

The board rejected certain black demands, vetoing transfer of lunchroom personnel and refusing to guarantee that no bus route would duplicate another. A compromise was eventually worked out, the board agreeing to accept ninety-two blacks at the Sparta School Center immediately, plus two black teachers, and to admit the remaining ninety-two blacks in the winter quarter. Most of the other demands were met: a black would be hired as coordinator of federal programs, a black would accompany the white visiting teacher, boycotting students would not be punished, buses would pick up children without regard to race, and old buses would not be assigned to black drivers.[12]

White reaction was strong, reflecting considerable emotion in the community. Years later, a white business leader recalled that he had kept his sons in the public school; the 20 percent integration they had at first did not bother him. "Then McCown got into the act. He led marchers down the street, marched into the white high school, and took it over. After that we took our children out of the public schools.

Until he came I considered myself a moderate in race relations. That's a hard spot. The blacks call you a redneck and the whites say you are a nigger lover."

"I stuck it out in the public schools until 1969," said another white leader. "The blacks started raising so much hell at Sparta I wouldn't send my children into that. Now it is a hardship as we are ten miles from Sparta and we have to pay that big tuition at the private school and send them down there and bring them back. The school bus used to pick them up at the road."

A white teacher spoke of her agony when she was assigned to a black school in 1969. She needed to stay in the public schools to get her retirement benefits. She dreaded the prospect of teaching in a black school so much she cried, but her son said, "Why run away from it?" So she went.

"I spent eight years there," she said, "and they were some of the best years I spent in school. I could never have had a better principal than the black principal at that school. No parent ever came to criticize me and everybody was nice to me.

"In recent years rural black children have been to more places and have seen more and there has been a big improvement in dress and hygiene. Everything is provided at the school, including free breakfasts and lunches. I feel sorry for the poor white children whose parents struggle to pay tuition, haul them to school, and have to feed them themselves."

A retired black teacher held a different view of school integration in the 1960s. "They first started sending a few black students to white schools. After that a few whites came to Central High School. They got along nicely and then the whites just pulled out their children. This past commencement there were one or two whites in the graduating class; the schools are just about all black again. They have no whites on the faculty. The assistant superintendent is white but she commutes from Macon or Milledgeville."

After the school board met the blacks' demands, McCown addressed a mass meeting at the county courthouse. Instead of conciliatory remarks that would have made the role of white mediators easier, he threatened, "Any time the board breaks the agreement we'll come back and do this town up right."

5

The Money Tree

"For centuries the black man
has sought and found his comfort
in Sweet Jesus. The vision
of ecstasy in the life hereafter
is no longer enough.
What about now?"
—British TV announcer in film
on Hancock County

When McCown came to Hancock County, he had never shown evidence of business ability. He had personality, courage, and a sense of theater. He excelled at debating and exhorting, but his work record and his credit record would not have won him a charge account at a well-run department store. Yet the United States government and major foundations entrusted him with millions of dollars. During the sixties, when the nation was urgently seeking a way out of its urban dilemma, McCown was able to peddle his ideas for training and employing rural blacks as a way of keeping them out of the slums of big cities. It was widely recognized that to reach this goal, the rural South would have to be made more attractive to blacks.

Among the many people who knew McCown, both close friends and enemies, no one ever said he was a good manager. He was universally described as unable and unwilling to delegate authority. He neither kept a good personal credit rating nor ever showed any record of managing financial affairs in an orderly way. His friends said he was careless about accounting. Others who knew him were more blunt and less charitable.

The American money tree reached full bloom in the late 1960s. Lyndon Johnson's War on Poverty produced the OEO, which continued to flower into the Nixon years. McCown found his way to that money tree and to the ones blooming in New York City, where big foundations had not yet cut back the spending boom.

McCown often preached green power. "I came here to do a job," he told British television reporters. "That job was to change the economic conditions for the people of Hancock County. That was all my concern—people. I did not come here for gradualism and stand-stillism and do-nothingism and I didn't come here to convert a lot of souls." He told the *New York Times*, "We hope to prove in Hancock County that the basic problems here are economic. We must pool our strengths, techniques and knowledge and bring talent back into the South and make it a viable and pleasant place to live. We don't need any more New Yorks, Chicagos and Philadelphias, where blacks are always ringing someone else's cash registers—we want blacks to own the cash registers."[1] The message sold well in New York in foundation suites and it was warmly received by bureaucrats in Washington.

The Georgia Council on Human Relations served McCown admirably as a channel for funds from the federal government and from foundations. The council set up the East Central Committee for Opportunity (ECCO) as an umbrella agency over the many projects that were popping up in Hancock County like mushrooms after a warm rain. The Presbyterian Church in New York promised a loan of up to $550,000 as seed money for a housing project. The board of directors named to a nonprofit housing corporation included McCown's friend John Glustrom and six other council members, including McCown himself, as well as three Hancock County men, all of whom were or became employees of McCown's various enterprises: George Lott, Nathaniel Dickson, and Robert Ingram.[2] The technique of naming people he controlled to boards was a key McCown device; eventually, almost everyone on any governmental board or agency in Hancock County worked in one of McCown's businesses. Lott was employed at the cement-block plant McCown set up; Dickson worked at the catfish farm when it got underway; Ingram ran a food program in neighboring Glascock County under the auspices of the council.

The centerpiece of McCown's program was to be the huge catfish farm at Mayfield, fed by the waters of the Ogeechee River. Southerners love catfish, a mainstay of "all-you-can-eat" fried fish places that line the highways in many parts of the South. Some successful catfish farms in the delta country of Mississippi and Arkansas encouraged the idea of a cheap source of food that could also supply incomes and jobs to impoverished rural areas, a combination which appealed to foundation executives. Catfish farms were trendy in the late 1960s, a project idea easy to sell. McCown was fascinated by the promise of catfish farming, becoming an expert on the subject. A friend described him as "sounding like he had a Ph.D. in catfish."

"Catfish farms were big and the Ford Foundation gave McCown one," said a New York foundation executive. "The Ford Foundation poured a lot of money into community development programs, selecting six or so sites on which to concentrate its efforts. Two of these were in the rural South, one in Mississippi and one in Hancock County. The Ford Foundation was as much a part of what happened in Hancock County as John McCown was. They did much of the planning and poured in the money. Ask McGeorge Bundy about it," he said. "He ought to remember. He had his picture made with McCown and it ran on the financial pages of the *New York Times*."

At the Georgia Council meeting in July 1969, "catfish" became the key word. Where they once discussed welfare rights and freedom-of-choice school plans, they now talked about Hancock County and catfish. Black ministers, Atlanta socialites, scholarly university professors all discussed catfish. Armed with stacks of charts and diagrams revealing how a catfish farm would look and operate, McCown enthusiastically addressed the council's board. He told them there was more money in growing catfish than in growing any row crop; a study showed demand for catfish in Georgia would exceed supply through the year 2010; the proposed farm would cover 320 acres of land to be divided into eight 40-acre ponds, each pond producing 2,200–3,000 catfish a year; the by-product from the catfish would be processed into pet food, creating additional jobs. In four to five months the fish would be ready to market.

McCown's ambitious proposals for a huge catfish operation ran into trouble at the state level. William H. Burson, then Georgia's state welfare director, called in an expert who raised some serious questions about the project. McCown and Marion Fraleigh attended a hearing at the state level and, according to McCown, proved that the statements made by the catfish expert were unsound. Catfish, so called because the barbels that project from the chin look like a cat's whiskers, became a topic in Washington's marble halls. The state catfish expert accompanied McCown and Fraleigh to OEO in Washington to discuss the project at a hearing also attended by Whitney Young of the National Urban League, a Mississippi catfish expert, OEO attorneys, and a field representative from the National Council of Negro Women.[3] McCown later received a telephone call (in the council minutes of July 3, 1969, he noted the exact hour—10:30 P.M., June 30, 1969) telling him his proposal had been approved but not yet announced because of some questions raised by the state.

Always full of energy and optimism, McCown had already figured the first year's net profit would be from $150,000 to $172,000 and he told the council a credit union would be established from the profit. He anticipated other pleasant side benefits, including a recreational area, some thirty acres for fishing with sleeping facilities for sportsmen. However, the realities of the business world already intruded on these enterprises. Somebody offered more money to the man who was to head a sewing plant McCown had begun, and the man left. Mrs. Arthur Reynolds, a large landowner, did not want the proposed cement-block plant to be in Mayfield, and it had to be moved to Granite Hill, a spot nearer Sparta on the Sparta-Warrenton highway; the relocation was costly.

Not all observers of the council shared McCown's optimism. One who had worked with the council said that when he first met McCown he felt "apprehensive," having grown suspicious of people suddenly appearing on the southern interracial scene. "Southern race relations are extremely delicate. You need to know more than 'White man, get out of my way.' I became leery of economic self-help schemes which were usually born of naiveté, so cruel to the poor black people whom they mobilized. I remember an old black woman who lost $300 in a food co-op. You come in as the Messiah and twelve months from now everybody will have the new version of forty acres and a mule.

"McCown came up with the fish farm. I was afraid John was a combination of a naive do-gooder and a demagogue. My fears weren't reduced when it turned out John was a master at going places and talking a great game," the man continued. "Foundations fell all over themselves giving. Soon there were tales that he used petty cash as if it were his own, that he took personal trips on the council's air travel card and charged two suits to the council on an American Express card. John wasn't the least interested in playing by the rules, moral or legal."

The council's bookkeeper was Curt Doernberg, a refugee from Hitler's Germany, who kept the books "for very little." Long after Frances Pauley had left her job, he called to talk to her, concerned about the bookkeeping as McCown expanded the council into many business operations in Hancock County. Doernberg told Pauley he would not keep the books any longer, even though they offered to pay him a large sum. "Curt told me he felt he needed to tell somebody about his concern for the integrity of the council," Pauley said. "He had resigned with the excuse of too little time."

"McCown was an incredibly charismatic man," declared one influential Atlanta woman who served on the council's board of directors. "He was so positive and so committed and so good at raising money. He was deeply committed to these people and unbelievably talented at going to New York City and playing with guilty liberal consciences. He seemed to have so clear a vision of where he was going."

"McCown was an operator," said another observer, a man involved in race relations work for many years. "He could sway the masses by talking of brotherhood. In the mid to late 1960s we developed a brand of southern demagogue who happened to be black, and I was very much afraid that McCown fitted into that new demagoguery. Economic development became the thing as people with hearts bigger than their heads began building houses, catfish ponds, food co-ops and all those things. McCown jumped in at a dangerous rate. We had cause to feel that his record keeping and spending habits were extremely sloppy. I had arguments with McCown and over McCown. He had the head to attract great sums of money but he saw that nothing was done that was not to his own interest."

McCown did not hesitate to lie when it served his purposes. One example appeared in his annual report to the council covering 1968, his first full year as executive director. In Dr. Philip Weltner's 1965 study of Hancock County, an error occurred indicating that three times as many whites were listed on the welfare rolls as blacks—an exact reversal of the true population ratio. Pauley, then executive director, complained to the Georgia Department of Family and Children's Services about this injustice to blacks. On March 28, 1967 Harold Parker of the state agency wrote her that someone had reversed the figures because the county's welfare rolls actually were 82.2 percent black and 17.8 percent white. Parker's letter was in the council's files, yet McCown in the 1968 report praised the work of his thirty-member welfare rights group for "astonishing results to say the least. For instance the welfare roles [*sic*] where whites outnumbered Negroes three to one was [*sic*] completely reversed."[4] He continued to use the falsehood in printed pieces during political campaigns. In a political letter addressed to all voters in the 1972 political campaign, McCown began, "In 1966, upon my arrival in Hancock County, I found that: Whites outnumbered Blacks on welfare three to one."

Even on the council, people held widely varying views of McCown. One of his strong supporters was Father Austin Ford, the Episcopal priest. "John McCown was convinced that the only way black people could enjoy full participation was through economic development," said Ford. "That was his main thrust. He wanted to get people into economic productivity. He was notably and passionately concerned about the interracial situation. He didn't want blacks to go it alone and was determined to keep whites and blacks working together. He didn't want to cause racial isolation; he liked white people, for one thing. He wanted to provide charismatic leadership and he felt it required an aggressive leader at the top, one who could control. He certainly didn't want people in his way or telling him what to do."

But there were always people in his way: state welfare directors, governors, auditors, people asking questions. "John told a person only what he wanted him to know," Ford had said. Some were beginning to speak out and ask for more. Among them was the Reverend Thomas M. Stubbs, Jr., a white minister from Columbus, then president of the Georgia Council. He had left a lucrative law practice to become an Episcopal priest. The letter Stubbs wrote came to be known in the council as the "July 31 AD 1969 letter." That was the way he dated it.

"The Georgia Council is in serious trouble in a number of areas," Stubbs warned the executive committee and directors to whom he addressed his letter.

In the past months there has been so much shifting of money from one project to another that I have been unable to understand or keep track of it. We get our money from various sources: from individuals, from foundations, from corporations, and from government. No one in the Council would knowingly violate any laws, regulations or trusts. And yet, we cannot tell either from our financial statements or from our Executive Director's reports whether our administration of these funds is in strict conformity with such laws, regulations, or trusts. To clarify what I mean by *trust*, let me say we have solicited and received from givers, money to be used on specific projects. Whether this has been carried out is unknown both to me and to you. But if in any one of these we have failed to keep faith with these givers, we are sure to suffer the penalty of not being found worthy of future trust—or worse. Even if we have the excuse of "pressing need" to shift funds, this will not save our reputation once it is lost.

Stubbs warned that the council had abandoned its traditional role in Georgia, that the executive director spent most of his time in Hancock County. By implication, he raised more questions about sources of income for McCown. "We need to have at least semi-annual reports of all income of all our paid employees. Only in that way may we know whether we are properly supporting the employee in his or her service to the people of Georgia, or whether in fact the employees are overpaid for the time spent for the Council." He leveled a final blast at McCown. "As matters now stand, neither your officers, nor Executive Board, nor the Board of Directors is permitted to do anything but discuss and then rubber-stamp the wishes and policies set forth by our Executive Director. No one seems to remember that he is in fact our most important and number one employee." With that parting shot, Stubbs tendered his resignation "with the sincere hope that the Council can quickly find a way to put its house in order before it is too late."

The board met to consider these charges. Stubbs, though invited, did not attend the meeting. McCown addressed the group, noting that in order to do an adequate job in the field, which sometimes required risking his life, he must know where he stood with his governing board. He assured the board that if Stubbs had spoken to him about any problem he felt existed, immediate action would have been taken and he insisted that one way or the other the board should take action on Stubbs's charges that day. As for the books, the Georgia Council was the only Human Relations Council in the country audited by a certified public accountant on a monthly basis, he added. "I and all of the employees of the council are bonded and should be expected to go to jail in the event of theft or fraud. In the past, organizations in the South have been surviving on philosophy alone, without one exhibit to justify their existence. The council decided it was time some group created a real, live exhibit of economic progress through human relations. We decided that Hancock County would be such an exhibit."

McCown went on to address the meeting at length. He thought the Southern Regional Council was better equipped to handle information work and the Georgia Council should go ahead with its new role that took it into fish farming, concrete-block plants, and other programs to help the poor. He reported that the Ford Foundation was favorably impressed with the Georgia Council's new direction in community organization and economic development. Other foundations were pleased also, he said.

McCown's strongest words came at the end. "There is one thing that board members must really consider at this point, particularly our white brothers and sisters. They've got to ask themselves from the depths of their hearts if they are really ready to set the black man free. I mean completely free, politically and economically, because if you are you must realize that when he reaches this degree of independence, he may very well tell you to go to hell."

The board voted to accept Stubbs's resignation and Mrs. Pendergrast moved that they give McCown a vote of confidence. Stubbs had said he would not meet together with McCown, that he would meet only with the board after they had accepted his (Stubbs's) resignation, adding that he had many more charges than the ones in his letter. As to that possibility, Marion Fraleigh commented, "I don't think the dialogue with Reverend Stubbs should be allowed to continue. The recommendations of this group should be sufficient." McCown had carried the day. He had other news for the board. "Even though we are not a political organization, we have been asked by leading civil rights groups to provide community organization and political education for John Lindsay in New York City and Carl Stokes in Cleveland, Ohio."[5]

Channels were now clear. McCown had the full backing of the board and was firmly in control. The Georgia Council was his instrument, one he used effectively as he gained complete dominance over a Georgia county. John Glustrom and Marion Fraleigh were his trusted aides.

The three were soon off to Washington and on that trip, $481,000 for the catfish project was approved by OEO. The money had not yet been released because accountants analyzed the project and found what they thought would be a shortage of funds around the sixth month of the project's operation. The Ford Foundation was asked for a $200,000 loan to eliminate that shortage. McCown met with Congressman Robert Stephens, whose district included Hancock County, to discuss the catfish project. The budget for the project was revised and submitted in person to James Draper of OEO. Later in the fall, Glustrom, McCown, and Becky Becker, incoming president of the council, went to New York to visit foundations. Glustrom told the council the Field Foundation had increased its grant from $15,000 to $25,000; the Norman Foundation was adding $2,000 to its grant. Becker found the fund-raising trip "a wonderful experience." She was "very proud of the way Mr. McCown and Mr. Glustrom handled themselves while talking to the key people of the foundations."[6]

By the time of the December 1969 meeting even the energetic McCown was beginning to falter a little. He explained that he had started many projects and had hired many people but the responsibility was always falling on him. He complained that OEO had given a small sum to start the concrete-block plant, but local blacks were not interested enough to take the initiative and "to the white people of Hancock County the plant stands as a failure. Many people in Hancock County, both black and white, are skeptical and discouraged about the progress and strength of the council in its activities to date." He suggested that the annual meeting of the council be held in Sparta as a show of strength.[7]

So, for the first time in its history the council held an annual meeting as guest of a local chapter. Sparta's white postmaster, R. A. McCaskill, gave the welcoming address as the sessions began in January 1970.[8] Historically, white postmasters, like black undertakers, have been freer than most citizens of local racial pressures in small Deep South towns. McCaskill served for a while on ECCO's board of directors. The white sheriff, J. T. Walton, was originally scheduled to make the address but did not do so for unexplained reasons. Walton had skillfully walked between the opposing black and white groups in the county and had survived, although many whites regarded him as a member of the McCown camp.

66

Among the more interesting speakers was the man chosen to get the catfish farm going, Robert Lindsay, a white Alabamian and catfish farmer for thirty-four years. He had come to Hancock County, he said, to do what he did best—"fish farming." McCown had used all his powers of persuasion, and some money too, to get him to come. Finally consenting to visit the site near the Ogeechee, Lindsay was convinced. "I believe in what Mr. McCown is trying to do and now I feel that I am ready to spend the rest of my life just helping people the best I can." A tall, blue-eyed man, Lindsay said he and a man in Cordele, Georgia, were the first two people in the South who catfish farmed. He had come that very month in the harsh January weather to live with his wife in a trailer at the catfish farm. "I'll stay until the farm is going, then leave," he later said.

Gilbert LaFon, county housing consultant, brought word that the city of Sparta had turned down a federal housing program of three hundred homes. His report did not say so, but local whites, having lost control of county government in the 1968 elections, had no intention of moving large numbers of blacks into the town of Sparta, where whites still had political control.

Glustrom took the occasion to write an open letter to members praising McCown.

Mr. McCown has provided us with superb creative leadership, dynamic, courageous, and effective. The magnitude of human relations in the South, as we all know, poses problems nearly overwhelming in scope. In spite of the threats to his safety, even to his life, and attempts to destroy his reputation, Mr. McCown steadily hewed to our goal of racial cooperation and a philosophy of brotherly love. He has not become unduly hostile or bitter even under the most serious provocations. He has shown a great drive to help the unfortunate and a beautiful creativity in ways to achieve these purposes.

Who else could have faced the enormous odds and achieve election in Hancock County? Who else could have seen the possibilities in the catfish breeding program? Who else could have operated the Georgia Council programs and have the time and ability to become one of the nation's most informed persons on catfish farming? Who else could have struggled, pleaded, and even forced funding of $481,000 for this program? Who else can now start it off successfully? Who else could have achieved such improvement of opportunity and life in Hancock County with benefits and effectiveness spreading to the Oconee District of seven counties and throughout the entire state of Georgia? I need not go on and on. At this point let us all join in thankfulness that John McCown is with us and that he has made so many of our desired goals into realities.[9]

The council, through McCown, was already involved in so many activities it could not keep up with them and at the Sparta meeting it added still more. The first step seemed simple enough. The executive committee, presided over by the new president, Becky Becker, voted to buy land to set up the ECCO program at a price not exceeding $200 an acre. It also voted to buy a theater building in Sparta for $15,000 and to transfer $25,000 to the general fund for the block plant.[10] A few months later at the March meeting, McCown reported that Mrs. Arthur Reynolds, who had earlier decided the block plant was too dusty for Mayfield, now wanted to sell some land. OEO would make the purchase, McCown said, but the land would belong to ECCO.[11] It was not until June that the executive committee approved specific land purchases: 358.5 acres of Reynolds land for $86,032, over 200 acres of land from Jesse A. Jackson, a white Hancock farmer and businessman, for $40,896, and 100 acres of Hill land for $17,500.[12]

The minutes did not show that the land had already been bought and in somewhat different circumstances from those indicated in the record. Apparently, members of the executive committee were not informed that the council had already bought the Reynolds land on April 21 from Rural Improvement Corporation, headed by Glustrom. According to records in the Hancock Clerk of Court's office, that corporation had bought it from Mrs. Reynolds. Nothing indicated that Glustrom made a profit on it. Jesse Jackson's land was another matter. Glustrom bought that land a year earlier, in 1969, as president of the R.L.B. Corporation. In January 1970 the R.L.B. Corporation changed its name to E.R.T. Inc., and the next month the new corporation sold the land to the council for $40,511. Jackson would not say what he was paid for it, according to the *Atlanta Constitution*. The warranty deed did not reveal, as required by Georgia law, a transfer tax reflecting a purchase price. Pioneer National Title Insurance insured the title for $20,145. Glustrom later denied profiting on his land dealings for the council. He said he had spent more in his work for the council and ECCO than he had received. He also told reporters he did not have the records from

1969 and could not say what the R.L.B. Corporation paid for the land.[13]

McCown's contacts in Washington, D.C., continued to pay off. He told the council he had just returned from the capital, having learned where two million dollars in unexpended funds were located. Representatives from the state OEO office were going with him to see if some of this money could be allocated to Georgia. ECCO would soon receive $100,000 from OEO for loans to catfish farmers, and the Ford Foundation expected to act on a $1.6 million loan to ECCO, he told the executive committee in June.

The money tree was in full bloom.

6

The Catfish Farm

"It was the biggest fish fry
in the area since the days
of Gene Talmadge, who told poor folks,
'You've got three friends—God,
Sears Roebuck and me.'"
—*Augusta Chronicle*

The catfish farm was built in a hurry on Reynolds land near May-field. It was supposed to be the largest catfish farm in the world and it lay near the Ogeechee River in one of the oldest settled parts of the county. The Reynolds family had been important in Hancock County a long time. Back in 1883, when few local people had any money, the Reynoldses joined David Dickson in helping finance the completion of the new courthouse. Dickson put up $12,000 for courthouse bonds, J. P. Reynolds bought $1,000 worth, and his brother Jesse $2,000 worth. Old tales say Dickson carried the courthouse key in his pocket until he was repaid. One of the Reynoldses' creations, a magnificent Victorian home built after the Civil War, was bought and restored in the 1970s by author Joe David Brown, whose book *Addie Pray* was made into the film *Paper Moon*. Now a commercial hunting preserve, the estate is called Covey Rise.

Mayfield flourished into the 1950s as the center for Reynolds activities. Clarence Reynolds and Arthur Reynolds, Sr., developed over the years a bustling community with cotton gins, cotton warehouses, saw-mills, and peach-packing sheds and kept the little station of the Georgia Railroad at Mayfield busy shipping cotton, lumber, and peaches. But when John McCown arrived on the scene, Mayfield was almost dead. The cotton fields were growing up in timber and the peach orchards had disappeared. Some whites were critical of Mrs. Arthur Reynolds's decision to sell land to McCown; others felt her motive was to help the people of the community.

McCown planned the fish farm as the cornerstone of his empire. It was typical of his casual business methods that although ECCO had been winning grants and running businesses for many months, the catfish farm was not incorporated until June 8, 1970, a few weeks before its grand opening.[1] The incorporators were Nathaniel Dickson and James Henry Jones, both black residents of Hancock County and employees of McCown. The main policy of the organization was to "revitalize a rural area through social and economic progress, stemming the flow of its people into cities."

Soon thereafter, ECCO caused the biggest traffic jam in Mayfield's history. Nearly three thousand people crowded into town on a blistering hot Sunday, July 26, 1970, for the widely advertised free catfish fry, which was supposed to have been held at the catfish ponds nearby. Plans had to be changed, however, after the tail-end of Hurricane Becky turned that area into a bog. A large banner strung across the front of the courthouse in Sparta had announced the free fish fry for days. *Atlanta Constitution* reporter Terrence Adamson noted that the *Sparta Ishmaelite* had limited its announcement of the event to three inches but had put it on the front page.[2] One reporter said it was the biggest fish fry in the area since the days of Gene Talmadge, who told poor folks, "You've got three friends—God, Sears Roebuck and me."[3]

John Glustrom was on hand, described in news account as an Atlanta businessman who had been treasurer of the Georgia Council for the past twenty-two years. He told reporters ECCO was a co-op venture "that people may join, owning a share in it and voting on the price paid for their product." According to the account in the *Augusta Chronicle* of July 29, 1970, McCown told the crowd, "This can put $325,000 yearly back into the county, into the credit union which is set up to lend money to farmers and small businessmen. You should join ECCO and work with others. Also this catfish farm is a goose and lays golden eggs, but you've got to take care of the goose and not kill it. If you do that it will lay golden eggs for years to come."

Dr. Earl Evans, a black advisor to the project, provided catfish for the first fish fry from his Arkansas farm, since the ECCO farm could not yet produce enough. The physical plant stood ready, including ponds and cages for breeding fish, five hundred raceways, and a thirty-acre reservoir capable of impounding twenty feet of water. The ponds were fed by the Ogeechee River and a creek. Robert Lindsay explained that the fish would be fed with protein pellets and harvested when they reached about twelve pounds. "We will build a processing plant with money loaned by the Ford Foundation," the Augusta paper reported Lindsay as saying. "It has approved a $500,000 grant. Some fish will be sold alive in tanks of water, others in frozen five or ten-pound packages, say to restaurants, and there will probably be small one-pound packages also. ECCO is in negotiation with a small food store for its product."

Hurricane Becky had cleared the air and the fish fry turned out to be a big success. The *New York Times* sent Thomas A. Johnson to cover it and on July 28 ran photographs of Harvey Evans in a black power T-shirt holding one of the blue catfish. Tom Rushing, a local white merchant, and Cleveland Dargan, black athletic coach at a nearby high school, displayed hush puppies and catfish for the camera. Dargan and Rushing cooked on the front porch of what had been Mayfield's general store. They told Johnson they were up the night before barbecuing two hogs, and they planned to cook 2,000 pounds of catfish before the festivities were over.

Earlier in the day, Edith Ingram cleaned the store with the aid of dungaree-clad local women, Johnson said. In addition to six pots of sizzling catfish and hush puppies, a small mountain of bread was piled on a nearby table, where young girls set up large buckets of potato salad. Three men manning a Coca-Cola truck worked steadily, filling paper cups with ice and Coke.

Other fish were frying that hot summer. After two years on the Hancock board of commissioners, McCown had decided he would not run for office again, telling reporter Terrence Adamson it was because of "battle-weariness."[4] As Father Ford, McCown's friend on the Georgia Council, once observed, McCown told people only what he wanted them to know. Local blacks said he decided not to run because holding political office conflicted with his job as executive director of the Georgia Council, a supposedly nonpolitical organization, and his overt political activity might create problems for other agencies such as the Ford Foundation. These agencies all enjoyed tax advantages under United States laws that might be lost. The large foundations often came under attack from various quarters and were sensitive to charges of using their tax-exempt grants for political purposes. It did not matter whether McCown served on the commission or not; he intended to run it anyway.

McCown told Adamson he was thinking about going to law school after retiring from public office that fall, but Hancock would still be his home. Meanwhile, he jumped into a bitter battle to defeat James Smith, the first black on the county commission, who had outraged him by accepting the chairmanship of the commission and by working too closely with the white community. He told the reporter that "Uncle Tom" was too nice a description for Smith. Edith Ingram said, "Smith turned white." McCown blamed his battle with Smith on disagreement over a corporation McCown organized to administer federal funds for low-cost housing.

Despite the conflict, McCown and Ingram assured Adamson of some real accomplishments as a result of black participation in county government. "For the first time blacks realize there is a county commission," Ingram declared. McCown said most Negroes never realized there was a relationship between the welfare department and the county commission. He gave Adamson a typical bit of McCown philosophy: "Instead of trying to change the heart of the lady at the welfare department, it's better to get in a position to be her boss." McCown also said he noticed a real change in attitudes toward the county sheriff's department. "Instead of here comes hell, people are beginning to think here comes help."

Writing in July, Adamson found a minimum of actual hostility and racial confrontation. Few, if any, white family groups had moved out of the county, and while one white official had heard some talk about it, he was not aware of any who actually had left. Most felt as the official did, "Everything I've got is right here."

Hancock was one of eighty-one school districts in Georgia ordered to discontinue a dual school system and to submit a plan by March 1, 1970. The white-dominated school board (whites were in the majority on it until 1971) offered essentially a freedom-of-choice plan similar to one the courts had earlier accepted for Caddo Parish, Louisiana. In order to keep the few remaining white students, the school board proposed that all whites be concentrated in the Sparta Center and blacks be limited to 42 percent of enrollment there. They pointed out that of Hancock's 2,642 pupils, 2,384 were black and 258 white. The proportion of blacks in the system stood then at 91.3 percent, the highest in Georgia. A total of 258 white and 153 Negro students attended Sparta School Center. White teachers at the school, the board explained, were either long-time residents of the county or else commuted from distances of more than twenty miles.

"Two white teachers do not plan to return to the system under any circumstances," the report added. "Twenty will not accept employment if assigned to other than the Sparta Center. The Hancock System has had immense problems securing white teachers who will teach in desegregated situations. The system could get white teachers for Hancock Central only through the College of Education at the University of Georgia and most of these whites did it as part of their graduate work." [5]

In July, as McCown was playing host at the first big fish fry at Mayfield and getting ready for a political campaign to oust Smith, the courts ordered a plan that basically accepted the school board's proposal. The court plan provided for retaining all whites in the Sparta School Center and integrating faculties in all three schools of the system. The United States Court for the Northern District of Georgia later denied objections filed against the plan, and the case was carried to the Fifth Circuit Court of Appeals, where it was again upheld. [6]

Residents of Hancock County, kept constantly stirred up and emotionally heated by McCown's tactics, even so were late building up to the national mood of intense racial feeling. Beginning with the Watts riots in Los Angeles in 1965, the United States suffered increasingly hot summers in the late 1960s. The world saw television films of smoke billowing over the nation's capital city as black ghettoes went up in flames. More than a hundred cities had riots by 1967, leaving eighty-three persons dead and 1,897 injured, with hundreds of millions of dollars in property damage. Though no one was killed in Hancock, feelings were more intensely personal in a small community, where everybody knew everybody else.

The federal court's decision allowed Hancock's handful of whites to stay together at the Sparta Center, where they would be a minority taught by blacks, but McCown said that would not be enough. He insisted that whites be parceled out, spread out through each classroom, one white raisin in each cake. Blacks demanded a unitary school system. The board replied that if they honored these demands, they would be in contempt of a federal court order.

When the United States Court of Appeals for the Fifth District affirmed the district court's dismissal of a complaint against the Hancock school plan, McCown got his youth group together and set in motion his carefully planned psychological warfare. First came a scattering of newspaper stories about young blacks meeting at Sparta and planning demonstrations. McCown informed the press of the "very dangerous and very tense" situation.[7]

Then he turned to his own image for, along with quite a few Georgia politicians before him, he knew the value of a little show business. Like Governor Eugene Talmadge, whose red suspenders brightened many a political rally in the depression years, John McCown understood about dressing for the occasion. He was known to disappear from a long meeting and return in a different suit, telling friends at the Georgia Council he needed to maintain an image of success. But for demonstrations he produced another costume, a pair of ragged overalls with one strap missing and the legs cut off like Li'l Abner's. McCown was heating up the fire, preparing for marches in August immediately before the 1970 primaries. He was cutting off the legs of his overalls that summer, getting ready to march.

Black employees of the school system told the board they would not report to work until their demands for a unitary system, as they defined it, were met. On August 22, a series of demonstrations began that continued for twenty-nine days. Three days after the demonstrations commenced, the board held an emergency meeting and voted to postpone school for two weeks. One white board member, subject to much financial pressure from the black community because of his business, resigned. He had been one of the more conciliatory whites, seeking mediation. At the end of the emergency meeting, the board dispatched the superintendent to announce its decision to a great gathering of citizens, black and white, at the courthouse.[8]

During the four years of confrontations since McCown's arrival in the county, he had always been the dominant figure representing the black community. There were plenty of leaders out there, men like Marvin Lewis, the principal at Hancock Central who had led the voter registration, but McCown managed to dominate the scene. If the black movement had to be personalized, it was McCown who did that. He provided the drama. On the white side, no one stood out in the confrontations. There were men like Marvin Moate, a veteran of twenty-

75

five years in the General Assembly and a former speaker of that body, and men like W. M. "Red" Andrews, school superintendent, and Dr. George F. Green, mayor and commissioner, but they did not symbolize a white position in the way that McCown represented the blacks. When confrontations moved to the streets, McCown found the antagonist he needed in Sparta's Mayor T. M. "Buck" Patterson, who succeeded Dr. Green in that post.

Hancock's white community is predominantly old and female, with relatively few vigorous white males in their middle years. Buck Patterson became the symbol for those who wanted somebody out on the streets to counter McCown's hundreds of young toughs. Patterson, like McCown, was of medium height and stocky, built like a fighter. Son of a building contractor, Patterson came to Sparta in the 1930s at age fourteen to join the local CCC camp (Franklin Roosevelt's Civilian Conservation Corps was designed to give jobs to unemployed young men and to do work like soil conservation). Like McCown, he was originally from South Carolina. He was much too young to join the CCC but his brother signed for him. A good athlete, he played baseball well enough to win a contract from the New York Yankees at age seventeen but, according to an interview he gave the *Macon Telegraph* (June 10, 1974), he jumped the contract after being sent to a minor league team in Montgomery, Alabama. He came back to Sparta to marry a local girl, Sarah Roberts, in 1938.

Eventually he returned to baseball for more than ten years. "He turned down offers to coach professional baseball clubs and an offer to become a professional fighter, but later he coached Little League teams in Sparta," the *Telegraph* said. During World War II, Patterson, a Marine sergeant, saw action in the Pacific, including the invasion of Guam. After the war he settled in Sparta, raising a son and three daughters and becoming a successful mortician. One of the founders of John Hancock Academy, the private school, he coached its girls' basketball team to many victories.

Patterson first remembered meeting McCown when Helen Miller, then county ordinary, called police to the courthouse where McCown had "cussed and raised hell," according to Patterson. Patterson described the incident in John Wayne terms. "I had a gun. McCown said if I would take it off he would take me on. I took it off and he backed down."

76

Patterson was willing to get out and mix it up on the streets, but most of the white community preferred to close their shops and go home, leaving Broad Street to the demonstrators. The marches occasionally provided a touch of comic opera. A man who served in the Sparta police department at the time said he learned about the first march a week before it was to happen and asked the mayor for his plans. He was told, "We will play it by ear." Sparta's four full-time policemen were to be supplemented by thirty-four auxiliaries, but only fifteen auxiliaries showed up on the day. After a big rally at the courthouse, some three hundred blacks gathered across the street. Four policemen and four auxiliaries went to observe while television cameras hired by McCown recorded the scene.

"McCown and the mayor exchanged shouts," the former policeman said. "The mayor said they could not march without a parade permit. McCown threw up his hands as a signal and they proceeded to sing and march. They walked right around us. The mayor had planned to use the fire hose on the crowd but the fire truck wouldn't start. Then he said to arrest McCown, so the police chief and I grabbed John and walked him down to the police station. When I asked if he was under arrest, nobody could tell me so I dropped his hand. As the tail end of the crowd went past, the firemen finally got the hose out. Just a trickle of water came out of the hose and that trickle fell on the police. It was a comical disaster."

The state ordered thirty troopers into Sparta following that first march. The Associated Press said the patrolmen were sent from nearby posts after Mayor Patterson telephoned Governor Lester Maddox's office to ask for help.[9] A State Patrol spokesman said the marchers pushed Patterson and two city policemen aside as the policemen attempted to read to them a city ordinance barring unauthorized public marches. After a scuffle the blacks, the spokesman said, marched down the main street, blocking traffic along the way. The *Atlanta Constitution* sent its education editor, Mike Bowler, to the scene. Bowler reported in the August 28 edition that several hundred blacks had marched Thursday for the sixth night in a row protesting a desegregation plan "that retains both Hancock County high schools and concentrates all the whites in one." He said the march from the courthouse through downtown Sparta appeared peaceful, though "several marchers wore holstered weapons." Sparta police and state troopers kept a watchful eye on the march through the deserted streets. The only whites who observed other than the police officers were two service station attendants in front of a sign: "Going out of business Sept. 19."

As they were calculated to do, the demonstrations, coupled with a boycott of the stores, closed down business in Sparta. Many demonstrators and organizers were employees of ECCO, the county government, and the school system. Sparta's merchants found themselves in the interesting position of financing, through their federal tax dollars, boycotts against themselves.

The fire hose that figured in that first march did more than drizzle a few drops on the Sparta police. It sprinkled one prominent white man's cook and left her so disgruntled he said she never smiled again. He thought McCown made her march; whites were reluctant to believe their long-time servants could turn militant. Another supposedly unwilling marcher, Marvin Lewis, then principal of Central High, walked in the parade but toward the end of the line. He supported moderate James Smith and had tried to stay out of McCown's total grasp. Police used a mild form of mace that day and, as someone said, it blinded Lewis temporarily but angered him permanently. A few days later all black teachers voted not to report to work on the appointed date, already delayed two weeks. Blacks, including principals, teachers, bus drivers, and students, said they would continue their boycott until the federal court-ordered plan was scrapped.

Superintendent Andrews, whose coffin was carried in the parades, told reporters, "Even the courts have recognized that whites would not remain in the public schools where the ratio is 28–2 black to white. Since the daily demonstrations began a significant number of whites have withdrawn their children from the public schools, trying to get them into private schools or sending them to live with relatives and attend school in other counties. We had only eight percent whites in the schools and that's diminishing." [10]

Marvin Lewis told the *Atlanta Constitution* (Sept. 3, 1970), "Thursday will be a dark day in Hancock County because we are not going back. It's time for educators to stop worrying about their paychecks and get concerned about the education of their children." Lewis told the reporter he had been sprayed with mace. McCown announced that blacks would use "physical force" if the board of education tried to replace black teachers in the boycott. Lewis, McCown, and Ingram charged that the black community had not been consulted in drawing up the plan. "We've always been ignored," said Lewis, according to the *Atlanta Journal* report (Sept. 3, 1970). "But we've been walked on too long and for the first time we are not afraid to express ourselves."

The month-long 1970 demonstrations came to an end at last when a federal three-judge panel ordered the schools to resume operations and named school officials and John McCown as codefendants in a United States Justice Department desegregation suit against Georgia (*Atlanta Constitution*, Sept. 15, 1970). The judges enjoined McCown and school officials from interfering with the court order and rejected a plan submitted by McCown's attorney which was the same McCown idea of a unitary school system. The orders were given in Atlanta before 150 blacks who came up from Hancock for the hearing. At the close of the hearing, McCown told reporters he could not say whether the court order would result in an end to the student-teacher Negro boycott of the schools.

McCown claimed that his goal was to oppose any form of segregation. What he accomplished was an exchange of partial integration for a return to total segregation. Surrounding counties, all with majority black populations in their public schools, were able to solve their school problems and retain a considerable segment of whites. McCown's efforts to move into Baldwin and Greene counties were rebuffed by local black leaders.

After they gave up on the public schools, Hancock's tiny white community eventually built a modern school on the outskirts of Sparta. Many of them in modest circumstances, they erected the school at great personal sacrifice and they continued to finance it with tuition, gifts, and dinners. The cost was a heavy burden for middle- and low-income families. In addition to tuition, parents also provided books and transportation, which were free in the public schools, where most pupils also received free lunches and breakfasts. The private academies that sprang up across the Black Belt in the 1960s were scornfully called "segregationist academies," and that was undeniably the principal reason for their existence, but there were other reasons. Many parents felt concern about the totally secular nature of the public schools as a result of Supreme Court decisions. In the Protestant rural South, by custom public schools had been partners of the Protestant churches and the return to private academies in the Black Belt was a return to a tradition the people had always believed in.

After whites had abandoned the public schools, McCown paid a call one day on John Dickens, headmaster at John Hancock Academy. "He came to see me to put his child in school," said Dickens. "McCown deliberately came at noon so the children would all see him. We were very polite to each other but I did ask who the man with him was and expressed my surprise when he said he was his bodyguard. I said I was not afraid of blacks or integration, having taught in integrated schools and having gone to school with blacks, and I felt safe in any neighborhood in Hancock County. I couldn't understand anybody's need for a bodyguard here.

"I told him I would be glad to accept his son's application but I felt it was unwise for a black leader to put his child in a private school. He said his child was as smart as any at John Hancock and he knew because he had seen grades white children made in public school before they transferred. I said I wished I hadn't heard that because such information was required by law to be kept private, and he and someone else had obviously violated the law. He said to forget about the grades. After he left I never heard any more about his child's application."

Blacks and whites in retrospect held widely varied opinions about the school troubles. A retired black teacher recalled the accomplishments of local blacks in the cruel days when nearly all of the tax money was spent on whites, and blacks walked to shanty schools and used textbooks already worn out by white students. "In those days Hancock County was noted over the state for blacks grasping for an education," she said. "Ben Hubert was president of Savannah State College. C. L. Harper was the executive secretary of the black teachers association for Georgia [GTEA] for many years. Henry Hunt founded Fort Valley State College. They were all raised right here."

"My grandchildren went to the integrated schools for two or three years," a retired white teacher recalled. "My son said we had to learn to live with Negroes. My grandchildren finally left the public schools because they had some colored teachers who could not teach. The children were afraid they would be so poorly taught they could not go to college. I'm still pessimistic about the public schools. I would not have minded teaching with black teachers but I want them to be capable."

80

A conservative black leader felt the demonstrations frightened whites and chased them into the private school. "If we had waited it would have been better, like in other counties. Sandersville is getting along with many of their middle class children in the public schools."

In the midst of the school disputes, McCown selected George Lott to run against James Smith for the commission in the 1970 election. Lott had been a leader in the school demonstrations and was later on McCown's payroll as assistant manager of the ECCO block plant. Johnny Warren, another ECCO employee, was chosen to have McCown's old seat. McCown's group won in the September 9 primary, with Lott defeating Smith and Warren getting more votes than a local druggist. During the campaign, the McCown faction was repeatedly accused of threatening to burn people out and to cut off their welfare.

"I went in with the idea that we could work together," Smith said later. "Dr. Green and I worked well together. We got more done for everybody in the county than has been done since. The first two years McCown trusted me but later he grew angry when I wouldn't go along with everything he wanted. We wanted to have a part in our local government. The new group wanted to have the entire government and they just put the whites out."

McCown was particularly vindictive toward Smith, calling his wife "Aunt Jane" at public gatherings and Smith an "Uncle Tom" at church meetings. McCown told officials at Central State Hospital in Milledgeville that Smith held public office and could not hold a job legally at the state-operated institution. Smith had to resign and was appointed night watchman at the Sparta hospital by Dr. Green. Later, when McCown gained control of the local hospital, he fired Smith, boasting he would "make a good nigger" out of him and have him crawling to him on his knees. The Smiths had to take their daughters out of the public schools and put them in a private academy out of the county because they were severely harassed by McCown supporters.

The minutes of the Georgia Council meeting in Sparta in November gave no hint of all this. Glustrom introduced McCown to the gathering saying, "What he has done is not surpassed in Georgia by anyone. He has performed small miracles in attracting huge sums of money to operate businesses in Hancock County. These businesses are owned and operated by the people of the county. If the people of Hancock County operate and take care of these businesses now, these same businesses will take care of them and their children in the years to come. If each county had a John McCown the state would find its way to brotherhood."[11]

McCown's lengthy report informed the group that ECCO was the umbrella over all of their projects and that articles about ECCO had appeared in the *Berlin Times*, the *New York Times* and *Newsweek*.[12] The articles had attracted the attention of a group from London, England, which came and did eight days of filming about the progress the county was making. He reported on the operation of the ECCO Theater, the only cinema in the county, and the ECCO American Service Station run by blacks on Sparta's main street. ECCO had bought the theater at McCown's insistence and over the objections of Paul Anthony, director of the Southern Regional Council, who thought food for hungry children was more important than buying the decrepit theater. The theater, however, had symbolic importance to McCown, who was strong on symbolism. It was in the heart of white man's territory on Broad Street, and it had for years segregated blacks in a steamy hot balcony. McCown also enjoyed telling how he had to go to the white owner's back door to negotiate the purchase.

The ECCO concrete-block plant was running in the red, McCown informed the gathering, because the city of Sparta refused to run the water line a few hundred feet to the plant. "At first the city said it did not have the money to run the water down there. We offered to loan the city the money; then they said they didn't have time to dig the needed trench; we offered to dig the trench but this offer has not been accepted. As a result we have no water at the plant." Sparta officials said later they were always willing to run a line to the plant but McCown refused to pay for the large size they insisted on.

ECCO had purchased a grocery store in Mayfield, which McCown said he planned to make the largest supermarket in the county, but his comment about it hinted at a problem. "We are now working on bringing our prices back in line" (they were probably too high). Everything else was going well. ECCO now owned 1,500 acres of land in Mayfield and the town was being developed "to show what can happen when blacks and whites are only concerned about people." McCown claimed that the ECCO Catfish Farm "is the largest inland catfish project in the United States." A new program with raceways and farm pond culture would increase profits enormously from the original goal of $325,000 a year to a projected $1,325,000 by 1973–74, he said.

McCown involved himself in every aspect of the community. "We tried to buy one of the local banks," he said, "but it was not for sale. We could not get a license to establish another bank because the county does not need another one." He had attempted to buy Sparta's second bank, the M. G. Pound Bank, then privately held. The Ford Foundation and the government were being generous and enthusiastic, he said. "The Ford Foundation gave $481,000 last month and signed an agreement for $850,000 in addition. They have already given $200,000 and any portion of the remainder may be acquired within seven days notice." Golden leaves were also falling from the money tree in Washington, D.C. (When you went with McCown to that big OEO building in Washington, everybody there knew his name, said a Georgia politician.) "The government wants to expand ECCO into seven other counties because of the general interest ECCO has generated. A proposal for a $600,000 expansion of the catfish project has already been approved," he said. "We have a loan fund of $250,000 for an eight-county area. We also have a proposal for a multi-purpose community center which will be valued at $1.5 million. An application for eight hundred homes in Hancock County has been approved on the regional level. I have applied for a license to operate an FM radio station in Hancock County and it has been approved on the local level and is being argued on the national level in Washington." (Carl Vinson, who served in Congress longer than any other man before retiring to his home in Milledgeville across the Oconee River, was said to have killed the radio project.)

The Ford Foundation made it possible to set up a MESBIC (Minority Enterprise Small Business Investment Corporation), McCown said, providing $200,000 and an additional $1,000 for overhead. The MESBIC and the Georgia Council office would be located in the Citizens Trust Building in Atlanta, he added. "It is now time for the state office to get involved in areas other than economic development," he concluded. "We are ready to do whatever is necessary to straighten out this sick society."

Back of the rosy forecasts were hints of a financial situation that would get worse, not better. As of September 30, 1970, auditors indicated the catfish farm had already lost $77,548, its expenses including

$10,313 for consultants and $20,721 for travel. All of the ECCO businesses, in fact, lost money.[13] The bewildering array of projects the council was involved in, principally through ECCO, was put together without much planning. The catfish farm was a faddish project popular with foundations and government agencies at the time, and the concrete-block plant made sense in terms of a local market only, because of transportation costs. The other businesses were acquired haphazardly; the theater, for instance, was bought for emotional reasons. McCown created some businesses as a tactic used, along with boycotts, to pressure white merchants. ECCO functioned somewhat like a chain letter; it survived only by expansion. It produced little or nothing and could survive only so long as grants and public relations efforts kept it afloat.

One of the most effective propaganda pieces of the McCown organization came about by accident. Attracted by publicity about ECCO, a British television company, Thames Productions, spent several days filming a program on the county. Months later two large metal containers arrived at the Sparta post office from London, one addressed to McCown and another to George Rives, conservative white landowner. Nothing remains secret in a small town. Edith Ingram knew that the whites had a copy of the film and she also knew that it was not shown or publicly talked about in the white community. Whites later claimed that the British television people had selected the most damaging quotes from them and the most favorable ones from the blacks. At any rate, the film was a highly unsympathetic portrayal of local whites. One of them said indignantly, "They went up to the north end of the county and found some old man nobody had ever heard of and used the most ignorant and vicious quotes from him."

Veterans of the old ECCO organizations remembered the film eight years later and most of them mentioned the man as if he spoke for the white community. Edith Ingram was among them. Al Horn spoke of him in Atlanta. For propaganda purposes, he proved to be the multipurpose image of a Hancock County white man. The London television crew filmed the farmer feeding his chickens and saying, "The niggers are taking over everything. If one comes and knocks on your door and says he is going to stay all night you can't do nothing about it. Would you want a nigger to come in and sleep with you? The son-of-a-bitch better not come in my front door. If he do he'll get a bullet in him." The London film makers led the old man on, having found the prize they sought. "What would happen if a member of the Klan were assaulted by a black man?" they asked. "I don't know," he replied. "They might lynch his ass. I don't know what they would do. And old John McCown, the lowdown son-of-a-bitch needs killing."

"They left out the important things we had to say," one white claimed. What was left was a propaganda film that McCown delighted in showing to newsmen, foundation officials, and other visitors to his headquarters at Mayfield. Some of the remarks local whites made to the Londoners resembled those heard earlier all over the region as the civil rights movement began. Said one, "I don't think they were born and raised here. I don't think they know anything about how the whites and blacks feel here. I have a maid that has worked for me almost forty-eight years that I love. They are just outsiders and should go back where they came from."

"The whole idea of integration was thought up to keep the Negro in the South," said a local man. "He is not wanted in the North. It is political, pure and simple. They are trying to make it so advantageous locally and anywhere south of the Mason-Dixon line he will want to stay here." "The problem is," said the British commentator, "that the white man sees little evidence that his interests are being protected in plans for the brave new tomorrow and he has reached the state where he regards every change as a change for the worse."

"They speak about black people as possessions," said Ingram, discussing the film. "They still think of us as possessions. . . . I know a lot of whites don't care for me but I believe they have more respect for me standing up for what I believe than they do for blacks who sell themselves and their people for a few dollars. They are using them and they are going to kick them in the ass and not care any more about them than they do the rest of us."

7

The Arms Race

"The dream shattered into a million pieces."
—*President of the Georgia Council
on Human Relations*

McCown loved theater. One of his first extracurricular activities in the Air Force was to perform in *The Caine Mutiny* at Mitchell Air Force Base.[1] He liked to put on a good show and he enjoyed bragging about his toughness, boasting to reporters, "We've got more guns and better people. We're meaner and we're smarter."[2] And so the great arms race started. In the spring of 1971, Mayor Buck Patterson announced that Sparta citizens had bought ten submachine guns for use by the city police department. Patterson said city officials frequently heard automatic weapons being fired at night and were concerned for the safety of citizens. Phil Gailey of the *Washington Star* recalled that when he was a reporter for the *Atlanta Constitution* and visited McCown at his brick ranch house in Sparta, "McCown went to the basement and showed me a submachine gun. I was frankly shocked. He went to his back yard and cut down a couple of pine saplings with it. This was at the beginning of the arms race."

"I'd get a lot of calls at night," said Patterson. "Thirty or forty blacks threatened to kill a policeman. There would be automatic weapons fire in different parts of town and the Georgia Bureau of Investigation and the FBI would come in. This was an armed camp but it was a standoff; we would protect blacks or whites. I had calls from all over the country, from sheriffs and police and businessmen saying, 'If you or your family get hurt we are coming in there.' We even had the Klan trying to come. I said no."

After a policeman was injured in a scuffle with a black, Patterson inserted a paid notice in the *Sparta Ishmaelite*. "Our police force is hired to protect the law-abiding citizens. . . . In the performance of

86

these duties, I do not intend to have them intimidated, slapped around or beaten. Policemen all over this country are putting their lives on the line each time they arrest a criminal and all this is for your protection." He said he had advised the police to "meet violence with full force."[3]

Private individuals contributed money for the machine guns. One man who gave told *Constitution* reporter Bill Shipp the money was originally collected to buy communications equipment for the Sparta police.[4] Never used for that purpose, it was eventually spent to buy the guns. McCown took full advantage of the propaganda value the guns brought him. He had the county order thirty submachine guns from a Florida arms dealer and leaked the story to the state press. Then he and Edith Ingram and Leroy S. Wiley, clerk of court, organized the Hancock County Sporting Rangers, sending out handbills to enlist members. The handbill encouraged the purchase of firearms and said financing could be arranged through Citizens Trust Bank, a black bank in Atlanta where McCown kept large amounts of government grant money on deposit. Among the guns the sportsmen were invited to purchase were M-1 rifles and 12-gauge automatic shotguns. While organizing this "sports" club, McCown and Ingram were still officers of the Georgia Council on Human Relations.

Ingram told Bill Shipp, "The Sporting Rangers is an organization to enhance sports such as hunting and fishing in the county since that is the only kind of recreation around here. I guess he [Mayor Patterson] thinks the Rangers were just organized to get him and his machine guns. That's the way most of the whites around here feel—anything you bring up that is new, they think it is just something to trap them" (*Atlanta Constitution*, Sept. 23, 1971). Later, Ingram said something quite different to Thomas A. Johnson of the *New York Times* (Oct. 17, 1971). "We couldn't have gotten the city to give up the guns if we had not pressured them with the threat of more guns, the hunting club and the boycott—not unless there was open warfare, of course."

Governor Jimmy Carter became involved when Patterson complained about the sporting organization and the thirty county submachine guns. Presumably under pressure from Carter, McCown gave up his guns on the condition that the city police would give up theirs. The county's guns had never been delivered. Many whites, including members of Sparta's city council, opposed the machine gun purchase by the city.

One councilman told the press he did not know about it until it was already done. Another young white businessman remarked, "We deeply regret all of this. It was an unwise decision—very bad. That isn't the kind of community this is" (AP story, *Atlanta Journal-Constitution*, Oct. 10, 1971). The Hancock County grand jury, with conservative whites among its leaders, asked the city aldermen to remove all machine guns from the city police force and to secure the services of proper authorities to find and remove all illegal submachine guns in the county (*Sparta Ishmaelite*, Oct. 7, 1971).

On October 1, 1971, the Sparta city council voted to give up the guns and Governor Carter announced that the arms race had ended, saying black and white leaders had met for several hours. "The County Commissioners have given us their purchase order for thirty machine guns and the City of Sparta has given the ten machine guns they had to the state patrol," he added (UPI in *New York Times*, Oct. 2, 1971). Patterson recalled later that he did not get a check immediately for the city's guns. He wrote to the governor and finally received the payment, which he donated to the private school.

Carter's efforts to end the gun race brought him a harsh letter from McCown. When under attack, McCown liked to wrap himself in the respectable robes of the Georgia Council and he wrote Carter on September 27, 1971, on Georgia Council stationery, signing as executive director. The letter went on for four pages of single-spaced typing, beginning: "I am writing in response to your letter of 22 September 1971 where you voiced your concern about the 'inflammatory situation' in Hancock County and to me as a responsible party. My reply is delayed for fear that I would speak out in anger, or in some way fail to give you the courtesy or proper respect deserved by the chief executive officer of the State of Georgia."

Carter had defeated Carl Sanders in the race for governor in the fall of 1970. He did it by sounding very much like a redneck candidate, even saying kind things about Alabama's segregationist Governor George Wallace, whom the Sanders group had given a very cold shoulder. Some of Carter's old friends complained during his campaign about its tenor; his reply to one was that he could not do much good if he did not get elected. Many Georgians were therefore understandably startled when the newly elected Governor Carter gave a very liberal inaugural address, promising a new day in Georgia with no place for segregation.

John McCown did not like to be kept waiting, and part of his annoyance with Carter dated from the time of his efforts to get an interview with the new governor right after the inauguration. He reminded the governor in his letter that he and "Mr. John Glustrom, treasurer of the Georgia Council for 19 years, . . . waited several weeks for the opportunity to visit with you early after your inauguration. . . ." McCown pointed out that he had given him his complete personal history and had asked Carter "to please use your influence on citizens of Hancock County in helping bridge the gap in communication that existed between black and white."

"Even though you have not made any contact with the Hancock County government or members of the black community, I wish to share the following facts with you," McCown wrote. The county government made no gun requests until it was "an established fact that at least 10 nine mm submachine guns were in the possession of Mayor T. M. 'Buck' Patterson without the authority of the City of Sparta and that these weapons were believed to have been used in violation of federal laws on peaceful demonstrators in Warren County, Georgia." McCown said he personally pleaded with officials of the city of Sparta to help avoid any trouble by returning the machine guns.

One paragraph in the McCown letter said,

News reports of your statement have implied that the Hancock County Sporting Rangers in some way provoked the gun situation. As a matter of fact its purpose of hunting, fishing and marksmanship was organized [*sic*] several months after the purchase of machine guns by the City of Sparta. It is not a violent oriented group in any way and I am sure that you are aware that hunting clubs are prevalent throughout the state "for whites only." However, our proposed club does not discriminate against race or sex. We used the term "Sporting rifles" while you insist upon the term "weapons." M-1 carbines are used quite frequently in connection with marksmanship competition and the ammunition is the least expensive on the market.

McCown went on to ask the governor:

Was an investigation not called for following the shooting of Warren County Negroes with submachine guns on loan from the Sparta police

89

department just a few months ago? These are the same guns that the press would lead the public to believe are still in their boxes and unused. I know better, sir, for I was awakened on the night of May 21, 1971 by leaders of the black community of Warren County, some crying that the sheriff and state troopers were firing at anything that moved, stating that their meeting place had been riddled by machine gun fire. I talked with one of these leaders again the next day after he had been beaten in jail with handcuffs used as brass knuckles. . . . Another young man, accused of leadership, was dragged from his mobile home and taken into town where he was beaten with fists and gun butts. He stated to me that he pleaded from a few feet away for his life as he was cut down by a charge of buckshot and a .38 slug from what he believed to be a state trooper's gun. With all these disturbing situations, sir, in Hancock County we somehow managed to keep our people under control, adhering to the principals [sic] of non-violence. Yet the white community is saying they see no wrong in their actions since their weapons were donated. What would your reaction have been, Sir, if the blacks in Hancock County had accepted a similar donation from the Black Panthers?

There was a final slap at Carter. "However, I cannot help but wonder, Governor Carter, if this entire problem might have been averted if my request of almost one year ago for your assistance in bridging the gap in communication in Hancock County had received the same priority as the present situation."[5]

If Carter or his staff had read the *New Republic* of March 6, 1971, they would have had a better understanding of McCown and the cynicism of his letter. The article in the *New Republic* was friendly to McCown, quoting him and Edith Ingram in a tone that could best be described as admiring. Explaining that the blacks were not going to oppose Sheriff J. T. "Slim" Walton, the article quoted Ingram as saying he was a reasonable man. It went on to say,

Sheriff Walton has one white and one black deputy and a score of other black deputized volunteers. This posse (ever heard of a black posse?) carrying a wild assortment of firearms, was sworn in at the height of desegregation demonstrations last fall by Judge Ingram. Miss Ingram also controls the issuing of gun licenses and has thus ended the traditional minority dominance of white over black in the Southern outback simply by reversing the preponderance of firepower. Judge Ingram herself keeps one pistol in her office, one in her car and two at home; she says she knows how to use them all. Yet only once have shots been fired in anger in Hancock, with no known casualties. "We got better people and more guns," grins John McCown, an articulate Atlanta-trained civil rightser who is de facto boss of the black movement in the county. "We're smarter and we're meaner." The blacks strut a lot, the whites scowl. The blacks have organized their own two-way radio network, with six base stations and fifteen mobile units; they fairly dare the State Patrol or Ku Klux Klan to start something in Hancock County.

The article continued,

The whites in Hancock, outnumbered as they are, have turned silent and angry and inward. Most of their children attend all-white John Hancock Academy instead of the public schools. Since they still control the town of Sparta, whites in store fronts openly insult outside reporters. The white-owned bank has begun refusing credit to blacks who demonstrated for a unitary school system last fall, and accelerated loan payments for others. John McCown and another black county official were forced to go to an Atlanta agency to obtain their bonds of office. Recently the Georgia Bureau of Investigation has been photographing election records in Judge Ingram's office and interviewing long-time black (and some other white) voters in what the Negro leadership calls an intimidation tactic.

No other persons were quoted in the article and the point of view of the McCown faction was apparently accepted without question. A local white expressed his feelings about the reporting. "McCown would talk to reporters but whites would chase them off. It was several years before we got a fair break. With some reporters you were guilty just because you were white. They swallowed McCown's propaganda whole."

Concerned about the deteriorating racial situation in the county, some fifty whites and one hundred and fifty blacks met at the courthouse. A local black who had lived in Philadelphia and had seen the hatred that developed from confrontation there spoke. He told the group how bad racial feelings had become in Philadelphia because of the stirring of hate. A white citizen described the meeting later as he remembered it. "John McCown came running in and took over the meeting," the man recalled. "He leaped up on the table and began to walk up and down shouting. He yelled at one of the white organizers, 'Why don't you move over there with your colored girl friend? You ain't nothing but a big fat buzzard, you ain't nothing but a son-of-a-bitch. Come on up here. I've been wanting to take a chunk out of your big fat ass ever since I came to Hancock.' He raved and ranted and screamed and shouted. A bunch of armed blacks came in with him. These boys [with him] were deputy sheriffs and if you burned one of them you burned the law. Finally the sheriff came in and broke up the meeting. It was the nearest to a jungle scene I have ever seen. That was my first and last biracial meeting. I had feeling for the black man I was raised up with but that night I lost it. I drove home with an empty feeling in my stomach. I felt like I was robbed and part of my life was taken away from me."

Struggles over the schools continued during the months of the arms race. On January 5, 1971, the Hancock school board met with two new black members elected in the fall, the Reverend R. E. Edwards, who became chairman, and James Hunt, an employee of McCown.[6] Robert Ingram was the only holdover. Two whites, G. B. Moore, Jr., and Sidney Trawick, now constituted a minority on the board. The federal courts in August turned down yet another "unitary plan" submitted by the black-controlled board. Hunt and Ingram pushed for an appeal, but Edwards, now wary and pulling away from McCown, did not go along.[7] McCown launched an effort to get Edwards thrown out of the pulpit at one of his churches, but he failed. He was the first black minister to leave the McCown organization.

McCown enlisted black preachers from the beginning. "John had a way about him," said one black who ended up in political opposition to him. "He just about ruined religious services. He broke up some churches when members who did not want their churches turned into political organizations pulled out. He had a few preachers so indoctrinated they thought he was God. He had been trained to talk and was very impressive. He didn't like Dr. Martin Luther King's non-violent ways and fell out with Dr. King."

Assistant Secretary of Labor Arthur Fletcher visited Hancock County in August 1971 and called it a national model for the development of rural America. Fletcher toured the catfish farm, the concrete-block factory, and other economic projects and said he would recommend that the federal government "assist this county because the nation needs this kind of success story." Fletcher said he was impressed with the attitude of McCown. "He wants whites to share in what's happening and that's the kind of attitude we need" (*Atlanta Constitution*, Aug. 7, 1971). Fletcher was not very well briefed; at the time of his visit, the arms race was raging and McCown had begun plans to build a shopping center to destroy the town of Sparta, which had served as a trading center since the early 1800s.

While claiming to be revitalizing the economy of the county, McCown actually was gradually destroying what was left of it. His threats to burn the town and his repeated demonstrations and boycotts badly damaged business. Dr. George Green, mayor of Sparta in the late 1960s, made strong efforts to attract industry. He told how Georgia Pacific inspected Sparta as a site for a plant that would employ several hundred. Land, gas, water were all available. As the inspection party and the mayor were driving back into Sparta, they encountered McCown holding one of his frequent demonstrations. "The plant went to Monticello where they didn't have any of these things," said Green. "About fifty Hancock County people commute there every day to work."

McCown's friend Glustrom was aware of the problem. "I went with McCown to try to interest a manufacturer of garments in opening a factory that would do certain minor sewing operations, towels and work clothes. This manufacturer was almost on the verge of opening a plant there and then he got frightened, he told me later, thinking there might be trouble with employees because they were easily controlled by McCown or whoever was running the county. He thought he might be in a situation where they would have all of his merchandise down there and quit working and sort of use the plant as hostage. It just seemed the situation would be risky for him, and I can understand his feelings." Others shared these feelings. No industry came to Hancock County after McCown arrived.

In late April of 1971, threats of competition with the white business community led to open friction. McCown told Vinnie Williams of the *Atlanta Journal* that blacks had bought fifteen acres of land at the junction of Highways 22, 15, and 16—in the middle of Sparta—for a shopping center. "The three roads lead to Greensboro, Eatonton and Milledgeville—and the shopping center, if it becomes a reality, will inevitably turn Sparta's Main Street into a desert of deserted white stores," the *Journal* reported on April 29, 1971, "for McCown and

ECCO envision a supermarket, clothing stores, a beauty shop—'the whole range of shopping center stores.'" McCown told the reporter, "This will badly hurt white merchants, but we don't know what other route to take, because we've gotten no cooperation from them at all."

McCown's dictatorial ways were starting to cause trouble even among his staunch supporters at the Georgia Council. Glustrom strongly supported him but others began to fall away. After their meeting with Governor Carter in May 1971, Glustrom said he had discussed McCown's becoming a Republican, explaining why he needed to be one during the Nixon administration, but none of that was mentioned in the letter Glustrom wrote Carter after the meeting.

> I know of no problem that could result from any investigation of McCown, financially or otherwise. I have known him intimately, personally and financially, over four years. I have known him to be investigated numerous times. In all of this there has never been anything to my knowledge of a dishonest or dishonorable nature concerning him. . . .
>
> In rural Georgia, even peaceful change in white-black relations is often maligned and the leaders are broadly accused in personal ways for doing things we all do and accept normally in our American free enterprise system. As a businessman I have always found fringe benefits to myself from every corporation I headed, all legal and ethical. I would lose the respect of my peers if I did not utilize them.
>
> McCown has used the same astuteness in managing his own affairs that he has used for public economic development in the state. If he did not develop his own affairs simultaneously and remained a poor man, I submit to you in our society it would harm him and his work. Such Christlike attitudes are so rare in history that people might regard him as odd or strange for practicing them.[8]

While the arms race continued in Hancock, a storm was gathering among the officers of the Georgia Council, where differences had been growing for some time. One Atlantan said she left the council not because she differed with its goals but because she felt the board was simply a rubber stamp and she was making no contribution. Others felt it was wrong to place too much emphasis on one county. Some began to ask questions about finances. The big blowup took place at the executive committee meeting of September 22, 1971, when one member arrived with a prepared list of questions about finances. The Reverend

James L. Hooten of Savannah wanted to know the nature of sums listed under "other costs." The Reverend Charles Wilhite asked to record in the minutes an agreement by McCown that an itemized statement would be made available. Glustrom objected that the minutes would indicate a basic distrust of McCown and the accountant, but the motion was carried with Glustrom dissenting. Following a heated discussion, McCown turned in his resignation. Marion Fraleigh marched out of the room to a typewriter and neatly typed hers. Loyal to the end, Glustrom moved for a vote of confidence in McCown and Fraleigh. The motion, expanded to include Glustrom, passed.[9]

McCown made his farewell address to the Georgia Council at its annual meeting October 30, 1971, at Jekyll Island. "The community must be shaken a little more to get a little more," he said. The board of directors ought to decide its role, he advised. There needed to be more white involvement, but he was concerned as to whether whites were willing to put their reputations on the line to deal with racial problems. "The entire board has not been against me but I could not find some of you when battles were being fought," he commented.[10]

McCown's direct involvement with the council thus ended, but for the next several years it struggled with legal and accounting problems he left behind. The *Atlanta Constitution* later reported (July 4, 1974) that the council paid two certified public accountants $10,000 to bring its books up to date as of January 15, 1972. The accountants quickly pointed out that the accounts were in a mess; for one thing, appropriate contracts defining relationships between the council and ECCO and the two major sources of funds, the OEO and the Ford Foundation, simply did not exist. Property titles were in a tangle or incomplete. Payments had been made from one agency to another without proper credits.[11]

As an example, the accountants found that an option on some additional land owned by Jesse A. Jackson was never exercised. In that connection, a $2,800 loan was made to Jackson. McCown erased the loan the last day he served as executive director of the council. McCown personally bought the additional 500 acres of land from Jackson shortly after the council took an option on it in late 1970. Through a complicated series of land deals, McCown apparently made a profit of more than $50,000 on the land by selling it to ECCO, and a housing project financed by Ford and by HUD-guaranteed mortgages was later built on the property (*Atlanta Constitution*, July 1, 2, 1974). The accountants found other interesting things. The federal information return for the fiscal year ending September 30, 1971 was incorrect, and no record existed of a return for the previous year.

Problems continued to turn up, including real estate transactions involving the "English" property in Warren County and a payment to a Land and Forest Service for it. The property ended up in McCown's hands under the name Mayfield Farms, an unincorporated company he owned. It included a site on the Ogeechee where he began building an elaborate home (*Atlanta Constitution*, July 1, 1974). Clouded titles to real estate and other property imposed a special kind of liability upon the council, the accountants warned. "Losses of these kinds may impose a serious financial drain." ECCO's profit-and-loss statement for the year ending September 30, 1971 showed mounting losses, much greater than those for the previous year. Losses on the catfish operation alone reached $292,892. Expenses included $73,526 for consultants and contracts and $47,337 for travel.[12]

"The dream shattered into a million pieces," said Becker, the council's president. "It gave me so many gray hairs. Frankly, I try not to think about it. The only financial reports the Board was getting were the computer printouts, statements we couldn't read. There were many questions unanswered. Where are the funds coming from? Who are they earmarked for? It bothered me more and more that I didn't know what was going on. At the meeting where the breakup occurred hard questions were being asked. McCown said if he was not trusted he would quit, but I was not sure I wanted Mr. McCown's resignation. Our bookkeepers, all hired by Mr. McCown, were going in and out like a revolving door. Frankly, I was disgusted. What was happening to the Georgia Council? Things looked great for ECCO but there were no funds for the council and the membership had been let go.

"Any time we asked about finances Mr. McCown reminded us we were monitored by Ford and ECCO, that everything had to be kept in great shape," she said. "It was a shock to discover that we were not. Mr. McCown was a many-faceted personality. I was impressed by the hard work he did. I would go out and follow him around for a day. It was exhausting and the pressures were enormous. He was not educated in a formal way to manage such an operation and the pressures got to him; sometimes he would pull away. I believed what he said about his concerns for poor people, black and white. I still believe he was sincere about that. Later I came to Atlanta several times for grand jury hearings but I was never called on to testify and charges were dropped. I felt that Mr. Glustrom and Mr. McCown had acted unethically but I did not know about illegally. At any rate, I was shocked and disillusioned. I felt that John McCown's contacts with the Ford Foundation had corrupted him; he learned about Lincoln Continentals and three hundred dollar suits. It gave him a view of a world he didn't know existed."

The council gradually faded away despite efforts to revive it. The Reverend James L. Hooten moved its headquarters to Savannah, keeping it barely alive.

Troubles abounded in Hancock County and in the Georgia Council, but according to the *New York Times*, McCown's programs were looking good. Thomas A. Johnson of the *Times*, who had written about the first big fish fry the summer before, was back. His story in the September 8, 1971 issue was headlined, "Blacks in Georgia Let White Minority Share Power: Strategy of Restraint Said to Gain Amity in Farm County." Johnson said the county was one of some thirty in the South where majority blacks had taken over the political apparatus and that it had attracted wide attention because its black population, numbering about 8,000, deliberately took no more than a controlling share of the offices from the 2,500 whites, thus allowing the white minority to retain a role in county power. The *New Republic* had a better grasp of what was actually happening some months before (March 6, 1971), when it reported, after interviewing McCown and Edith Ingram, that the school superintendent and the tax commissioner are white "but only because those jobs are not up for election until 1972." Every white officeholder was to be challenged in the 1972 elections, but anti-McCown blacks joined with whites to keep a few whites in office.

As for the fish farm, which was losing thousands of dollars, Johnson reported it was to provide some $250,000 worth of catfish annually. McCown told Johnson the fifteen-month-old fish farm "expects to harvest some 350,000 pounds of catfish this fall, set up a processing and freezing plant on the grounds and then open at least six fish-and-chip houses in Georgia and Florida in the next few months" (*New York Times*, Sept. 8, 1971).

Times were changing. Where Hancock once grew cotton, it now

97

grew pine trees and government checks. In the fall of 1971, Sam Carpenter, owner of the only cotton gin still operating in the county, announced he would not open because of a short crop. For the first time in more than a century, farmers would have to go out of the county to get their cotton ginned. A few days after the announcement, Carpenter was accidentally killed when his tractor ran over him.

The year 1971 marked a turning point. It saw McCown's break with the Georgia Council but no real solution to the growth in hostility between the races in Hancock County. By year's end, the minority of whites who tried to work with McCown had given up. Hancock citizens in 1971 had seen the bitterness of an arms race and had heard McCown's threats to destroy Sparta by building a new shopping center because "Sparta's merchants wouldn't cooperate with him." McCown gave up his idea of controlling whites through "green power" and began to consider building his own town. With his eye on federal funds, he decided to carry Hancock County for Richard Nixon.

8

The Revolution Goes Republican

*"McCown wasn't a saint
but he did know how to get things done."
—Georgia's State Republican Chairman*

ancock County had never gone Republican, even during Reconstruction. Before the Civil War it was a Whig county, its politics dominated by planters and lawyers, key men in the state. After the war, it became solidly Democratic and never left the fold, even though many of its conservative whites approved of no Democratic president after Woodrow Wilson. Since John McCown had upset most Hancock County traditions, it was to be expected that in the 1972 election campaign he would attempt to overturn still another one.

The Voting Rights Act of 1965 caused the 1970 United States Census to be of more than usual interest to politicians. The *New York Times* reported July 6, 1971, "The Bureau of the Census released today data that reaffirm the immense political power of Negroes in the South. The latest findings, drawn from the 1970 census, show that 102 counties in the nation are at least 50 percent black, all of them in 11 Southern states. The states are Virginia, North and South Carolina, Florida, Georgia, Tennessee, Alabama, Arkansas, Mississippi, Louisiana and Texas." The accompanying map in the *Times* showed that the band of black majority counties swept down from the old tobacco country of eastern Virginia into the cotton plantation country of eastern South Carolina, central Georgia, and Alabama, and on to the Mississippi River delta, with heavy concentrations along the river in Mississippi, Louisiana, and Arkansas.

The black community across the country demonstrated little enthusiasm for the Republican party or for President Nixon and his Southern strategy, but some pragmatic blacks made alliances with the Nixon administration, McCown among them. McCown explained to Governor Carter that he had to be a Republican while the Republicans were in power because Washington was where the money was. He told a Sparta businessman that a chance meeting when he sat beside Donald Nixon, the president's brother, on an airplane trip started him on his career as a Republican. Bob Shaw, who was chairman of the Georgia Republican party at the time, described McCown as a practical person who knew what it would mean to be allied with the party in power in Washington. In 1972, McCown met Sonny Walker, regional OEO director, who came from Little Rock, Arkansas, where he was the first black in the South to serve in a governor's cabinet, that of Republican Winthrop Rockefeller. Walker also took pride in the fact that he had taught five of the famous "Little Rock Nine" who integrated Little Rock's Central High School during the Eisenhower years. Walker was urging blacks, particularly blacks in Hancock County, to support the Republican party.

The office of the state chairman sent out a letter about it June 21, 1972, addressed to Hancock County Republicans, written by Administrative Assistant Susan Piha. McCown had already begun his moves to take over Hancock's party organization and Piha was trying to explain to the few white Republicans in the county that the state organization still wanted them:

> State Chairman Bob Shaw was called by Regional OEO Director Sonny Walker and advised that he had been talking with local blacks about their supporting the Republican party. Mr. Shaw was asked to talk with Mr. McCown but was unable to do so because of his activities in candidate recruitment across the state. We were later informed that Mr. McCown wanted to offer all Hancock County candidates on the Republican ticket, but we had no official Republican organization in Hancock County.
>
> . . . I advised McCown that I would ask our Tenth District Chairman from Augusta to come through town at 11:00 on Wednesday, June 14, and qualify his candidates. However, the Chairman, Mr. Bill Sams, qualified for the State House of Representatives, and was holding a press conference and could not arrive in time to handle the qualifications. Therefore, McCown had the candidates qualify with the ordinary of the

county and through a conference telephone hook-up with me and the Secretary of State informed us as to what he had done.[1]

A little reading between the lines suggests that Georgia's regular Republican organization felt just a little skittish about lining up with McCown too publicly; he had to do his qualifying by phone. Piha pointed out in her letter that the action did not mean the Republican party organization had changed hands, "because a county convention must still be held in order to have a legal county party." Sams was working on arrangements for holding a county convention, Piha said. "I hope this explanation will assure you that we do not wish to lose any of our faithful Republicans in Hancock County."

McCown was far ahead of Hancock's handful of regular Republicans. He needed political help to build the new town he planned at Mayfield. It was the season for new towns. They were as currently fashionable as catfish farms, and the Nixon administration was handing them out to its more important friends. Floyd McKissick's Soul City in North Carolina was the outstanding example of these towns. McKissick, another civil rights leader who found it profitable to be in the Nixon camp, achieved national prominence in the 1960s as the leader of the Congress of Racial Equality (CORE). He got his town approved by the Department of Housing and Urban Development (HUD) in 1971. Some eight years and $29 million later, HUD announced withdrawal of its support. At that time, 124 persons were living in thirty-three houses in Soul City.[2]

McCown got the political year off to a good start in January by telling the press about plans for his $7 million new town that would be financed by the Ford Foundation and government agencies. The proposed town was to occupy one thousand acres and would include eight hundred housing units, an industrial park, a convention hall, a radio station, and the county's first airport. The *Atlanta Constitution* reported January 27, 1972, that blacks had given up trying to win the cooperation of Hancock whites and were striking out on their own—a move that could seriously hurt white businesses in the county. McCown complained the story made it seem that Ford and the others were being duped into building a town for blacks by killing a white town (Sparta).

The story jeopardized the new town, McCown said, denying that his

101

project was a separatist movement by blacks and accusing the *Constitution* of negative journalism. He said the project had been biracial from the beginning, "as everything we've undertaken in this county has been." He accused the press of trying to show that blacks and whites were at each other's throats since the black-white arms race of the previous year. Newspaper stories about the new town introduced another name into the Hancock County saga. Already important behind the scenes as the Ford Foundation's monitor for Hancock County projects, Bryant George was quoted as confirming that the foundation was working with Hancock County blacks on a major program but "would not discuss the details." The program would make Hancock County a national showcase for blacks, the spokesman said.

After the first story appeared, George denied any knowledge of the project when questioned by reporters. Robert Tolls, another Ford Foundation official, was quoted as saying his organization had not made any financial commitment to McCown's project but "refused to say it will not become involved." There was apparently more thinking about the program at the Ford Foundation. The *Constitution* said in its February 1, 1972 issue that it got a third set of answers when it called the New York office the following Monday. George was quoted as saying "such a town is not planned now nor has it ever been planned." Tolls said, "We're at a loss to know what McCown is talking about. He could be confusing us with some government grant." McCown's complete town never did materialize, but eventually he got help to build a housing development near Mayfield containing 150 units in two sections. Ogeechee Estates and Lakeview Village were built with HUD-guaranteed loans plus some Ford Foundation money for items such as land. In April 1972, ECCO amended its charter to enable it to develop a water and sewerage system and low-cost housing projects, and in June, HUD awarded a contract to the Hancock Housing Authority for 108 low-rent housing units (*Sparta Ishmaelite*, April 8 and June 29, 1972).

Much of Lyndon Johnson's antipoverty program was dismantled during the Nixon years, but disproportionate parts of what funds remained were channeled into key areas as part of a Nixon strategy to get black votes in 1972. "McCown was Georgia's counterpart of Floyd McKissick," declared a former regional OEO officer. "Nixon saw to it that McCown did not suffer. McKissick and McCown had connections that made it difficult to say no to them. My opposition was not to their ideas but to the extraordinary kind of waste and the people they surrounded themselves with."

Black bureaucrats in Washington frequently got on the phone to tell McCown about programs and money available. "He got the word on the money and how to get it," said Republican chairman Shaw. "McCown wasn't a saint but he did know how to get things done. He always played on the up and up with me. He said, 'If you need me, use me. If you don't, disown me. If it helps, disavow me.'" Shaw said McCown was well taken care of himself and he took care of his people. "He saw a way to help himself and those around him too."

McCown completely outmaneuvered Hancock's small group of traditional Republicans, who were naive enough to think that loyalty to the party had meaning. They gathered up a file on McCown and sent it to Nixon's attorney general, John Mitchell. Later, they learned the file was immediately sent to McCown. "It got back to him before it was hardly in the mail," said one. They firmly believed that Marion Fraleigh provided strong Republican connections for McCown through New York's Senator Jacob Javits. Fraleigh was a native New Yorker and stories circulated in Sparta that she had political clout. When asked about it, she laughed at the idea.

Marion Fraleigh first came to Hancock County in 1966. In the beginning, she did not spend much time in the county, she said, because of her other duties as program coordinator for the Georgia Council on Human Relations. Her brief stays gradually grew longer and the county became her home for more than a decade. She experienced some cultural shock coming from New York to rural Georgia; life was so much more relaxed than she was used to. When the Georgia Council adopted Hancock as an area of major concern, she became interested in social issues. "One of John McCown's prime theses was you couldn't have true social development without economic development," she said. Fraleigh, in interviews, often sounded like a sociology textbook.

Bright, efficient, pleasant, and understated, she hardly seemed to fit into McCown's flamboyant way of living. The circle of women in McCown's life provided interesting contrasts. Fraleigh was certainly, on the surface, the primmest of the lot. Bob Shaw, who often visited the ECCO projects, spoke of what a fine person Marion Fraleigh was.

Highly intelligent, she knew every detail of the operation and kept everything going behind the scenes.

At key moments in McCown's career in Georgia, Fraleigh seemed to be always at his side. When he resigned in anger from the Georgia Council, she marched out with him. When he went hunting grants in Washington and New York, she accompanied him. When he met with a reporter at an Atlanta motel, charging that Sparta whites had plotted to kill him, she was present. She kept pictures of their twin sons in her office at ECCO headquarters, and a reporter remembered years later being kicked under the table by his colleague when he innocently asked who the children were. Hancock whites were particularly disturbed by this enigmatic woman, who came in their midst violating rules they considered fundamental.

Despite the belief of local whites that Marion Fraleigh provided McCown's Republican connections, no evidence exists to support it. McCown knew how to make friends in important places. He became a Republican to get government funds. His increasing arrogance and his decision to go Republican caused dissension in the ranks, and the 1972 elections marked the beginning of a break between McCown and some of his supporters. These people constituted part of the inner circle that was accustomed to meeting and discussing a slate of candidates; this time, McCown came in and simply told them what the slate would be. They took their resentment to a group of whites headed by George Eisel, a retired Air Force major and Californian who owned a cattle ranch in the county. One of the defecting black leaders was the Reverend R. E. Edwards, whose son had been the first black to attend the white school in Sparta.

At first, the blacks were very frightened, Eisel said. "They were afraid for their safety. They would park their cars behind my house in the country and then go to another white man's farm in Greene County in different cars. We put out a clandestine letter. We were so late we had to come up with write-in candidates. We got about twelve hundred votes in the county and got blacks to come out publicly, though they were still nervous and timid. The other side used aides who greeted people at the polls and went into the polls with them. The code was violated so openly it was pathetic. There were federal observers in 1970 but none in 1972."

The *Sparta Ishmaelite*, alert to the land mines and quagmires of small-town politics, had survived by staying out of most issues. A reader of that paper would never have known that a revolution was taking place in the county. Reports were bare-bones listings of election results with no comment, but the paper abandoned its noncommittal policy briefly in its August 3 issue with a rare front-page editorial, boxed and prominently displayed with a headline, "Tuesday's Election Holds Hancock County's Future." Said the editorial,

A few years ago Black leaders worked hard to promote integration of Georgia Public Schools and the county government. Their efforts were successful and Hancock County was among the first to integrate schools and government. More recently a Black Power group has worked and is working hard to capitalize on gains made by people of good intent.

The power hungry group is determined to elect a hand-picked slate of candidates and by doing so it will control all the offices, all the County's money; all the County's properties; all the County's decision-making; all the County's public works; all the County zoning (or lack of it) and as a result all the County's future. No one, Black or White, (outside the power hungry group) could expect any degree of security unless he agreed to the group's demands. THE RIGHT DIRECTION. Voters in Hancock County have an opportunity next Tuesday, August 8th to secure and insure a good future—a future in which people of different races and beliefs can be free to work together to improve their home county. Let's go to the polls Tuesday, August 8th and vote to make sure we don't "blow" that chance.

McCown provided plenty of symbolism in the 1972 elections. He often emphasized in newspaper interviews his desire to keep whites involved in the government as public officials, but he demonstrated his firm grip on the political process by announcing where candidates might qualify in Hancock primaries. Prospective Republican candidates were invited to see McCown at ECCO headquarters; Democrats were dispatched to a black funeral home. To further discourage whites, he placed all the polling places at spots traditionally thought of as black controlled. One of his many jobs was county administrator, and he boasted that through the county police cars and radio system he could locate anybody in the county in ten minutes. So powerful and feared was his network that a white candidate's cook told the man she had

105

voted against him because she feared the McCown crowd would burn her out if she did not.

McCown did not totally succeed in the primaries. Although the white sheriff had allied himself with most efforts of the black movement and had even gotten in a fight with Sparta's mayor during the school demonstrations, McCown decided to run a black against him. He failed to oust the sheriff. He also failed in his effort to remove the white tax commissioner. Marvin Lewis, principal of the former black high school, Hancock Central, did defeat W. M. Andrews, the white school superintendent. The November minutes of the Hancock County school board revealed that a political rally favoring local Republican candidates had been sanctioned and authorized by Principal Lewis at the Hancock Central School on October 27. The report said classes at the senior high level were dismissed and students directed into the gymnasium, where Republican candidates for offices in the general election were permitted to make statements.[3]

Dwain Andrews, a white candidate, won election to the county commission, which thereafter consisted of Andrews and two blacks, both employees of McCown's ECCO operations. During the 1970–72 period, George Lott served as chairman of the commission. Following the 1972 elections, McCown fell out with Lott and arranged for Johnny Warren to be chairman. With Warren, McCown had such complete control of the county's affairs that he kept the county's official stationery at ECCO headquarters, writing letters and calling Warren in to sign them.

Opposition candidates, as they had done in 1970, challenged the election in the courts, asking for a recount of votes cast in the Democratic primary. Secretary of State Ben Fortson refused to intervene in the contest, thereby winning the enmity of a considerable number of Hancock whites who, in their frustration, felt that state officials had made them the token sacrificial lamb. Some of them charged that Judge Hal Bell of Macon, who heard the case, seemed more concerned with the local political situation in Macon than with the merits of the case and that he released his decision to the leaders of the NAACP in Macon before it was officially announced. In truth, the problems of the tiny white community no longer interested politicians at the state level. These politicians had to look at a wider picture and a growing black vote across the state, which they did not want to alienate.

Traditionally, the Democratic primary in Hancock County decided elections and the general elections in November were simply a ritual required by law. McCown's seizure of both parties gave him two chances in the election; he had slates in both primaries. Bob Shaw remembered years later how it was done. "The same names appeared on both slates, Democratic and Republican, except for the presidential electors. McCown carried Hancock County for Nixon and elected the ordinary, the sheriff and two county commissioners as Republicans."

Although McCown brought Hancock County into the Republican column for the first time, the victory cost him dearly by splitting his supporters. The victory for Nixon was a narrow one, 1,595 votes to 1,502 for the Democrats.[4]

9

Labor Trouble

"Poverty program officials
are afraid McCown is becoming
a black emperor,
no different from a benevolent
white plantation owner,
except he is black."
—*News reporter*

McCown was immensely frustrated by anything he could not control. Even in high school in South Carolina, he had sought to command. "If you tried to take the lead role away from him he would fight you," said his uncle. "He was just that aggressive." It angered McCown that the little town of Sparta eluded him and that he could not buy one of its banks. The town had only two industries of any size, a garment plant and a furniture factory, and he decided he would control them by controlling their labor force.

In 1972, Defiance Manufacturing Company of New York owned plants at Sparta and at Greensboro and Gibson in neighboring counties. Defiance employed four hundred of Hancock's nine thousand people. McCown founded a union that attempted to organize the Greensboro and Sparta plants. He brought the owner of the plants to a meeting at Sparta that the New Yorker later described as one of the worst moments of his life. For whites who became the focal point of McCown's mass meetings, even for hardened reporters and labor negotiators, it was a wrenching emotional experience they never forgot. The plant owner, described as a sensitive man who understood the well-springs of the black movement and wished it success, found the rhythmic shouting and chants of the McCown mass meeting a new and unnerving experience.

"Finally there was a mass walkout at the Greensboro and Sparta plants," said John Bacheller, Jr., an Atlanta labor lawyer who was involved in the negotiations. "The central activity was at the Greensboro plant where the owner was. John McCown brought up a busload of workers. His group pulled some nonstrikers out of cars. The supervisors who were still working saw that and took off to the woods near the plant. They had a seventy-five-yard lead but the McCown group followed them. Everyone got out of the plant except the owner and me. McCown only wanted to talk to us but it didn't seem like a good idea at the time. We chose not to have McCown come in."

While the chase was going on, the labor lawyer's partner was trying to get an injunction against the mass picketing. Meanwhile, the Georgia State Patrol had fifteen cars on the other side of town. The Greene County sheriff asked what he could do to help and the lawyer urged him to get the State Patrol out of the picture. "The sheriff later brought us fried chicken from his restaurant," said the attorney. "When the sun went down John loaded up his bus and went on back to Sparta and that night we got the injunction." The conservative blacks in Greene County did not want McCown around. They told the factory owner and his lawyer they did not need McCown there.

The rural bushwhacking ended in the Ford Foundation's elegant board room in New York City. The owner of the Sparta plant had found a sensitive nerve and he pressed it, pointing out to the foundation that tax-exempt funds were being used for purposes not exempt under federal laws. The foundation gathered McCown and the factory owner and his lawyer in a meeting and suggested that they make peace. Eventually, McCown disbanded his union and abandoned the two men he had brought in to organize it.

Bacheller, despite his role at the opposite side of the bargaining table from McCown, was fond of him. "I really liked John," he said. "We could get a bottle of whiskey and sit around for two or three hours at a time telling war stories or talking about ideas. McCown was a sophisticated, intelligent negotiator, as good a negotiator as I ever dealt with." Even so, Bacheller recognized that McCown was no administrator. "When you went into ECCO's headquarters there were people rushing around and a lot of activity, but if you watched you realized most of them weren't really doing anything. John's office was mammoth with a big desk and a deep carpet. At noon we went over to the big house next door where lunch was served." The guest-house cook had worked for Mayfield's grande dame, Mrs. Clarence Reynolds, until McCown hired her away. "John always talked in terms of big ideas. He was an effective spokesman but he needed a manager."

McCown's style fascinated Bacheller. He remembered their first meeting, which occurred at the Atlanta airport. McCown came flying in from Jacksonville in his own plane, apologizing for being late but explaining he was delayed by a weather front. "He was wearing that jacket that would cost five hundred dollars now," Bacheller said. "It was a sport coat made of the finest leather—like an expensive wallet might be made of." Bacheller recalled that at other airport meetings, McCown's aides served vodka and orange juice at five o'clock in the afternoon.

John Taylor, the union organizer McCown brought in and later abandoned, incorporated the basic McCown theme into his message to workers at the Sparta plant. "If our brothers and sisters could see how worried those white folks are they would vote for a union. Anytime a colored man gets a white man worried that's reason enough to vote for a union." McCown won a few benefits for workers at the Sparta plant, but his efforts to unionize Sparta's small furniture factory killed plans to enlarge it.

A flourishing enterprise in Hancock County and one in which the entire community took great pride was the Hancock Memorial Hospital. It opened in 1967, built with local funds (no federal dollars, they proudly said), and operated in the black. As McCown gained control of the government he also took control of the hospital. At one meeting, the elderly white chairman of the board, in reply to a remark from McCown, threw up his hands and resigned, saying, "I've had all I can take of it." The by-laws decreed that the vice-chairman, who was white, should step up. McCown snapped, "I said elect a chairman." The whites walked out and Elmer Warren, a black, was elected. McCown told the resigning white chairman, "You all built the hospital and we are going to run it with your money."

As the McCown group took over the hospital, they used it as a place to employ friends. The staff changed drastically. One observer said, "Dr. Green found out one night not a single licensed person was on duty, so he and Dr. Ferrell moved their patients to Eatonton. Then the county commission promised all sorts of change. The doctors moved their patients back but none of the promises were kept, so they moved them out again."

"The hospital in Hancock County was a workshop for two white doctors. They dominated the medical service and did not want the new administration to be in charge of the hospital," said Dr. Lee Shelton, a black physician from Atlanta who worked there briefly after the whites left. Dr. Shelton felt the hospital had no reason for existence except for the local doctors. "It was a striking example of the ability of physicians to generate hospitalization and lab services. The hospital was the product of the ingenuity and imagination of those doctors. The county government was naive when they meddled with the doctors; the last thing was to meddle. That hospital was their workshop and when they went it lost its meaning." A local businessman looked at it another way. "They destroyed it," he said. "It ought to be filled up with hay. That's the last thing you do with a building before it dies."

At last, in June 1975, the hospital, propped up by county funds though virtually empty, sent its only patient away and told employees there were no longer any jobs (*Atlanta Constitution*, June 28, 1975). For many months, the once thriving hospital had been a disaster, a monument to McCown's intransigence. A nurse who left the hospital two months before it closed said nurses frequently failed to show up for duty, leaving the hospital empty at night except for the patients, who had to fend for themselves. She also declared there had been no oxygen in the wards or emergency room for three months; the only microscope had been stolen, and nurses had to bring their own blood-pressure kits to work. Once, she charged, when the hospital was out of catheters, untrained nurses used a plastic sandwich bag and rubber bands, causing a patient to suffer gangrene. On one occasion, the only way the staff could feed an unexpected accident victim was to send out for meals from a fast-food place.

While McCown was stopping expansion at the furniture plant and destroying jobs at the hospital, he was expanding his ECCO-related businesses. As a result of his wide connections, he received grants when no one else could get them. "You'd tell him he couldn't have something and he would get on the plane to Washington and get it," said one state administrator. Joseph Luttrell, the ECCO attorney, applied for articles of incorporation for many businesses in 1973. In April, he incorporated the Hancock Water and Sewer Authority at Mayfield and the Soul Brothers Citizen Band Radio Club with Leroy Wiley, Hancock clerk of court, as the registered agent. In May came ECCO Wood Products and in August, ECCO Transportation Services. Countywide Security Agency, Inc., appeared in September, with Wiley again as agent for what was described as "a private detective and private security agency business." By December, ECCO's new attorney, Roosevelt Warren, sought articles of incorporation for the Worldwide Furniture Company.[1]

The LaFayette Hotel, successor to the old Eagle Tavern and the Drummer's Home, in continuous operation for 133 years, was closed in November, another sad victim of the county's racial disputes. Its antique pieces were taken from the hotel and sold in Atlanta (*Sparta Ishmaelite*, Nov. 22, 29, 1973). Owner LaFayette Chupp had tried to mediate between McCown and the whites, and the white community had boycotted him.

Bryant George, later with the State Department's Agency for International Development, who served as program officer for ECCO programs during the period in which Ford was involved, said he wrote the first program Ford undertook in Hancock. "The Ford Foundation had helped the Southern Regional Council and through that the state councils," he explained. "The Georgia Council came up with this program of economic development at the same time Ford said it was going to do such a program. In the South, Ford chose Mississippi MACE–Delta, Southeast Alabama Self-Help Association and a group in Durham, North Carolina, called Fund for Community Development (FCD). All of the ones in the Southeast were black. The Georgia Council came to us and we made a grant for a MESBIC. Our second grant was for a fish farm. We made another grant for housing; housing was the permanent thing."

Asked why the Ford Foundation had entrusted such large sums to McCown's management when he had no previous business experience, George explained, "John was the best community organizer I ever saw and the worst businessman. It is rare you find both in the same person. Henry Ford was the rare person who could design and make the car and then market it. John McCown could organize anything. John could organize people who didn't like him.

112

"In the original plan," said George, "the fish farm was to be the hub around which 250 farm families would work, a centralized source of supply and marketing and technical help. It never worked. The technology didn't come on stream as people might have expected. OEO was trying to put people out front of technology. The only way you could have organized it was to have had John McCown. All of the others at MACE-Delta and the other places could not have unified Hancock County; they were managers, not organizers. McCown had to break up the alliance of black leaders and white patrons. He couldn't wait. It would have taken years the other way."

George admired McCown. "He was an American who pulled himself up by his bootstraps. All of us on the boards had the cream of American education, yet it was he who was able to go into a county like that and get people to follow him into breaking up a pattern that had existed over two hundred years."

The Ford Foundation supported McCown's programs with millions of dollars. Millions more came from various government agencies, particularly from the OEO, which was served by Sonny Walker as regional director. Walker had been busy during the Nixon years recruiting black supporters for the Republicans in the South. He remembered that he first met McCown during the summer of 1972 at the annual ECCO fish fry. Walker was the second Arkansan to become involved with ECCO; Dr. Earl Evans had served as an advisor to the ECCO fish farm and provided the catfish for the first big fry.

When he talked about McCown and ECCO, Walker was careful to explain that they were not funded out of his office but received their grants from the OED in Washington, D.C., because they were a Title Seven community development corporation. Walker said he was impressed by McCown's ability "to relate to people around their needs as he perceived them." Noting McCown's persuasiveness, he had also heard stories about the county's undergoing "a fantastic change." He said it had evolved from a county where "the majority of the population had been dominated by a minority to a situation where blacks were exerting themselves through some help from the Ford Foundation and some OEO grants and had begun to establish an economic base that was independent of the traditional structure in the county."

He came away from his first meeting "impressed with the courage and determination of the man, John McCown." Later, Walker went to

Hancock County with Alvin J. Arnett, then national director of OEO. McCown had invited them to talk about his plans to expand some of his activities into surrounding counties. However, the last thing black leadership in surrounding counties wanted was help from McCown. "Arnett made some funds available," said Walker, "for us to begin to try to expand some of the concepts that were taking place in Hancock County into other counties. We did make a small grant for that purpose to McCown."

His close friendship with McCown finally made Walker a principal figure in a controversy between McCown and Governor Carter. Walker said the issue came about because "the county government came to us for some assistance in elevating the ability of the county officials to administer county operations." What he meant, apparently, was that the county had asked for money to train its unskilled new officials. Hancock County had, no doubt, elected many incompetent officials in its long history, but no one had thought in the previous 180 years from 1793 to 1973 to ask the government for money to remedy the errors of the voters.

What brought the big flareup involving Carter was an OEO recommendation that the new county commissioners be paid a salary out of federal funds. They proposed a $300,000 grant to the county. This was to be done because, in Walker's words, "there had been a transition in the county from whites to blacks who did not have an economic base." Walker said some persons in the county took exception to this and "Governor Carter had some questions about it." Carter had the authority to veto funds coming into Georgia through regular channels, but he could do nothing about Title Seven grants that came directly from Washington. Carter asked to see an audit of OEO operations in Hancock County and said he would not allow salaries to be paid to the county commissioners.

"The grant we were making was more or less held hostage," said Walker. "I did not have the audit that the governor wanted. McCown had the audit and Washington had the audit. McCown, ultimately, at my request made the audit available to the governor. In the meantime, Frank Moore of the governor's office and Benny Solomon of mine worked out the concerns the governor had about the grant. I was very pleased with the way the governor worked this out."

Carter wrote Walker on April 5, 1974 that he was vetoing the

$300,000 grant to the Hancock County Board of Commissioners, carefully explaining that he had usually supported programs to aid the poor. "Throughout my public life," he wrote, "I have supported the OEO Community Action Programs and other programs designed to give the disadvantaged an opportunity to live satisfying and productive lives. . . . During my term as Governor, I have approved millions of dollars in grants to community action agencies in Georgia, even when these programs were under attack from politicians at the local and national level."[2]

The project had some worthwhile portions, Carter said, but the total effect "would only furnish additional ammunition to those who seek constantly to discredit and dismember any plan designed to benefit the poor and the disadvantaged." He went on to point out that more than 60 percent of the funds would be used for salaries and other administrative costs. "Three county commissioners in a county with less than 10,000 total population will be paid salaries far in excess of those paid to the commissioners of our most populous county and ninety percent of the other commissioners in our State. I cannot justify salaries of $8,000 a year for three county commissioners, $15,000 for a county manager, and $10,000 each for two assistants to the county manager in a county with a median [family] income of less than $5,000 a year."

So firmly entrenched had McCown become with powerful friends in OEO in Washington that he felt free to thumb his nose at Governor Carter, who noted in his letter to Walker (with copies to McCown and his employee, Johnny Warren, chairman of the Hancock commission): "Many of the existing programs in Hancock County are no doubt worthwhile; however, requests from my office and our Department of Human Resources for information which could be used to evaluate these programs have been evaded or flatly rejected. Specifically, we requested copies of audits of previous OEO grants to Hancock County. We were told that these audits were in the National OEO Office, but were 'unavailable' to us. We can only assume that any attempt to evaluate this proposal will be met by similar rebuffs."

McCown, spending millions in taxpayers' funds, refused to let the governor see the audits until considerable pressure was put on him. Walker's wording is interesting in this connection. "McCown, *ultimately*, at my request made the audit available to the governor."

115

A state OEO official said of ECCO, "They ripped off where they could. This was his chief objective. John had delusions of grandeur. When he started the project, his idea of a catfish farm seemed to be good, but the mechanics just couldn't get by. We took him to Washington on this and Washington changed it. We then recommended the project to the governor. We believed we were right and defended it. McCown was supposed to take in surrounding counties but what I found out was they didn't follow through; they did not get representatives from other counties. They were more interested in getting control and keeping it for John McCown. . . . You ought to see some of those project proposals. I felt too vulnerable and I didn't feel like it could last with the government throwing money away, being stolen blind, people ripping them off. John was on the inside of all of these things. If I said 'John, we can't buy that,' he would get on the plane and go to Washington and get it done."

Considerable disagreement with Walker's decisions existed within the regional OEO office. Reports were leaked that the team from that office studying the Hancock situation recommended the $300,000 grant not be made. Disturbed that news accounts indicated the grants met with staff approval, the team reportedly insisted that Hancock had already received the highest per capita OEO grants in the country and that a number of questionable matters with regard to the existing program in Hancock would be exposed to a thorough General Accounting Office (GAO) audit. The OEO team suggested that if any grant were made, it should be allocated for technical advice to the Hancock County program to shore up its weaknesses. They said the decision to make the grant was solely that of Walker and Arnett, the national director.

At a news conference, Governor Carter said he objected most to the plan to place elected Georgia officials on the federal payroll on a full-time basis, describing this as a radical departure from state procedures. Carter said he had been informed that "Mr. McCown has already obtained a commitment through the state Republican chairman that my veto will be overridden by the Nixon administration" (*Atlanta Constitution*, April 10, 1974). McCown told the press he had discussed the pending grant with Carter and agreed that county commissioners should not be paid federal salaries. McCown did not tell Carter or the press that in a sense the commissioners already were on federal salaries, at least the two of them who were employees of ECCO.

116

Hancock County's elegant Victorian courthouse, built in the 1880s, dominates the town of Sparta from its site where roads leading into the county seat converge on a high hill. John McCown took control of the courthouse in the late 1960s and it became the focal point of his activities.

Above: John McCown strikes a pose beside the Confederate monument on Sparta's courthouse square. A reporter who was on the scene when this photograph was taken asked McCown to look belligerent, "because that's what you are." (Courtesy of the *Atlanta Constitution.*)

Right: In 1971 Hancock County witnessed a virtual arms race as whites and blacks eyed each other with fear and suspicion. Ordinary (County Probate Judge) Edith Ingram and Clerk of Court Leroy S. Wiley, shown here, helped John McCown organize a group called the Sporting Rangers. A teacher before she was recruited to run for political office, Miss Ingram was an important ally of McCown. (Courtesy of the *Atlanta Constitution.*)

In 1966 McCown arrived in Hancock County driving a broken-down Chrysler. He was broke but he had ambitions, one perhaps being to live in a house such as the one that he later built for himself on the Ogeechee River. In order to photograph the house, two reporters paddled down the Ogeechee in a canoe. (Courtesy of the *Atlanta Constitution*.)

On the night of May 11, 1974, while McCown was in jail in Sparta, the antebellum Clinch house was burned to the ground in a blaze set by arsonists.

On May 20, 1974, Jimmy Carter, then governor of Georgia, came to Sparta in an effort to ease the tension between blacks and whites that threatened to erupt into violence. He is shown here conversing with McCown, who earlier had frustrated Carter's efforts to obtain an audit of federal funds being channeled into Hancock County. (Courtesy of the *Atlanta Constitution*.)

On his visit to Sparta, Governor Carter met first with the mayor and a
largely white group at a local bank before moving on to the courthouse where
he spoke to McCown and his followers.
(Courtesy of the *Atlanta Constitution*.)

On the night of January 30, 1976, John McCown and two of three others who
were with him died in the crash of a single-engine Cessna 182 McCown was
piloting. The plane took off from an unattended landing strip and then
dived into a wooded area a few minutes later.

Carter said he had been informed that Georgia Republican leaders were trying to pull strings in Washington to get the plan approved over his objections. Georgia Republican Chairman Bob Shaw retorted that he had never heard of the plan and OEO did not ask him when to approve a grant. He said Carter was unhappy, not with the content of the plan, but with the fact that it was developed by a Republican. "He's unhappy because Mr. McCown has done such an outstanding job in Hancock County and Mr. McCown is a Republican." He accused Carter of playing politics with the program (*Atlanta Constitution*, April 10, 1974).

Shaw, the only white Georgia politician at the state level to speak out openly for McCown, had become his good friend during the 1972 election campaign. Shaw genuinely liked him. "McCown was a genius at meeting with government representatives and determining what funds were available and working at putting together projects. His friends in Washington, mostly black, would call and tell him what was available," said Shaw. "I've been down to Hancock County and have found two or three from Washington there telling him about programs. His contacts were very good. He was also close to the people in Hancock County. You could go anywhere with him and they would invite you in to eat with them." Shaw's pilot was also a friend of McCown's. Tired of landing at the field at Thomson, some miles away, the pilot persuaded McCown to take earth-moving equipment being used to build the housing project at Mayfield and smooth out a landing strip. Shaw's plane was the second to land there and the first to take off from there.

Glustrom thought Carter stopped the OEO grant and then approved it because he wanted something. "He was trying to get McCown to come into the Democratic party and come into the Carter orbit politically and McCown felt that since Republicans were running the government he should be a Republican if he wanted a grant, and so he resisted."

What caused a real furor was a front-page story in the *Atlanta Constitution* on April 18, 1974, headlined, "Nightclub Getting Hancock Poverty Funds." Reporter Jeff Nesmith wrote that a Hancock County development company (ECCO MESBIC) "recently obtained more than $1 million in U.S. Office of Economic Opportunity grant funds, some of which was being used to finance a nightclub and to buy two air-

117

planes and a helicopter." McCown and Walker were infuriated because the story did not make it clear that money for the businesses came from ECCO MESBIC and that MESBICS were designed under federal law to help small minority businesses. The nightclub, as it turned out, was one of the few things ECCO touched that prospered. As for the airline, one of its two planes soon crashed and it never had a helicopter.

Nesmith noted in his story that he had been unable to reach McCown, saying later that McCown did not return his calls. Bob Shaw called Nesmith when the story appeared and accompanied him to Walker's office; then he went into another room, Nesmith recalled. "McCown was there and he just screamed at me. 'You wrote that and you ain't never been there.'" So McCown invited Nesmith to Mayfield, where he showed him around the catfish farm, then returned to a conference room where they all sat around a large table. McCown called in a group to tell what ECCO had meant to each of them. One was Roosevelt Warren, a young black attorney. Another was an old black man who described how blacks had suffered from racism in Hancock County and how McCown had come as the Messiah. This was Deacon Ed Andrews, who was trotted out regularly for newsmen, as he had been for the British television film. Nesmith, it seems, was getting the treatment McCown normally gave reporters. Another McCown ploy was to visit Sparta merchants with a reporter in tow and ask them how things were and what they thought about him (McCown). Reporters usually failed to note the cynicism involved; McCown had, and frequently exercised, the power to shut down these merchants' businesses.

The *Constitution* reported on April 18, 1974 that a financial statement issued by ECCO showed that between May 1, 1972 and September 30, 1973 the company received OEO grants totalling $1,150,000, approximately $1,000 for every identified poor family in the county. The funds included $615,000 for the administrative budget and $535,000 for venture capital. Expenditures included $257,476 for salaries and wages, $22,328 for telephones, $4,843 for public relations, and $36,072 for travel.

On April 19, the day after the story about the nightclub and the airline appeared, the *Constitution* ran another story and another headline, "Carter Fears Leaders Get OEO Aid." It quoted Carter as saying at a press conference that he feared the funds pouring into Hancock County were being used "to maintain a few leaders and for the profit of some private entrepreneurs." Carter repeated the charge that he had not been able to get an accounting of how federal funds were being spent in the county, saying he doubted very seriously if it was proper to use OEO funds to finance a nightclub and an airline. McCown replied that ECCO MESBIC had lent $80,000 to Academy Lounge and Associated Airways. He said the owners of Associated Airways were two black pilots "who flew B-52 bombers all over Vietnam but couldn't get jobs with the airlines because they were black."

A few days later, on April 22, the *Constitution* published the results of Nesmith's visits to McCown's headquarters at Mayfield. The headline was "Blacks Laud ECCO Chief; Whites Hit 'Black Emperor.'" From Sparta, Nesmith wrote,

> In 1966 John McCown came to this sleepy town in poverty-ridden Hancock County as a black civil rights worker, supported by a wage that provided just enough to live on. Today he owns 525 acres of Hancock County farmland, is building a house that will cost nearly $60,000, holds the title to several pieces of commercial property in Sparta and flies his own twin-engine airplane, price tag $33,000. How in eight years a hungry black civil rights worker could become that prosperous in a rural Georgia county where poverty and racism have maintained an iron grip since the Civil War has become a question a lot of people want answered.

"McCown refers darkly to political connections between the governor and some members of the Sparta white power structure," said Nesmith. Carter had added fuel to the fire by asking how a county of nine thousand people, nearly half of whom lived on incomes below the poverty level, could use an international airline. McCown admitted under Nesmith's questioning about Associated Airways that a company plane had been making regular flights to Bimini in the Bahamas and to Haiti. He claimed that the flights were part of an elaborate commercial fishing deal he was negotiating with top government officials in the Bahamas. Later, some of his black associates who fell out with him complained that they had not been taken to the parties in Bimini and Atlanta and had not dined on the shrimp and lobster flown back to Mayfield from the Caribbean.

The key statement in the Nesmith article came in another paragraph. "Poverty program officials, men who openly admire McCown's work in bringing housing, jobs and political authority to Hancock's disad-

119

vantaged blacks, are afraid he is becoming a black emperor, 'no different from a benevolent white plantation owner, except he is black.'"

McCown's natural arrogance grew as his power grew. No longer content to humiliate local whites and blacks who opposed him, he was now willing to take on the state's governor. Even Al Horn, the ACLU lawyer and devoted friend, described him as "imperious" and losing some people by the very nature of his style. "It was very difficult to deal with John," he said. "He was being very effective and for that reason I and others continued to support him."

10

A Symbol Burns

"The sky was red. We got word the blacks
were burning the town. My father, husband and brother
took their guns and went. My mother and I
took pistols and stood watching the sky,
not knowing whether the men would return."
—*Young white woman*

The Clinch house, as most Spartans called it, was almost as much a community symbol as the courthouse. It stood high on a hill at the north entrance to town with a commanding view of the surrounding countryside. Down the hill to the south, the village of Sparta appeared, Dr. William Terrell's handsome Federal house to the right, the Victorian courthouse ahead. William G. Springer built the house in 1823. Over the years it was home to many families, but Colonel Henry Atkinson Clinch, a New Orleans attorney, fixed his name to it for more than a century when he came in 1865 to live there.

"A place that ever was lived in is like a fire that never goes out," Eudora Welty once wrote. "It flares up, it smolders for a time, it is fanned or smothered by circumstance, but its being is intact, forever fluttering within it, the result of some original ignition. It sometimes gives out glory, sometimes its light must be sought out to be seen, small and tender as a candle flame, but as certain." [1]

The massive house with its six huge columns gave out glory in the dark days after the Civil War. The Clinches made it a social center for the town and it was alive with music and dancing. The story was that Colonel Clinch, after serving in the Confederate army with a Louisiana command, had returned to the practice of law in New Orleans when that city was under the control of General Benjamin F. Butler. He refused Butler's order to address twelve blacks as "gentlemen of the jury" and fled the state. Like her husband, Mrs. Clinch was a strong-minded leader. She helped start Sparta's first public library and led the fund-raising effort to build the severely plain Confederate monument that stands in front of the courthouse.

At times the candle flame at the Clinch house almost flickered out. The shutters came off, the columns sagged, the gardens disappeared. Houses across the highway fell into disrepair while the surrounding groves were sold for timber. Finally, the Georgia Power Company acquired the land on which it stood and gave the house to the Hancock County Foundation for Historical Preservation, which set about acquiring funds to restore it. The foundation had spent much effort and considerable sums on it, raising money through home tours, antique shows, and contributions (*Sparta Ishmaelite*, April 27, 1972, Nov. 29, 1973). The refurbished home was preserved as a reminder of the county's past, a symbol of its traditions.

On Wednesday, May 8, 1974, Beatrice Thomas, an ECCO employee, parked in Sparta, blocking a sidewalk in violation of city ordinances. Police Chief Walter Garrett III said it was Thomas's third offense in recent days (*Augusta Chronicle*, May 13, 1974). In late April, the town's meter maid had issued a parking ticket to Thomas who, Garrett said, tore it up, threw it down, and used abusive language to an officer. On May 1 the woman had parked and failed to put money in a meter, according to Garrett, who personally gave her a ticket. He asked her to take care of the illegal parking and meter violations and she failed to do so. After the third incident, Garrett took her to the police station and made a case against her. Under the law she had several options: putting up a cash bond, a signed bond, or her driver's license instead of bond. She could not decide what to do and called McCown, who advised her not to give up her driver's license. McCown told Garrett to release her on her word.

McCown, now under attack in the newspapers for several strange businesses' being financed with public funds, had lost some of his black support. He had staged many successful demonstrations to arouse support during election periods. He thought he could control the law at the county level, and the parking ticket offered him a chance to rally his supporters once more in an emotional battle with Sparta officials. The Sparta business community, worn down by many demonstrations and boycotts, did not want further confrontations with McCown. Even Mayor Patterson confessed he had given up trying to do anything about the black leader, charging that he sometimes came to town at night drunk, with shotguns pointed from his car window, and that the state patrol had said to leave him alone.

McCown went to the police station threatening to protest when Chief Garrett would not follow his orders. A group of some fifty to seventy-five persons converged on Sparta's city hall, blocking the main street with cars and trucks. Many protesters were, through ECCO, on the public payroll, and some of the vehicles were public ones. Thomas, after two hours of protesting, signed the bond and the Wednesday demonstration broke up (*Macon Telegraph*, May 14, 1974). Thomas was never jailed; she was detained at City Hall while deciding whether she wanted to post a fifty-dollar bond. If she had paid the parking fines immediately, the cost would have been three dollars, police said. A black woman, leader of a group opposing McCown, said she thought it was a planned thing. "She's done this several times. Why would you wreck the county and have some of the things we've had this week for a dollar parking ticket?"

McCown was charged with interfering with an officer, unlawful assembly, and failure to disperse. His bond was set at $3,000 by the justice of the peace, who bound him over to a state court. McCown refused to post bond and was placed in jail Friday morning. James Hunt, executive vice-president of ECCO, charged that McCown's arrest exemplified the kind of justice the city of Sparta continually meted out to the black community.

City officials said they never locked McCown's cell during the daytime, that he could have left on his signature at any time, but that he chose to stay for propaganda purposes. McCown, holding press conferences from his unlocked cell, said the whole thing was a "deliberate attempt to find what would happen to the Hancock black community if it was stripped of a major portion of its leadership." A gathering of armed ECCO employees encircled the jail the entire time McCown was there. McCown told a reporter that they guarded his cell because "blacks have been known to be shot while in the jail and they weren't about to let that happen to me."

It suited him to stay in confinement for a while. The jail made a convenient place to hold interviews and he cheerfully posed looking through the bars for a black newspaper in Augusta (*The Mirror*, May 19, 1974). While McCown held court at the Sparta jail, his ECCO aides busied themselves organizing another of their boycotts of Sparta stores for Saturday. This boycott, later described as halfhearted, was accompanied by the usual march of some two hundred to three hundred hard-core supporters through town (*Macon Telegraph and News*, May 12, 1974).

That warm May Saturday night, while McCown was still in jail, two fires were set. One damaged an unoccupied house out from town. It was set as a decoy, attracting Sparta's one fire truck. While the firemen were occupied there, the real target of the arsonists burst into flame and was completely destroyed. The Clinch house, built of heart pine seasoned for more than a century and a half, almost exploded into flames. With its classical Greek columns lit up like giant torches, the fiery mansion on the hill reddened the night sky for miles around.

"We were at our home several miles from Sparta," said a young white woman. "The sky was red. We got word the blacks were burning the town. My father and my husband and brother took their guns and went. My mother and I took pistols and stood watching the sky, not knowing whether the men would return."

Rex Epps, president of the Sparta Chamber of Commerce and a volunteer fireman, was one of the first on the scene. He told a reporter, "When I saw what it was, Clinch Terrace was already covered in the back with flames. As we unrolled the hoses off the truck, I was saying then we couldn't do anything . . . but we went ahead and hooked it up . . . it was sickening. . . . I knew how much they [the historical foundation] had put in it. The blaze lit up this whole area. It was red all over. Folks several miles out in the country could see it" (*Macon Telegraph and News*, May 19, 1974). A saddened official of the historical society said, "You couldn't build it back for a million dollars."

A fire in a town as small as Sparta is a social event; a large crowd usually gathers. The Clinch house fire was a spectacular show and, despite their fears, many citizens, black and white, turned out to see it. The burning house set off a flood of emotions. Arson is a powerful weapon in the country, where most people live far from effective fire-fighting equipment. McCown had frequently talked about arson and his followers had threatened to burn the town on several occasions.

124

McCown himself told a friendly reporter how he had gotten access to the site of his river house when a timbering company threatened to stop him from building a road across its holdings to his property. He said, "Okay, but we won't be putting out any forest fires we might happen to see."[2] A few days before the Clinch house fire, he spoke to another reporter about a white political figure. "I don't know why he is mad at me. When I saw I couldn't lick him I didn't burn his house down."

Although McCown had always used threats of force, intimidation, economic blackmail, and similar tactics to get his way, he kept a strong hand on the reins. The burning of a symbol like the Clinch house did not fit his usual pattern; it was more his style to threaten. If, as was suspected, some of his overzealous followers burned the house without his knowledge, they did his cause tremendous harm, focusing even more unwelcome attention on his business activities. That night, John McCown signed his own bond and left the jail shortly after midnight.

Another fire broke out early Sunday morning, only hours later. It destroyed the home and automobile of a black woman who sympathized with local whites and had said so. The police chief said the town had three phones to the police along the two blocks of Sparta's business district, all extensions to the one line. The woman used one phone to call and say how sorry she was about the fire. Someone heard her on another line, the police chief speculated, and as a result her home was destroyed also. In each case, the state fire marshal found that arson was involved, but nobody was ever charged.

The town of Sparta had issued another parade permit for the blacks on Sunday from 3:00 to 7:00 P.M. McCown sent word he would parade when he chose, and at 7:05 P.M., after the permit expired, he led a group out of the courthouse, assembling in front of it and blocking the main street. The marchers then walked through the business district and on to the Sparta Baptist Church, where they entered, posted armed guards, and held their own service. Following the takeover of the church, they went out to the main street and lay down, blocking it. After listening to a speech by McCown, the marchers returned to the Confederate park facing the courthouse, where they destroyed a newly planted lawn and began to shout demands that Mayor Patterson resign.

McCown had already violated almost every traditional taboo in the rural Deep South. The last one was the violation of the white man's church—the final and unacceptable humiliation. Most news accounts skipped over the event, as Georgia news media were trying not to inflame the situation further, but an understated account in the *Christian Index* of June 6, 1974 told thousands of members of the powerful Georgia Baptist Convention about the incident. Georgia politicians began to hear from people over the state wanting to know what was going on. The message was no longer coming from a group of diehard Hancock County whites but from many others curious to know what kind of Georgia community it was where a congregation could not hold church services undisturbed.

"That started McCown's downfall when he commandeered the Sparta Baptist Church with armed men," said a local farmer. "Then people across the state finally understood what had been going on here."

"Sparta Church Scene of Black Takeover," the *Christian Index* headline read.

> Sparta Baptist Church in racially troubled Hancock County was the scene of a usurpation of facilities by blacks during a turbulent weekend in May.
>
> Sparta church, a 400-plus-member Georgia Baptist Church, had to forego evening services May 12 because about 150 black and three white persons took over the church's sanctuary and conducted their own "service."
>
> James Hartley, pastor for 2.5 years of the church, told *The Christian Index* that on a Sunday morning nine black persons, including John McCown, a "black power figure," entered the services in three groups at various times. One member of the group left before the service was over.
>
> Mr. Hartley said that on Sunday night, during the Training Union period, the group of 150 persons "marched from the courthouse to the church . . . coming in without saying anything to anyone.
>
> "They had their own service planned with preachers and all. One of the 'preachers' was a local black pastor. Also posted around the church building on the outside were several blacks wearing guns," he said.
>
> Continuing, Mr. Hartley said that "after staying about 20 to 25 minutes, the group left with one person stating that they would 'meet back here tomorrow.'
>
> "After leaving the church the group made their way back down main street, blocking the highway by lying down in the road," the pastor said.

McCown's response to public outrage over the church takeover was to charge Mayor Patterson with knowing something about the fire. Al Horn, McCown's attorney, said it might have been like the Reichstag fire. When the town posted a reward for information about the Clinch house fire, a letter postmarked New York City came from a Sparta black who said he saw two McCown aides running from the fire. The letter giving their names was turned over to the state fire marshal, but nothing was ever proved. Both men later became Hancock County officials. One was described by a reporter who had several encounters with him as "a fanatic, always armed and dangerous to himself and the community."

No marches took place on Monday following the traumatic weekend, but McCown held impromptu press conferences up and down the street as reporters and cameramen flooded into town. He told the *Augusta Chronicle* (May 14, 1974), "I'm not a violent man but if someone stands in my way I believe I should kill him. We don't need anybody to pray for us anymore." The *Chronicle* reported that a representative from the United States Justice Department along with a top official from the Georgia State Highway Patrol and a representative from the governor's Civil Disorder Task Force were attempting to arrange a meeting between McCown and city officials late Monday night to negotiate a settlement.

When the television cameras rolled into town on Monday, McCown abandoned his usual public relations performance. For a brief moment cameras recorded a side reserved for those who opposed him, not the image he displayed in foundation board rooms. McCown, guarded by four ECCO employees with pistols tucked in their belts, raged and threatened, "I'll destroy the town of Sparta," he shouted. "I don't give a damn about whites."

That Monday was an unusually busy day for McCown. He caused a disturbance at Sparta's only downtown restaurant by insulting two women. He told the police chief the only way to deal with him was with a baseball bat or a bullet. McCown informed newsmen that after "seven or eight years here trying to work with the whites there's just no hope." He said the mayor believed "God put blacks and whites separate and until the mayor is dealt with there's just no hope here. . . . If they leave me alone, I'll leave them alone, but if they bother me I'll knock hell out of them" (*Macon Telegraph*, May 14, 1974). Monday night, shots were fired into the home of a former Sparta policeman, breaking a large picture window but not injuring the sleeping family. Later, three or four shots from an automatic shotgun broke a window in a store owned by the police chief's brother (*Atlanta Constitution*, May 15, 1974).

Hancock blacks opposing McCown ran an advertisement in the May 16 *Sparta Ishmaelite* following the tumultuous weekend.

> We take this time to write a note to all law-abiding citizens to express our views on the conditions of our county. As you know, things are being destroyed in our county by outsiders who are here on big payrolls. This money is supposed to be for the betterment of the poor people. . . . They parade in front of the stores and tell you where to spend your money, but they don't give you a damn dime. What happened to the hospital when the so-called "black power" took over? We had a good hospital providing jobs for about 70 people. . . . More blacks are beginning to realize who is getting the money. We are still poor and black. . . . We have been living under black power eight years. No new industry will dare come this way because we have been grandstanding and head-lining too long. . . . No one will spend one dime to build factories in Hancock County because "Big John" wants to control everything. He takes care of a few, but many suffer. . . . That damn nightclub and those airplanes won't pay your bills or feed your family. . . . There are hot-headed people beginning to burn houses and trailers. Now is the time for good men of both races to come together and work things out for the betterment of all our citizens.

One of McCown's black opponents told the *Macon Telegraph* (May 14, 1974) that the protesting was political, not racial. "He [McCown] upsets the people and frightens them until they're almost afraid not to go the way he wants them to. You've got to be strong to stand up against him. I mean strong. He is the Hancock County boss. He runs the commission and the hospital. He tells us what to do and we're sick of it," she said.

The troubles in Hancock caused considerable embarrassment to Governor Jimmy Carter. He was already making plans to run for the presidency and black voters formed a key part of his strategy. Hancock County was a potential disaster area for any Georgia politician and most of them stayed away. Hancock's small white minority had little or no political influence and had gained a reputation for right-wing extremism. They were continually frustrated that nobody seemed to understand what was happening in their community.

Caught between the violent bombast of McCown, abetted by the ignorance of much of the black community, and the primitive racial concepts of some whites, moderates in each racial group were silenced. There were many clues that Carter understood the real nature of McCown but it was not politically advantageous to act on what he knew. Carter's unframed picture is pasted to the wall in the Hancock County courthouse alongside that of Dr. Martin Luther King, Jr. No photo of Carter is likely to adorn the walls of Sparta's city hall.

Governor Carter announced that he would make a personal visit to the county on Monday, May 20, to try to ease tensions, a visit some observers believed was simply a campaign gambit. Before coming, he issued a statement to the press expressing his concern about recent confrontations between the races and "the inexcusable destruction of property and violations of the law." Carter said McCown had already agreed to meet with him but Mayor Patterson at that time had not. Later, Carter promised to meet with each man separately. "There is no magic solution for the problems in that county," he said. "They have been building for years. But maybe we can at least make a beginning [to finding solutions] today" (both *Atlanta Constitution* and *Journal*, May 17, 1974).

The *Atlanta Constitution* (May 20) praised Carter editorially, saying, "He deserves a full measure of praise for making the effort to intervene personally to head off further racial strife." The *Atlanta Journal* (May 22) also praised him for going, adding, "But the important aspect is that he did so without taking sides." The *Journal* was particularly reserved in its coverage of the Hancock County situation, adopting what it considered to be a responsible and moderate position. The *Augusta Chronicle* (May 15) took what turned out to be a more realistic view when it endorsed efforts at a peaceful solution "provided it was not a mere cover for capitulation to threats, intimidation and force." The *Macon Telegraph* (May 19), nearest to the scene, found it difficult to believe blacks were discriminated against in a county where they held most of the offices and noted that it was McCown's style to gain political power in the streets with demonstrations every election year since 1966.

Arriving in Sparta, Carter met first with Mayor Patterson and a group composed largely of white citizens at the Bank of Hancock County. He was greeted by a placard-bearing crowd, predominantly women, carrying signs that said "Arson Must Not Pay," "We Back Our Mayor," "Fight Nazi Rule." Carter told whites (and a few blacks) at the bank he would send state election supervisors down for the fall primaries. Then, before a large gathering of blacks at the courthouse, he promised to lift his objections to the $300,000 OEO grant to the county. Afterward, the governor visited Mayfield and the ECCO projects there.

The *Constitution* and the *Journal* (May 21) quoted Mayor Patterson as saying to Carter, "We need your help and if we don't get it we'll put Lester Maddox in. He's my buddy." Patterson said years later, "Jimmy Carter wore me out calling me up trying to get me to meet with McCown and cool things down. He got elected president of the United States on civil rights right here." Another city official added, "Carter said he never told a lie. He told three here that one day."

Many embittered Sparta whites felt that Carter was using them. Said one, "He went over in the bank building and told them he wasn't going to give McCown any more money. When the books were audited they showed that he gave it to McCown the day he was here." Actually, news accounts quoted the governor as saying before the meeting that his objection had been met and he was going to release the $300,000 grant.

There was no question that Carter alienated the whites in Sparta when he talked to them, said a *Constitution* reporter who covered the meeting. "He was pretty hard line with the whites. I got the impression he was saying, 'You are not going to get any favors out of me.' Instead of sending in state troopers he sent in a small racial unrest unit."

The reporter remembered that it was "bloody hot" at the courthouse when Carter addressed the blacks. "He made a strong speech for being peaceful; he was really trying to be responsible. It was unusual for a governor to meddle in local affairs. I didn't feel any fear of violence. There is something intimidating about having the governor in town. There was no fighting for turf."

A young Englishwoman, wife of a member of Parliament, accompanied the Atlanta reporter when he covered the Carter visit. They went to see the mayor and found him and his people very hostile. The Englishwoman asked, "Isn't it true you keep all blacks here in a state of slavery?" Her remark reveals an attitude Hancock whites met often, one that had already embittered them.

A black minister thought whites misinterpreted what Carter had done. "The whites were angry at Governor Carter for going to Mayfield and for speaking to the blacks. Actually, he was going to learn. At the courthouse he told the blacks the world had its eyes on Hancock County to see how blacks can operate and be fair. He told them 'I regret to say you haven't done such a good job in that respect.'" The minister's version of Carter's speech was not reflected in news accounts that quoted him as telling blacks, "I didn't come here as a judge to tell you how to run your business." He was applauded when he said he had found no illegal use of OEO funds as a result of audits of ECCO operations. Carter reminded the crowd, "I have the ability as governor to send 11,000 troops into your county," adding that he did not want to do that. "I can't come over here and run your business for you."

McCown calmed down when the governor came, telling Carter that Sparta officials needed help desperately but that "they won't accept help from us." McCown praised Carter for trying to open the doors of communication. A reporter who covered several McCown incidents before the Carter visit described McCown's usual attitude. "John swaggered around the county with a gun on his hip. He had his photo taken sitting on the Confederate monument chewing a straw. I asked him to pose standing in the street looking belligerent 'because that's what you are.' He did pose and even had the film driven to Atlanta."

"The ruling whites in Sparta were basically not quite as mean as in Sandersville [a neighboring town that also had some racial trouble]," said another Atlanta reporter, "but would want to keep blacks in their place. I would agree with McCown that he should shake them up. . . . McCown was an example of what Lord Acton said; power corrupts. . . . Hancock and Sparta were a depressing place to me. I spent the nights in Milledgeville and the Holiday Inn was a cheerful sight. Sparta's main street with its vacant stores and the distrustful whites who wouldn't speak to you was upsetting. There was a tinge of meanness in Sparta."

The calm following Carter's visit did not last long. McCown, getting ready for the late summer primaries, invited Stokely Carmichael, then traveling the United States on a Ugandan passport, to speak at the Hancock County courthouse. Carmichael was described as a Ugandan diplomat, though the Ugandan desk at the State Department said he had only a regular passport from that country. Jeff Nesmith and Jim Rankin of the *Constitution*, who were on hand at the courthouse when Carmichael spoke June 4, found it an unbelievable and frightening experience. Only two other whites were present in the crowded room. Rankin described it as a "get whitey" evening. One speaker, recently returned from a visit to Africa and wearing a dashiki, said they were handling the situation in Africa by killing whites. This was greeted by strong applause.

Nesmith remembered that when McCown got up, he started in on whites, shouting that whites had mistreated blacks for hundreds of years. Then he began shouting rhythmically, "Who killed Martin Luther King?" and the crowd would reply, "Whites!" This chant continued for a while, getting louder and louder. McCown then pointed out the reporters and said they had been examining land deeds in the courthouse. "We got white reporters going around beating us over the head with pencils like they used to beat us over the head with sticks, and I'm going to put a stop to it," McCown yelled.

When McCown brought Carmichael into the volatile Hancock County situation, introducing him as a Ugandan diplomat, it was almost precisely the date the International Commission of Jurists issued one of the most scathing reports it had produced in twenty-two years of investigating injustice. After examining evidence for three years, the jurists concluded that Uganda had seen "a total breakdown of the rule of law."[3] Carmichael, a native of Trinidad, was one of the most rhetorically violent of the black spokesmen during the 1960s and 1970s; he would talk of smashing the entire nation, or all of western civilization, crying, "To hell with the laws of the United States!"[4]

The Carmichael visit was a typical McCown device to stir up racial feelings before election campaigns. McCown used demonstrations and threats in every election, beginning in 1968. The vicious verbal attack on whites at the courthouse June 4 was simply an opening gun in the election campaigns for the summer. Atlanta news media played down the Carmichael visit. No violence followed and Carmichael quickly disappeared from the Hancock scene.

132

In early July, the OEO announced a $2 million grant for McCown. Thousands of Georgians had seen his threats on television during the May riots and when the OEO grant was announced, the governor's office was besieged by telephone callers demanding that he veto it. Since it came directly from Washington rather than from the regional office, he could not.

The burning of the Clinch house and the violent rhetoric it unleashed increased the uneasiness in the white community. Dr. Olin Shivers, Atlanta physician who had restored Rock Mill, the old Shivers plantation near Mayfield, became concerned for the safety of his house and thought he should call on McCown. "I decided to talk to McCown about getting some of his people to live in the house as caretakers, since it was only two miles from his fishpond," Dr. Shivers said. "I drove my truck to a black filling station in Sparta where they directed me to the county ordinary's house. I found McCown there, a fairly short, nice-looking black man, and told him I was looking for a couple to live at my place. He said he had to go immediately to a meeting, so I invited him to come by later that afternoon and I would fix him a drink. We were desperate to get someone to watch the house.

"McCown came and had his drink," Dr. Shivers recalled, "and then he wanted to show us what he was doing and we went out to his car. There was an enormous pistol on the seat. He said he carried it around because he knew everybody was after him and if they tried anything he would get a shot at them. He showed me the catfish farm and then came back to the house and had a couple more drinks before telling me he wouldn't think of having any of his people live in what used to be a plantation. He said he planned to buy up all the store fronts in Sparta and that he already owned most of them. 'We are going to build a showcase city in Mayfield,' he said. 'We are going to close up Sparta.'

"I told him he ought to let Sparta die a natural death if competition brought that about, but it was not fair to do what he said. McCown replied, 'We are going to kill it. You know that square in front of the courthouse they call Confederate Square? We are going to name it Martin Luther King Square.'"

It was late in the afternoon and McCown said he had to go to Atlanta. Dr. Shivers warned him to be careful driving.

"Oh, I'll take my driver with me," he replied.

"You have a chauffeur?" Dr. Shivers inquired.

As he put the car in gear and raced down the curving driveway, McCown waved a hand out of the window in a dramatic gesture, calling back, "Somebody has to do the work."

11

A Time for Questions

"Now after nearly eight years and several million
dollars from the federal government
and tax-exempt foundations, Hancock County is
still poor. But John McCown is not."
—*Atlanta Constitution*

After the events in May, the burning of the Clinch house and the takeover of the Sparta Baptist Church, the state's most powerful newspaper, the *Atlanta Constitution*, began a serious study of the situation in Hancock County, as did the *Macon Telegraph*, the leading newspaper in Middle Georgia.[1] United States Senator Sam Nunn, great-nephew of Middle Georgia's long-time congressman Carl Vinson, also began to take note of McCown's affairs.

The *Telegraph* series started June 9, reporting, "It's not too unusual, in fact, for McCown to stop county business and his own federally-supported operations to carry out demonstrations—sometimes using two buses purchased with federal Small Business Administration loans to carry his followers to the protest scene." Describing the first of the demonstrations in May, the article said, "Although it was Wednesday, a working day in Hancock, employees at his government-financed minority businesses and black county employees who work for him, including Ordinary Edith Ingram and Superior Court Clerk Leroy Wiley, left their jobs and joined in."

Widely varying views were expressed about the demonstrations. The *Telegraph* said McCown marched on City Hall with an estimated one hundred and fifty followers—"some armed as is customary in his protests." Al Horn, McCown's attorney, observed, "When they had that rumpus in town when they arrested some of the ECCO workers for just nit-shit stuff, I tried those cases and believe me, they were just absolute nit-shit. John was over in Mayfield when the thing broke out, and a genuine little downtown mini-riot started. John came there and

135

they arrested him and charged him with several things. He hadn't created the situation and he saw no reason to break it up, suggesting it would break up real quickly if they would release the woman from jail. [Actually, she was never jailed.] They ended up arresting John and he refused to make bond. They had no business arresting the woman. It was a total harassment arrest. The arrest of John was even worse because he hadn't done anything.

"We got acquittal on both charges that they tried John on," said Horn. "They couldn't have won the case anyway. I had an all-black jury. By the time we finished picking the jury it was a foregone conclusion," Horn said. "The most they could have done was hung the jury. We won it on the merits as well, as they had no case. They should have dismissed it on a motion to dismiss." The jury found McCown not guilty in fourteen minutes. For many years during the McCown era and thereafter, no Hancock jury brought a guilty verdict in a criminal case. Enforcement of the law had become so firmly ingrained in local black consciousness as a white man's thing, that it was thought antiblack to carry out normal legal processes.

Although the trouble had quieted down, the *Telegraph* quoted a state agent assigned to the community as saying, "There's nothing to compare with this situation in the state and perhaps in the nation." Discussing the "countless incidents" over the eight years McCown had been in the county, the article said, "McCown does not deny that such incidents are, at times, deliberately provoked to solidify the black community, and it is commonly believed in town that he begins agitating at election time. Once before, several burnings occurred—in 1970, when McCown and his slate of black candidates took control of county government.

"McCown owns four homes around Hancock County, including a $60,000 residence on which he owes $58,000 near his Mayfield complex and which he says he plans to turn over to ECCO soon; and some neglected acreage. He has neglected to pay property taxes for three years, 1970, 1971 and 1973, totaling about $3,500 without any apparent threat of being penalized.

"One potential black candidate not aligned with McCown has withdrawn from the fall county commission race because of telephoned warnings that harm might befall his family," said the *Telegraph*. The man said the calls "centered around my children and grandchildren. Within myself, it didn't scare me. But I was afraid for my children."

On June 12, a few days after the *Telegraph* series began, Senator Sam Nunn wrote Elmer B. Staats, comptroller general of the United States, requesting that "the General Accounting Office undertake to monitor the ongoing OEO audit and make such additional audit of other federal funds received by ECCO, Inc., as you deem necessary after your investigation." Nunn complained to Staats, "Despite the fact that sufficient questions existed to justify this in-house audit, the OEO informed me last week of its intention to award ECCO an additional two million dollars well before the completion of the ongoing audit. Public confidence in government, and in the ECCO project in particular, can only be further eroded by such administrative action." Nunn said that despite his opposition to making the grant before the audit had been completed and reviewed, OEO officials had advised him they still intended to do it. He added that since he did not have all of the relevant facts he was making no judgment "as to alleged improprieties."

A month later, on July 24, 1974, Senator Nunn's office issued a press release that was front-page news in Georgia. To it he attached his letter to Staats and a letter dated July 22 from Gregory J. Ahart, director of GAO. Ahart said discussions with OEO officials showed necessary reviews and approvals were made prior to awarding the $2 million grant and that ECCO had already received $500,000 of it. The release said GAO had briefed Nunn in his Washington office and "their initial report indicates that the OEO external audit will show substantial discrepancies." Nunn's attitude was that there was ample smoke to suspect a fire at ECCO and that sensible people would act accordingly. A Justice Department official based in Atlanta recalled meeting with Senator Nunn in Washington; the GAO and the FBI were represented. Nunn urged a swift investigation, saying, "If something is wrong, find out and punish. If not, say so and let them go about their business." The Internal Revenue Service put a special agent and a full-time revenue agent on the job.

Ernest Moore, an articulate young black then on Nunn's staff, had been dealing with McCown for several years, beginning in 1968 when he served on the governor's staff and had to work out disputes involving the area community development agency at Milledgeville. At one meeting, McCown and Moore engaged in a shouting match and later McCown called to apologize. "He was just testing me," Moore said. "He had a habit of testing everyone. He would check you out to see if he could use you." When Senator Nunn became involved, McCown asked for a meeting with the senator in Washington. "John and I had a big argument there," Moore recalled. "He called Senator Nunn and said he ought to fire me. I later arranged a meeting in Macon between Senator Nunn and some black moderates from Hancock County but we never really cleared it up. The way McCown handled himself raised a lot of questions," Moore continued. "I never saw anything that indicated he really stole. He had a bad habit of thinking you were an enemy if you didn't agree with him. His personality had an awful effect on what happened there. Doing it differently would have been more successful. It's so sad. I avoid that place."

The *Constitution* was widely criticized over the years by conservative Southern whites because of its liberal stand on the race question. Many whites hated Ralph McGill, the *Constitution's* crusading editor and later its publisher, who strongly advocated equal rights for blacks. McGill was dead by the time of the Sparta trouble, but his reputation lingered and it seemed strange to hear his newspaper charged with racism when it began to show a marked interest in McCown's activities. McCown called reporter Jeff Nesmith a racist. When Carter held up the OEO grant, asking to see an audit, the *Constitution* turned its attention to developments in Hancock County. "I thought there wasn't a story down there," said Nesmith. "McCown had a good image and was highly regarded as a black figure who wanted to do away with welfare through jobs. Hancock County whites had acquired a bad image in race relations. The managing editor kept saying there was a story and pushed me and Jim Rankin down there to do it."

McCown's organization followed them around the county wherever they went, Nesmith said. "They had a system of radio-equipped cars and kept a check on us. When we were in the county clerk's office checking records we heard him say to the caller, 'Yeah, two of 'em just walked in.' We made a very thorough study of the deed records, tracking down all of the names and firms involved. That's how we began to discover the self-dealing. We found out about McCown's land dealings and his involvement with the Georgia Human Relations Council. He bought land with a mortgage against the council. The last day he was employed there he marked the mortgage as satisfied. We made notes from the deeds and compared them to the records of the council. We also talked to the people in the council and they told us a good bit. It was difficult to deal with Hancock County sources as they were all too emotional."

One of the tales circulating about McCown involved an elaborate house he was building on the Ogeechee River. At first it was to be McCown's home; it was always described that way in the early stages of its construction. Later, when it became involved in court charges, it was described as a conference center. The house was remote and few people had seen it when Nesmith and Rankin began their investigations. The two reporters decided they would like a photograph. They got their pictures, but it took a canoe trip down the Ogeechee River. The Ogeechee is unspoiled and wild and on a hot June day in Middle Georgia it is alive with cottonmouth moccasins. "I was scared to death," Nesmith recalled. "Not of John McCown, but of all those cottonmouths."

The photograph appeared in the *Constitution* July 1, 1974, along with an article describing the house as "a large brick home at the river's edge. The architecture of the sprawling home is more befitting Miami's Biscayne Bay than a Hancock County river swamp. The house is being built of bricks manufactured at a concrete-block plant owned by ECCO. . . . A short canal has been dredged from the river to a flight of wide concrete steps that descend from a backyard terrace directly into the water. A winding dirt road leads through timber company lands for more than a mile before it ends at an imposing pair of concrete pillars (also made of ECCO bricks) and a high wrought iron gate."

Questions were asked about the land the house was located on and why an initial down payment had been made with a check from the Georgia Council when the land title was held by Mayfield Farms, an unincorporated company owned by McCown. The *Constitution* wrote, "McCown once said he had borrowed $56,000 from the Citizens Trust Bank in Atlanta to build the home. He said it would cost that much to build 'the kind of house I want.' . . . Of the few persons who have viewed McCown's river home, most insist that it will cost far more than $56,000 to build."

The *Constitution* probe of McCown led to a series of articles that brought on a federal investigation of his programs. The first story said:

> Now after nearly eight years and several million dollars from the federal government and tax-exempt foundations, Hancock County is still poor.
>
> But John McCown is not.
>
> During those eight years, McCown has wheeled and dealed and profiteered and used poverty funds for his own benefit. By Hancock County standards, he has become a rich man.
>
> When he drives around the county, John McCown usually drives a Cadillac Eldorado. When he visits Atlanta, he usually flies a twin-engined airplane which he says he owns and borrowed $33,000 to buy. In Atlanta, an apartment at the expensive Peachtree Towers in Peachtree Center is listed in his name.
>
> A search of property deeds in the courthouse here revealed that McCown now personally owns over 600 acres of land in Hancock County, all of it purchased since 1966. The property has a value estimated at $200,000. . . .
>
> With one hand he ran Hancock County. With the other he ran the Georgia Council on Human Relations. . . .
>
> The East Central Committee for Opportunity (ECCO) was established under the council to administer individual anti-poverty programs.
>
> Through ECCO, McCown established a 358-acre catfish farm, a concrete block plant, a wood pallet plant, and a sheet metal products factory, all aimed at providing jobs. He vowed to drive welfare out of the county by bringing jobs and prosperity to the people, both black and white.
>
> However, none of his antipoverty enterprises has yet made a profit. The sheet metal plant was inactive when *Journal-Constitution* reporters visited it. So were the wood pallet plant and the concrete block plant.

During the McCown era welfare cases in the county increased 673 percent and unemployment 20 percent, the article said. When an inflation factor was applied, retail sales decreased 7 percent. ECCO had received funds averaging more than $5,000 for each poverty-level family in the county with "no readily apparent" impact.

"The Atlanta newspapers are, in my opinion, a reactionary crowd," said Al Horn. "The reporters were not sent down to do an impartial investigating job. They were sent down to prove a point: that the blacks were incompetent and stealing and that McCown was a crook. The blacks were having a hard time. The general problem was acquiring managerial talents. Running the government and business is difficult and if you've got no training it is even more so."

Horn was not the only person who believed that McCown was the victim of racist, reactionary forces. Sonny Walker felt he was "put in his place because he was a black who was a symbol of power and influence and authority and he got too big for his britches." Walker said McCown made some political enemies and because he was courageous and persuasive "and, to a certain extent, dominating and controlling," the decision was made to stop him, and he was stopped. "We use all of the agencies that are available to us in this country to stop people," Walker said. "That can be done on a neighborhood level, city level, state level, whatever."

Federal agencies investigating themselves are not always productive, and OEO's probing ECCO was somewhat like an indulgent parent's investigating a spoiled child. Walker said that he found "John McCown and ECCO were operating programs a lot differently from the way I had been accustomed to seeing programs operate. John was more or less paying bills out of his pocket, out of petty cash. The audit took a lot of exceptions to the way things were happening. We didn't see any signs of any money being siphoned off or stolen or anything of that nature, especially in our funds, but we just saw some very questionable management practices."

The OEO audit begun by Walker's agency found some embarrassing sloppiness, but no illegality. McCown was drawing $50,000 a year in salary in a county where the median family income was $5,000. ECCO was renting apartments in Atlanta, including one occupied by McCown's son, who was attending college there. Three ECCO employees were using ECCO credit cards to charge airline tickets, motel rooms, and other expenses in excess of amounts allowed by OEO. One of McCown's top assistants was paid living expenses by ECCO. The auditors noted that ECCO's system of financial management was "inadequate" to properly keep track of the use of federal funds (*Atlanta Constitution*, Aug. 3, 1974). Such findings would normally result in a freeze of funds, but OEO Washington announced an additional $2 million ECCO grant in the middle of the investigations (*Constitution*, Aug. 3).

The people who worked with McCown almost unanimously condemned his business practices while defending his motivation and character. Glustrom, who had been closely associated with him for several years, said he "operated out of his hip pocket," a statement commonly made of him. More interestingly, in view of later developments, he said McCown was not at all a record keeper "and that may or may not have been calculated by him." Glustrom added that he had resigned from the board of ECCO because he was too far away to keep tabs on things and he knew "certain irregularities were taking place and the program was him [McCown] and without him there couldn't be anything and nothing could continue."

Glustrom thought McCown had to be very brave to go into Hancock County as he did. He said he had heard McCown's life threatened, and McCown told him the reason he had such an expense with automobiles was the possibility of attack.

"He always felt that he would die in a violent way," Glustrom added. "Anybody who would stick his head down in Hancock County, a black man trying to get political power, would have to have some sort of psychological bent. Something would have to be driving him. Very few people would do that; I don't know anybody else who would except McCown. He would have to be a very brave man or a fool and he would have to want something mighty bad." McCown wasn't idealistic in a Christlike way, Glustrom thought, starving himself to death for an ideal. He wanted to take care of himself "according to the American ideal" along with taking care of the situation in Hancock County. McCown was making a large salary so he had money to do a lot of things most people in Hancock County did not have money to do. "A lot of what appeared to be stealing was actually a part of his income," Glustrom said.

Al Horn thought "a lot of the frustrations of the government in pinpointing John's misfeasances, if any, was they thought a lot of this stuff was embezzlement or diversion of funds when in fact all it was was just shifting from one thing to another. John took care of his lieutenants and took care of his people. I'm sure he diverted money from time to time from the overall process of what he was doing."

McCown had some very respectable connections and he made use of them. He maintained ties with Atlanta University and much of his Ford Foundation money was channeled through that reputable black institution. Dr. Robert Vowels, then dean of its business school, took a strong

142

interest in the work in Hancock County and recruited some of his faculty to go down and help ECCO. Dr. G. G. Neffinger, a white professor of business administration on Vowels's staff, was one of a team from the school that worked with McCown in the early stages, well before the investigations of 1974.

"ECCO had problems meeting the requirements of the government and the Ford Foundation," said Dr. Neffinger. "We went down and looked at the accounting system and found that it was in a terrible mess. We spent a lot of time getting it into shape, but we got it all reconciled. I was back there after that and the system was operating correctly as we set it up." Neffinger later worked on straightening out ECCO records for the Georgia Council on Human Relations. He thought there was serious mismanagement, but he saw no evidence of illegalities. "Because these various corporations weren't generating funds on their own and because you had to meet payrolls, they kept shifting money from one fund to another. They didn't keep records of how these shifts were done. It was all OK but they did it the wrong way. They didn't keep a control account of all these things. It was a terrible, terrible mess."

McCown offered Neffinger a job with ECCO, but he refused because he could see it was not going to succeed. The people operating the fish farm were not doing a good job, Neffinger thought. They were not trying to get markets and they were not producing well. He felt the major problem was a lack of management skill. "They didn't have the technical experience to do it." Part of the problem lay in McCown. "He had a very dominant personality. He was stubborn and once he made up his mind it was very difficult to change it. He had a tendency to make poor decisions because he didn't have complete knowledge of the facts. He should have continued to be the head man and hired an assistant to run the day-to-day operations. He made every decision about every single thing that went on down there. He could not delegate authority and as a result he was like a juggler with ten balls in the air all the time."

A black management expert hired by the Ford Foundation believed if McCown had followed his firm's recommendations, his program could have been saved. "We couldn't ever pin down what happened to the money," he said. "McCown had a Messiah complex. He gave away catfish—some $50,000 worth disappeared like the loaves and fishes.

143

They made management mistakes, not taking care of the temperature of the water and killing thousands of fingerlings. McCown valued loyalty above business acumen and knowledge.

"The records were so confused we couldn't create an audit trail. We could not discern any evidence John had taken money. He would keep programs going that were no longer funded, saying, 'What the hell, I'm keeping fifty black folks going.' He let people live rent-free in the housing project. He had that kind of Messiah complex; he didn't feel that rules applied.

"He would try you. Once he walked me real fast for several miles hoping I would puff and pant and have to sit down. I stayed with him and finally he had to sit down. He liked to test you and put you on the spot," the black management expert said.

"He was undisciplined. John didn't feel bound to conventions or rules.

"You are in danger when you start getting close to the bottom line of what makes stuff happen in an area. John did that. 'If they shoot at me they are going to get the ball right back,' he would say. Senator Talmadge is supposed to have made a phone call to the head of OEO threatening that if he gave a dime more to ECCO he would be fired. Absentee owners of large tracts of land were taxed at the level of the 1930s. John started dipping into that. He was talking about taxing it at a rate favorable to the county. He was getting close to what this country is about—money, privilege, power. It was a Greek tragedy.

"John McCown came along at a time when he was able to attract support to challenge the status quo," the management man said. "He upset a lot of people. ECCO was upsetting the political ecology not only of that county but of the region. It got the attention of Governor Carter and Senators Talmadge and Nunn and pressure was put on the Atlanta University School of Business. Most people involved were audited by the IRS and my people were investigated by the United States district attorney. We had one hell of a time with the FBI, being treated as if we were part of a plot. Some of my people got very distressed about it."

Another black man had a different story to tell. In rural Georgia they talk about "public" jobs. When a man leaves his farm to take a job elsewhere, he says he is doing public work. This Hancock farmer had never done public work until McCown came. He had always worked on his pleasant, well-tended farm. "The fish farm was one of the nicest things that could have happened," he believed. "I was hired out there by a fellow named B. R. Lindsay from Alabama who was brought by McCown. They started as good a project as could be put in the county, except for the raceways. Water had to be pumped half a mile from the river to feed the raceways and the electricity bill was over our heads. Lindsay told McCown from the beginning he was going overhead on the raceways but McCown didn't care. He didn't take an idea from nobody. He fired Mr. Lindsay, who was a fine fellow. Lindsay's got a fish farm of his own in Alabama and still operates it."

Lindsay said he was not fired by McCown but that he managed the fish farm at Mayfield for thirteen months and left hurriedly because the man running his own fish farm in Alabama had a heart attack. Lindsay said he got along with McCown, but he did oppose the expensive raceways and thought the farm could have been a success operated his way. His opinion about the expensive consultants was less positive.

"McCown didn't like white people," said the black farmer. "We've got a lot of whites in the city and county here, I mean well-off people, but they didn't fit McCown's bracket no way. Look like he just didn't want no whites involved in nothing, so the federal government began to crack down. He was planning to put a black in charge. I don't know this but this was some reports we heard. But then we had to turn around and get another white fellow, Jim Hall. I think he was out of Mississippi. He had been in the fish farm business years and years and was well experienced but he could not get McCown to leave those raceways alone.

"He [McCown] had orders carrying fish to Alabama and the Carolinas in all sizes," the black farmer said. "At one while it [the fish farm] was bringing in some money. At the time Mr. Lindsay left it was. Finally Mr. Hall left too. I never knew why Mr. Hall left, what happened or nothing. McCown put another guy in charge of it and he knew everything, but he didn't know nothing concerning fish compared to neither one of the other two. He was black. If somebody with business experience had been in charge I believe it would be operating today."

Charges circulated that whites had poisoned the pond and killed thousands of catfish. Al Horn said it happened twice. Later, asked if anyone had been killed in Hancock's racial disputes, Horn smiled and said, "Only those poor old catfish."

145

The farmer who worked at the catfish farm was not sure about who killed the fish. He came to work one morning, he said, and the water had turned a different color. "Every fish in there was dead. The land was cleared around the pond and the only way was to come up through the thickest part of the swamp. It was impossible for anybody to throw anything from the road into this pond. I don't think the whites had a thing to do with it, I think it was an inside job. I didn't know what type insurance they had or anything. The biologist was there and that same morning he took some fish and cut them open and took them to Alabama or Mississippi to an experiment station. We haven't heard that report to this day."

McCown's fish fries became famous, attracting black leaders like Atlanta's Mayor Maynard Jackson. A prominent black Atlanta attorney, a friend of McCown's, told about the time Jackson was there and the real terror a local black showed when his car horn stuck during the ceremonies. "He got out of his car and ran away in fright, shouting 'I didn't do it, Mr. McCown.' McCown really intimidated those people down there. They made him a kingfish. He slept with all the women around him." A reporter gave more insights into McCown's relationship with local blacks when he wrote in *Esquire*, "On one occasion he dealt with some Washington officials from a gas-station pay phone in Hancock, then walked right out the door to buttonhole an elderly Step-in Fetchit black who had been seen preparing a barbecue for the white Sparta police chief. 'Yes, John, yessir, brother,' the old man said. 'I won't do it again.' "[2]

"When we first went down there John McCown was looked on by the natives, the black people of Hancock County, as the incarnation of Christ himself," said Dr. Neffinger. "John was the driving force, the thing that put it together and kept it together and the thing that eventually made it fall apart, too." A black man, once a top aide in the McCown organization, felt "the concept of McCown's project was terrific but the administration of it was not good. It was not designed to be a political springboard, it was designed to help poor people."

As for McCown's economic development programs, a Sparta businessman wrote the *Macon Telegraph* July 3, 1974: "We raised from local merchants and interested people here in Hancock County over the last few years, a nucleus of $84,850. With this we started a garment plant, an addition to a local furniture plant, and bought the ground the lumber plant is on. These three operations employ 344 blacks and 73 whites. Mr. McCown states he has spent many times more and has fifty employees." The seed money they used to create more than four hundred jobs was less than the amount spent for consultants and travel in nine months at one ECCO project, the catfish farm.

Some criticisms of McCown came from veterans in the civil rights field. The flood of money into civil rights work caused considerable tension between old-timers and newcomers. A former director of the Southern Regional Council (SRC) was particularly dubious of "do-gooders" who took on business projects like co-ops and also very sensitive about propriety. "We old-timers knew we were on the spot just because we worked for a sensitive agency dealing in race relations. We were very careful that money was spent for the purpose for which it was given, and we used ironclad accounting methods. You had better be like Caesar's wife." Differences in style existed, too. Experienced workers felt that extravagant living, even if one could afford it, was not the best symbol for people who were working with the downtrodden. It annoyed the former SRC man when four Ford Foundation officials chartered a plane to take them the hundred miles from Atlanta to Mc-Cown's landing strip at Mayfield, a distance that could have been traveled quickly by automobile.

"People never had any trouble here," said one black leader. "Hancock County was a good county. John did it for the money. He first came in here with an ACTION group to help the poor and then he changed when he found out he could get money by making Hancock blacks seem mistreated." Another Hancock County man who accompanied McCown to a foundation in New York City said he made Hancock blacks sound like slaves.

Teams of reporters, accountants, auditors, FBI men, IRS agents, and others went over the jumbled empire McCown built, and various estimates of the money he received were published, ranging from $5 million to $12 million. The total amount of money McCown received from various agencies may never be known. In a letter to the voters of Hancock County in the early 1970s (the mimeographed letter was undated), McCown claimed to have brought $10,582,000 to the county. It was typical of his bookkeeping that the figures in his letter totaled

$8,782,000 rather than the figure he gave. He listed housing development—$3 million, other funding sources—$1.5 million, Minority Enterprise Small Business Company—$600,000, Ford Foundation—$372,000, water and sewerage system—$300,000, real and other properties—$210,000, heavy construction equipment—$200,000, block and concrete company—$150,000, office buildings—$150,000, processing plant—$125,000, buses—$60,000, warehouses—$60,000, guest house—$30,000, theater—$25,000. He added $2 million, presumably for the fish farm.

The Ford Foundation put millions into the county, much of it through Atlanta University ($1,812,131). In addition to $250,000 handled by the Georgia Council, $850,000 was granted directly to ECCO for the catfish farm.[3] Various government agencies were even more generous. The controversial $2 million OEO grant announced in the middle of the 1974 investigations was supposed to carry ECCO until April 30, 1976. The grant was an extension of a previous one for $1.3 million, an OEO spokesman said.[4] The Ford Foundation and government agencies put large sums into McCown's housing project at Mayfield, with a $400,000 government grant for the sewerage system alone. In addition, HUD guaranteed two mortgages for nearly $2.5 million. The mortgages were in default and were again the responsibility of HUD within a short time. Most tenants paid one-fourth of their incomes for rent and utilities and, since many of them had little or no income, they paid little or no rent. The all-electric homes were heated in the most expensive way. With few tenants paying their electric bills, there was no incentive to conserve so costs were very high. The 150 housing units were built in a remote corner of the county at the opposite end from Milledgeville, where jobs were available.[5] United States taxpayers paid for the waste and bad planning.

The range of ECCO-related activities was wide. The ECCO airline flew principally to the Bahamas and Haiti, supposedly hauling seafood from the Bahamas to complement the marketing of catfish. Federal narcotics agents watched the ECCO airstrip many nights but would never admit it officially and nothing ever came of it. John McCown was imaginative and creative. What other poverty agency had spawned a night club, an international airline, a detective agency, and a sporting club with M-1 rifles?

12

The Money Chests Close

*"Some of the things were not monumentally successful,
for instance the fish farm."*
—*Ford Foundation executive*

One of McCown's lieutenants who fell out with him described the 1974 elections as being a time "when all you had to do was raise your fist and say 'I'm black and I'm proud' and you would be elected." William H. Jackson (Billy Jack), a black pool-room operator, was a candidate for the Hancock County commission. "This guy can barely read his name," said the ex-McCown man. McCown had planned for Jackson to vote for Johnny Warren as chairman, a post Warren had held for the past two years, but instead Jackson voted for George Lott. An observer said McCown nearly had a fit. "He had wined them and dined them and usually got them to do his bidding, but having Lott as chairman was a thorn in his side."

The whites did not protest Hancock County elections in 1968 when blacks won key posts because whites were still in charge of the voting, but beginning in 1970 they regularly protested elections. Several lawsuits were filed by groups of whites and blacks united in opposition to McCown. They generally charged that by using hundreds of absentee ballots, posting armed deputies at polling places, and using a system of aides who stepped forward and assisted voters, the McCown group was stealing elections. Dr. Green said he challenged twenty absentee ballots because he had signed the death certificates for all twenty voters.

The practice of forcing assistance on voters became so prevalent that in 1974 the Hancock Concerned Citizens Group mailed a letter to all voters explaining,

149

Remember, when you are in the voting booth, whether you are using the new voting machines or the paper ballots, NOBODY knows how you vote unless you are one of those who require assistance.

Incidentally, if you are qualified to receive assistance in voting, the Georgia Election Code says you are supposed to *ask* someone. You don't have to accept help from someone who grabs your arm and says they are going to help you.[1]

A team of observers from the State Elections Board recommended that voting irregularities in Hancock County during the August 13, 1974 primaries be investigated by a grand jury. The team reported a number of violations of the Georgia Elections Code, including a proliferation of unsupervised voting "helpers," partisan workers within 250 yards of the polling place, as well as the unauthorized counting of the absentee ballots. They also noted that some of the "helpers" were armed with revolvers (*Atlanta Constitution*, Sept. 4, 1974).

"Another problem with the helpers," said the report, "was that a number of them were illegally offering their help to the voters and even arguing about who would help which voter." In the Devereux precinct, 86 of the 450 voters required help. One observer said the ballots, when challenged, were counted anyway. The state observers' report, directed to the Hancock County grand jury, stated that the primary was conducted in a tense and undesirable atmosphere caused in part by the presence in polling places of persons carrying handguns.

Requesting a Hancock County grand jury in 1974 to do anything about electoral frauds was either cynical or naive. McCown totally dominated the county's jury system and that particular grand jury included James Henry ("Hen") Jones, McCown's employee and bodyguard, and Marion Fraleigh and other McCown employees (*Sparta Ishmaelite*, Oct. 3, 1974). Edith Ingram and McCown welcomed federal observers to the county in 1966, but when observers came to the 1974 elections, Ingram declared, "My job is to run elections in this county and I do it as the law prescribes. When those nine carloads of FBI men showed up, I knew it was Gestapo tactics. They just tried to intimidate folks" (*Washington Star*, May 9, 1977).

George Eisel, a leader of the Concerned Citizens group opposing the McCown slate, said that because all the federal observers could do was to report civil rights violations, unfortunately they were no help with

150

the kinds of frauds that went on. "The State Elections Board sent in three observers to watch our seven polling places. They saw so many violations of this assisting business they got an injunction to cease. By that time it was afternoon and most of the damage had been done. It was the first year we used voting machines and a lot of assistance was given to those who didn't know how to operate them. There were armed people at the polls as an intimidation tactic."

The McCown-controlled Hancock County grand jury ignored the recommendations of the state observers. It answered all of the charges in a paragraph. "The grand jury would like to thank our ordinary, Miss Edith Ingram, and other poll workers for doing a most outstanding job in the 1974 August primary election. Furthermore, we would like to state that we resent the Gestapo tactics used by the FBI during their investigation of the election. Our citizens should not have been subjected to such actions."

One of the opposition said the federal observers noted so many violations they were responsible for sending in an FBI team later. He said that when the FBI showed up, ECCO officials advised everybody not to talk, and nothing happened. Georgia's Secretary of State Ben Fortson refused to send observers to the general election in November, saying that the state did not have funds, but federal observers were sent again. A *Macon Telegraph* reporter was told he could not enter a polling place to observe and his way was physically blocked by an armed man, Robert Ingram, Jr., Edith Ingram's brother. As the reporter protested, McCown appeared, grabbed Ingram, and jerked him away, giving him a thorough tongue-lashing.

In the election, McCown candidate Johnny Warren defeated Dr. George Green 1,782 to 1,454. A total of 648 absentee ballots were cast, again causing criticism of the electoral process (*Macon Telegraph*, Nov. 7, 1974). McCown himself added a little spice to the turmoil at the polling places. When a woman at the Sparta polls challenged a voter because she knew he had a record as a felon, McCown shouted across the crowded gymnasium, addressing her by her first name and asking, "Who do you think you are—Jesus Christ?"

Word of unpaid bills and mounting financial difficulties at ECCO began to circulate. Nonetheless, in mid-July, at the height of the furor raised by the newspaper publicity, McCown bought a 32-foot boat and paid $5,500 cash as a down payment, signing a note for the $16,000 balance (*Macon Telegraph*, Oct. 11, 1974). As the investigations started, McCown counterattacked with charges that more than $74,000 had been sent into Hancock County from as far away as Mississippi to end black control of the county. He warned of rumors that "more money will be available if something of a violent nature happens to some of us" (*Augusta Chronicle*, July 31, 1974).

McCown had obviously become overextended and the publicity about his activities was beginning to hurt. Two of his many property purchases ended up in court because of nonpayment, and it was even reported that he had paid only $55 on a $127 personal telephone bill (*Macon Telegraph*, Oct. 11, 1974). Relief for ECCO came in October when $175,000 of the $500,000 OEO money held in escrow pending an audit review was released "to tide them over," according to an OEO spokesman. Meanwhile, McCown and ECCO were dipping into Hancock County revenue-sharing funds to keep afloat. ECCO received $13,500 for "social services" and "recreation," while McCown got $4,318 for a down payment on the Ferguson Building in Sparta.

In November, McCown sought to suppress subpoenas issued by a federal grand jury that was investigating his financial activities. Justice Department lawyers said that they had evidence of illegal kickbacks to McCown, and that former OEO officials responsible for approving grants to McCown subsequently received money from him (*Atlanta Constitution*, Nov. 12, 1974). McCown said he was eager to be tried so he could prove himself innocent and could justify $280,000 in expenditures questioned by federal officials. With customary bravado, he called on black congressmen to launch a probe of those investigating him and threatened to sue newspapers for writing "half truths" (*Macon Telegraph*, Nov. 14, 1974).

Six months after the Clinch house burning, another fire threatened Sparta's business district, again the work of arsonists. Fire departments from two neighboring towns, Sandersville and Eatonton, came to help fight the blaze, which began in a furniture store, Worldwide Furniture, financed by ECCO MESBIC. Owners said the records of the store, subpoenaed by the federal grand jury which was investigating McCown, were saved. The police chief told the newspapers that there was no evidence racial animosities were involved in the fire at the black-owned business (*Macon Telegraph*, Nov. 2, 1974).

In December, the county's major taxpayers, including many black landowners, began a tax strike, indignantly protesting McCown's threats to sell their property for taxes when he owed back taxes for three years. They expressed resentment of a 16 percent increase in county taxes, charging that the county had poured more than that amount into the unoccupied hospital to keep it open. They also complained that the county had not published a financial statement in more than a year (*Macon Telegraph*, Dec. 14, 1974).

That same month, McCown was sued for failure to keep up payments on 258 acres of land he had bought in the Powelton area—the third civil suit in the year against him involving Hancock County property (*Sparta Ishmaelite*, Dec. 12, 1974, and *Augusta Chronicle*, Jan. 7, 1975). His lawyers charged that the United States attorney and the federal government had devised an harassment scheme against McCown and the black businesses he helped originate. The charge was included in a motion to quash subpoenas served against several housing and construction firms associated with ECCO. The motion accused federal officials of acting in conjunction with "the former white power structure of Hancock County now centered in Sparta, Georgia."

This second effort to quash subpoenas followed a pattern that McCown's attorneys pursued throughout the long investigation. They insisted that the government's efforts were directed not at theft or wrongdoing but at shutting down the civil rights movement in the county. The motion described the government's probing as "a dragnet investigation" conducted in "an oppressive and publicity-seeking manner." The lawyers said the investigation had substantially retarded McCown's efforts to promote employment in Hancock County (*Atlanta Journal*, Jan. 14, 1975).

McCown had often threatened to sue the newspapers and when he finally did it, he chose April Fool's Day. He and twenty-five supporters journeyed to Atlanta to hold a press conference in front of the *Atlanta Journal* and *Constitution* building on Marietta Street. Attorneys for ECCO, McCown, and Ed Andrews announced a $60 million lawsuit against a string of defendants, including two United States attorneys, the *Atlanta Constitution*, and several of its employees. Also named were some Sparta officials as well as the Concerned Citizens of Hancock County (Group B) and its president, George Eisel (*Atlanta Constitution*, April 2, 1975). The suit omitted the black group of Concerned

153

Citizens (Group A) for reasons interesting to speculate about. Its members had participated in all of the actions of Group B, but because of the charge that the defendants had acted to enforce racial discrimination and to maintain white dominance over the City of Sparta, the appearance of black defendants might have seemed incongruous. The suit also omitted the Macon newspapers, which had been as diligent as the Atlanta newspapers in investigating McCown.

McCown lost the suit against the federal attorneys and the Atlanta newspapers. Judge Newell Edenfield then transferred the case to the Middle District of Georgia, where the remaining defendants lived, while each side accused the other of delaying tactics. At one point, Judge Edenfield ruled that a government-employed doctor might examine Robert L. Ingram, who said he did not respond to a federal grand jury subpoena because his knee had been injured in an automobile accident and he was unable to travel to Atlanta. The hearing brought on what approached a shouting match between the judge and Al Horn, who asked the judge, "Why are you always picking on me and never on them?" (*Atlanta Constitution*, June 13, 1975).

The federal grand jury that had been digging into McCown's affairs indicted Jesse A. Jackson on nine counts of perjury for statements made about disposition of money from land sales to McCown (*Atlanta Constitution*, July 30, 1975). He was subsequently found not guilty. Meanwhile, the sheriff levied on property near the Clinch house, bought by McCown as a site for the shopping center he envisioned to put Sparta merchants out of business (*Sparta Ishmaelite*, April 3, 1975).

A few months later came another sign of growing weakness in the McCown camp. McCown signed bonds totaling $100,000 for two men arrested in drug raids, but Superior Court Judge George Jackson refused to accept them, because the sheriff told him McCown was not worth that much money (*Macon Telegraph*, Oct. 10, 13, 1975). (When the investigations of ECCO began a year earlier, the regional OEO public relations officer had rushed to McCown's defense, issuing a statement that McCown had a negative net worth.) McCown had signed the bonds for Hancock Deputy Sheriff Frederick Gary Lewis and for service station manager Otis Glover following the raid and arrests made by the Oconee Regional Narcotics Squad. Lewis, a white, had been hired by the Hancock County sheriff one day after being fired by the Sparta Police Department. Glover, a black, was a long-time ally of

154

McCown and one of his most vocal supporters in the riots of May 1974.

In October, the Ford Foundation announced it would end financial support of ECCO at the close of the year. Bryant George explained that "Ford's ability to fund was shrinking. We cut a Chicano group in Denver and then we cut ECCO. We retained three black organizations we were funding before we went into Hancock County. All three had more staff strength and more programs going. There was always some opinion that Hancock County was too small. The criticisms of the Hancock program did add weight to our decision but each of these organizations had some firestorms of criticisms." George said he felt ECCO had accomplished a great deal, such as the 150-unit housing project, "but some of the things were not monumentally successful, for instance the fish farm."

Even though the businesses failed, George felt they had accomplished some notable results. "You've got more people in Hancock County trained to run housing, to run businesses, to do accounting, to do secretarial work. How many black secretaries, bookkeepers and other skilled persons would you find in the usual poor rural black community?"

Told that McCown had boasted when his funds were cut off that he had sources of funds in Africa, George laughed and said he had never heard of an African nation giving anybody a nickel, so he thought McCown's statement was rhetoric. George did not mention that McCown had once accompanied him on a trip to Tanzania. Touching on McCown's honesty, George said he thought "there was woeful mismanagement but no stealing. As an economic development model ECCO failed. As a community development model it was monumentally successful. John never intended it to be anything but a community development model. He was willing to break a lot of rules and sacrifice you to do it. He embraced other people only to get funds." [2]

In December, Judge Jackson ordered McCown and two Hancock commissioners, Johnny Warren and William H. Jackson, to stop interfering with George Lott in the conduct of his responsibilities as chairman of the commission (*Macon Telegraph and News*, Dec. 20, 1975). McCown and his two supporters had called a meeting over Lott's protest and Warren, supported by Jackson, nominated himself for chairman. When Lott walked out, McCown, not a member of the commission, took over and directed Warren to order County Manager Ernest

Ingram out of the meeting also. Ingram said Warren and Jackson closed the meeting and evicted him but allowed two men introduced as representatives of the *New York Times* to remain. Lott and Ingram said McCown was trying to oust them because they would not follow his orders after they had decided to do certain things that "would help the county progress" and aid all Hancock citizens. McCown opposed any measures benefiting white citizens, they declared. Ingram and Lott said McCown wanted the county to buy machines and help pay rent for a wood products firm, a subsidiary of ECCO, but Lott told McCown he could not use county taxpayers' money for a private company.

On December 31, a few days after the *New York Times* reporters were allowed to stay in the meeting, a story favorable to McCown appeared in the *Times* written by Thomas A. Johnson. The article did not mention the commission meeting, beginning instead with the often-quoted Deacon Ed Andrews. "This county was right smart pitiful eight years ago—the colored peoples had no rights, and we didn't even know we should have them," said Deacon Ed Andrews, "a graying, stocky man of 66 whose hands are gnarled from decades of chopping cotton and hauling logs."

Johnson pinned rural blacks' future to McCown, writing, "And it appears that the direction taken by blacks here in rural Georgia will be determined by what happens to Mr. McCown." Johnson quoted Edith Ingram as saying that the federal investigation was part of a nationwide attempt to discredit black leadership. He also wrote that ECCO had 150 employees at its peak and generated hundreds of other jobs.

The federal grand jury in Atlanta that had been investigating McCown and ECCO brought a second indictment, this one against Leroy S. Wiley, clerk of the Hancock Superior Court, who was charged with perjury and embezzlement in connection with a loan he received from ECCO's MESBIC to buy a laundromat (*Atlanta Journal-Constitution*, Nov. 27, 1975). He was later found not guilty.

Another in a series of legal notices of nonpayment on property in which McCown was involved appeared in the *Sparta Ishmaelite* (Dec. 11, 1975; Jan. 22, 1976). This dealt with one of several homes McCown had bought, one he later conveyed to Edith Ingram. It was followed closely by a notice that eighty-three acres belonging to McCown's Mayfield Farms were to be sold because of debt to the Citizens Trust Bank. A political advertisement concerning McCown appeared in the *Sparta Ishmaelite* January 29, 1976, from "Citizens for Support of Mr. George Lott, chairman of the Hancock County Commission." The writers complained that at a January 19 meeting of the county commissioners at which McCown was present, they had asked him to permit the elected officers to take care of county affairs without his interference. They complained that McCown refused to let Commissioner Johnny Warren speak for himself "almost without exception."

That same day Warren was indicted on three counts of perjuring himself before a federal grand jury (*Atlanta Constitution*, Jan. 30, 1976). One of the statements related to a $4,318 check drawn on Hancock County accounts, signed by Warren and made payable to McCown. Warren said it was for a down payment on the Ferguson Building, which the county commission had decided to buy. The building was one of many pieces of property McCown bought and lost for failure to make payments.

On January 25, the *Macon Telegraph* began a series of three articles about a new mood in Hancock County. George Lott and Mayor Patterson were working together, the paper said, and were making visible progress. For the first time, city and county government were cooperating. In addition, Sparta's business district was getting a face-lift with federal funds. "We've got several joint projects going with the county," said Patterson. "The county needs us and we need the county. Since George [Lott] has been elected chairman this time, we have worked as close as two people can work."

Said the *Telegraph* in an editorial on January 30, "Hancock County and its county seat, the city of Sparta, are on the verge of racial cooperation and progress that could be a model for other communities where blacks are in the majority. And this is in spite of—not because of— John McCown." On Saturday morning, January 31, the *Telegraph* ran a front-page story headlined "McCown's Empire Nearing Collapse." The last dozen employees of ECCO had been told by letter that Saturday was their final day of employment, the article said. OEO funds ran out on January 31. Of many ECCO-funded projects, only the Academy Lounge and the housing program remained in operation.

13

The Plane Crash

"Lord, our black Jesus is gone."
—An old black man

McCown had been drinking heavily for two weeks. His associates were being indicted, one by one. He told his wife, "They are saving me for last." "He was a cat far back in the corner," said a black preacher. "He was going to be sent to prison." "He was staying drunk all the time," declared a local businessman. "He was drinking heavy. He was going to have to tell those folks on the ECCO payroll the next morning that there would be no more checks. I don't believe he was as afraid of the federal agencies checking him as he was of getting the wrath of those people losing those soft jobs."

It was Friday night, January 30, 1976. At the Academy Lounge, where McCown had been drinking at the bar, he and several of his youthful followers decided to go up in his plane. They left his four-door blue and white Cadillac sedan fifty yards from the runway with its parking lights on. The night was dark but the sky was clear with the temperature at forty-one degrees. The air was still, the wind hardly more than four miles an hour.

The single-engine white, yellow, and black Cessna 182 took off from the unattended landing strip at 8:15 P.M.[1] McCown, flying the plane without a pilot's license, simply took off without communicating with anyone. About fifteen minutes later, witnesses observed the aircraft dive into a wooded area southwest of the airstrip. A witness at the airport saw the plane approaching from a southerly direction and reported that it appeared to be in level flight before entering a left bank. The plane then continued in the left bank until it descended below the trees. The witness, a former U.S. Air Force pilot, said he noticed nothing unusual in the sound of the engine.

158

Another witness located about two-and-a-half miles east of the crash site observed the plane flying near treetop level. He said, "It sounded like the pilot applied full throttle and the aircraft looked as though it went into a straight up vertical climb. At the top of the climb the aircraft abruptly rotated to a straight nosedown attitude and it sounded as though the throttle was retarded. The plane continued straight down until it disappeared below the tree line and I heard a crash."

Three young black men accompanied McCown on the flight. The plane crashed into a dense pine forest about two miles from the airstrip. Gerald Poe, McCown's pilot, just coming out of the Academy Lounge, saw the aircraft go down. Sheriff Walton started a search that eventually involved some two hundred deputies, Sparta police, Hancock County police, State Patrol troopers, and volunteers. A spotlight-equipped helicopter from Stewart-Hunter Army Airfield in Savannah spotted the wreckage at 4:45 A.M. and the sheriff and a deputy reached the fallen plane by 5:20 A.M. McCown and two of the other men were slumped on top of each other, dead, still strapped in their seats. The sheriff cut their seat belts to get them out. The lone survivor was found one hundred feet from the plane (*Macon Telegraph and News*, Feb. 1, 1976).

The FAA's Civil Aeromedical Institute in Oklahoma City later did toxicological studies. "Their studies were negative for drugs and carbon monoxide but showed a blood/alcohol level of 0.198 percent for the pilot," said the accident report. The alcohol level registered far beyond the .10 level at which a person can be charged with driving under the influence of intoxicants under Georgia law. Tom Watson, chief investigator for the National Transportation Safety Board at the site, said the plane was structurally sound and no evidence indicated that mechanical failure contributed to the crash. A representative of Cessna assisted with the investigation (*Atlanta Constitution*, Feb. 7, 1976).

"No record was found to show that the pilot [McCown] possessed a valid pilot's license or medical certificate," the investigators reported. "An expired student pilot certificate and combination third class medical certificate dated March 1, 1973 was found in his personal effects. His previous flight experience was not received. The autopsy was conducted by Dr. L. Howard, State of Georgia Crime Laboratory, Atlanta,

Georgia. Dr. Howard related that his studies showed no evidence of human factors involvement."

The ownership of the plane proved to be as confusing as everything else about McCown's affairs. The plane was referred to as McCown's plane; he used it for his purposes. But when investigators checked, they found records indicating it belonged to a black college in Mississippi that had once given McCown an honorary degree.

The investigators wrote, "An aircraft logbook entry dated December 5, 1973 was as follows: 'This airplane donated this date with 1529.18 hours on Hobbs meter to Mary Holmes College. . . .' The FAA's aircraft records branch in Oklahoma City, Oklahoma received correspondence stating that the aircraft had been donated to the college in Mississippi but an application for a change in aircraft registration was not received. The FAA received no reply to their correspondence to the college of 12–17–73 and 6–6–75 concerning the registration certificate for the aircraft. The certificate of registration for the aircraft was revoked by the FAA on October 2, 1974 for non-compliance with the provisions of Part 47.44 of the Federal Aviation Regulations."

At its annual commencement exercises May 13, 1973, Mary Holmes College had given McCown an honorary doctor of laws degree, citing him for his work toward "the economic development of the black man in the rural South" and for "the organizing of a political structure in Hancock County, Georgia, where blacks control all elements of the government of the county." The commencement speaker that year was Charles Reynolds, president of Citizens Trust Bank in Atlanta, where McCown and ECCO did their banking.

Years after the crash, a number of prominent blacks still felt that his enemies caused McCown's fatal accident, but no evidence exists to indicate this is true. An elaborate investigation showed that all parts of the plane were working when it crashed. Some people—even friends of his—suggested that McCown's crash was a suicide. His wife was particularly indignant at the thought. "Suicide is a form of cowardice. Anybody that knew John McCown knew he didn't commit suicide. He never showed any cowardice," she said. "Anybody knowing John McCown would know that he would not have crashed the plane with three others in it," said Marion Fraleigh, whose admiration for him still showed years after his death.

160

"He died the day before he was going to be indicted," said a former business associate. "I'm fully convinced that he committed suicide. He couldn't stand the idea that he was about to go to court as a felon. He had failed in his project which was so dynamic and important to the community and I just don't think he could adjust his thinking to that."

Even in death, John McCown led a march down Sparta's Broad Street. His followers marched by the hundreds in the funeral procession. Walking with them were such veterans of the civil rights movement as Ralph Abernathy and Hosea Williams. The crowd overflowed the Hancock Central High School gymnasium for the final rites. The Reverend Elijah Johnson, who had followed McCown in his labor battles, brought his congregation to sing; the choirs of Macedonia and Hickory Grove raised their voices in the old familiar hymns. The Reverend Joe Boone, another old-time civil rights activist, came from Atlanta to read the Scripture. Sonny Walker of the OEO, Fulton County Commissioner H. D. Dodson, Hancock Commissioner Johnny Warren, and Deacon Ed Andrews were among those making remarks. Other speakers were Roosevelt Warren, Atlanta Mayor Maynard Jackson, Hosea Williams, and Ralph Abernathy.

The printed program included McCown's favorite poem, Rudyard Kipling's "If."

> If you can keep your head when all about you
> Are losing theirs and blaming it on you;
> If you can trust yourself when all men doubt you,
> But make allowance for their doubting too;
> If you can wait and not be tired by waiting,
> Or being lied about, don't deal in lies,
> Or, being hated, don't give way to hating,
> And yet don't look too good, nor talk too wise: . . .

The program also repeated the text of his favorite song, "The Impossible Dream."

McCown was buried at Mayfield back of the old Birdsong place, which he had made ECCO's guest house. A simple marker is ringed with small green shrubs in the back lawn fringed with pecan trees. The fading ECCO headquarters stand a few yards up the street.

In death as in life, McCown provoked controversy. Hosea Williams,

161

a representative in the Georgia House from DeKalb County, was attacked verbally by Jones Lane, white legislator from Statesboro, for his remarks at the funeral. Lane quoted news reports that Williams said, "If you don't think white folks would put us back in slavery, you're crazy." Williams defended himself by declaring he also said, "Don't ever think all black folks are angels and all white folks are devils" (*Atlanta Constitution*, Feb. 6, 1976).

Al Horn wrote a blistering letter to the *Atlanta Inquirer* (Feb. 21, 1976), a black newspaper, accusing the *Atlanta Journal* and *Constitution* of failing to cover the funeral where the mayor of Atlanta and numerous other dignitaries were present and the crowd was so great Horn could not even get in. He complained that they found space to report McCown had been drinking at the time of the crash.

"McCown dying the way he did was the best thing that could have happened to the county," a white man commented. "If he had been assassinated he would have been a martyr. It was pathetic the way he exploited the blacks."

"Lord, our black Jesus is gone," cried an old black man. "What are we going to do?"

14

The Trials

*"It [ECCO] planted the seed of its own destruction
and the government watered it."*
—Sidney Moore

Despite John McCown's death in the winter of 1976, federal authorities continued to investigate him and his associates. The survivors of the wreckage of ECCO viewed the investigation as harassment. They and their attorneys sought to paint the investigators as malign racists, not interested in prosecuting wrongdoing but, rather, seeking to stop the spread of the black political movement out of Hancock and into neighboring counties.

This propaganda effort was even reflected in McCown's obituary in the *New York Times* (Feb. 4, 1976). Sent as "a special to the New York Times" and datelined Sparta, the story noted McCown had sued the *Atlanta Constitution* for $60 million, declaring, "I have handled millions for others, but I have taken nothing for myself." "Nonetheless," said the *Times*, "the Justice Department opened a full inquiry into the activities of the East Central Committee for Opportunity." The story did not add that the suit against the *Constitution* had been decided against McCown by a federal judge.

Shortly after McCown's death, Assistant United States Attorney Owen Forrester told the *Macon Telegraph* (March 19, 1976) the federal probe into his activities was winding down because "grand juries seldom indict deceased people." Forrester "did not say whether McCown would have been charged had he lived," the article said. "However, a grand jury in Atlanta will continue to take testimony concerning the anti-poverty agency because 'there are a few loose ends that ought to be tacked down,' Forrester said." In the same report, Al Horn commented that since McCown had died in a plane crash the federal officials were happy. "To spend this much time on harassment is pure politics," he said, charging that the investigation was aimed at discouraging blacks from organizing in Baldwin County and elsewhere.

One of the first of McCown's aides to come to trial was Johnny Warren, Hancock County commissioner and social coordinator for ECCO, who was indicted for perjury on several counts. One count charged that he lied when he testified that he had cashed $14,000 in checks made out to Hancock County to pay cash for services rendered by doctors and nurses at Hancock Memorial Hospital in 1973. The testimony revealed management practices that were at best unorthodox, including payment in cash to doctors and nurses at a county-operated hospital (*Atlanta Constitution*, Jan. 30, 1976).

Marion Fraleigh, testifying on Warren's behalf, told the jury that the money he said he paid in cash to the doctors and nurses came from a Ford Foundation grant to ECCO. She said no specific restraints were placed on the Ford funds and no accounting procedures were required by ECCO (*Atlanta Constitution*, July 20, 21, 1976). Warren endorsed and cashed the checks. The clerk to the Hancock County commissioners testified it was not normal for the chairman to cash checks made out to the county, adding that she had no knowledge Warren used the money to pay doctors and nurses. Warren testified that he used "eight or ten thousand dollars" to pay for mass meetings, which he called "parties" (AP report, *Atlanta Journal*, July 22, 1976). Testimony at the trial also showed Hancock County paid McCown $4,300 as a down payment for the Ferguson Building in Sparta, but the county never took possession of the building and never got its money back (*Creative Loafing* [Atlanta], Aug. 14, 1976). Warren was convicted of perjury in July. Sentenced to six months and five years probation, he served forty-five days and returned to Hancock County, where he was then employed as county planner, a job created for him since he could no longer seek an elective office.

Shortly after his conviction, Warren defeated George Lott in the Hancock primary elections in August. The losing candidates brought suit, pointing out that a voting machine in the Devereux precinct failed to register any votes for George Lott (some said it was defective, some said it was rigged) and that an extraordinarily large percentage of the vote was cast by absentee ballot.

Governor George Busbee appointed Fulton Superior Court Judge Charles Weltner to hear the charges. Weltner, liberal congressman from

Atlanta, had given up a safe seat in Congress rather than run on the same ticket with Georgia's segregationist governor, Lester Maddox. Weltner decided the defective machine could have been decisive in the commission races and ordered a run-off between George Lott and Johnny Warren (*Atlanta Constitution*, Sept. 22, 1976). Subsequently, because of his conviction of a felony, Warren could not compete in a run-off election and Lott ran against Jimmy Blanchard, a white businessman who came in third in the original race. Lott won in the final contest.

"The McCown faction made a tactical mistake," said Al Horn. "They tried to stick with Warren, who was a popular figure. If they had qualified someone else for the spot they could have won. We had a primary election in which Johnny got just over fifty percent of the votes, but one box was under challenge because the machine was defective. That was enough to potentially throw him below the fifty percent. The other candidates who had each received about twenty-five percent of the vote were then declared to be the only eligible candidates. I urged the McCown faction to support the white man on the theory he would be easier to get rid of and also he would be more inclined to make alliances with the McCown faction, but they were not able to prevail. Some of them supported the white man but the black man won."

Blanchard felt that he had really won the run-off election. "Going into the last precinct I was leading by thirty-one votes. Mayfield came in with sixty-six votes and my opponent was elected," he said.

The federal grand jury handed down six more indictments September 16, 1976. The indictments charged with conspiracy to defraud the government the late John McCown, Marion Fraleigh, Edith J. Ingram, John Glustrom, James H. "Hen" Jones, and Dr. Earl Evans. Assistant United States Attorney Robert H. McKnight, Jr., said the government's investigation into the alleged misuse of government money would continue at least into October. "We're continuing the investigation, and this indictment was returned at this time solely to stop the statute of limitations from expiring with regard to certain offenses," McKnight said (*Atlanta Journal-Constitution*, Sept. 18, 1976). Almost a year later, United States District Judge Charles A. Moye, Jr., concluded that the federal grand jury had brought the indictments one day after the five-year statute of limitations had run out (*Atlanta Journal*, Aug. 31, 1977).

In November 1976 the grand jury indicted Roosevelt Warren, ECCO lawyer and Hancock County attorney, Marion Fraleigh, and five other persons with conspiracy to defraud the government. The five were John Glustrom, Gerald F. Poe, Edith Ingram, Gloria Gardner, and Charles J. Solomon, an Atlanta contractor. Roosevelt Warren was also charged with conspiring to obstruct justice by making false declarations and by procuring others to make false declarations before the grand jury. Similarly charged were Poe, president of the airline, and John Askew, who ran the housing office. The indictment named as a conspirator, but did not charge, the late John McCown (*Atlanta Journal-Constitution*, Nov. 13, 1976).

Jimmy Carter in May 1974 had announced he found no illegal use of OEO funds as a result of audits of ECCO operations. Consequently, defense attorneys for the ECCO group tried to involve Carter in the trials. Shortly after Carter was elected president, he received a letter from the attorneys asking for an investigation of the government's "obsessive crusade to recapture an archaic hierarchy for Hancock County."

John W. Stokes, Jr., then United States district attorney, answered the charges March 3, 1977 in a letter to Marvin Arrington, one of the ECCO attorneys. Stokes apologized for his delay in answering Arrington's letter of January 20 to President Carter

> but the attorney handling the cases . . . has a very heavy case load and has provided me with the following as soon as he could possibly do so.
>
> Your letter mentioned a request of . . . ECCO for an investigation of the activities of myself and my office in connection with a recently-concluded Federal Grand Jury investigation into alleged illegal activity of ECCO related programs and individuals. In other words you are asking that a Federal Grand Jury which investigated alleged federal crimes in this district, be itself investigated as having allegedly been "used to harass and persecute innocent people because of their political or reformative activities." To the contrary, it is our position that the U.S. Attorney's Office and the grand jury referred to conducted a lawful, appropriate and fully justified investigation into these matters and that indeed it would have been in abrogation of their duties to have failed to do so.[1]

Stokes wrote Arrington that the investigations were begun concurrently by the FBI and the IRS around July 1974 "as the result of several events," which he said included the *Atlanta Constitution* series that started June 30, an OEO audit of ECCO which "ultimately questioned expenditures of over $280,000," and "information from other sources." As a result of the OEO audit of July 25, 1974, and the preliminary investigation by the FBI and the IRS, the grand jury began receiving records of ECCO and related enterprises October 8, Stokes wrote. These records had been subpoenaed.

The government collected records during the fall and winter; then an analysis by "a number of accountants and special agents" followed that took six months. Stokes said that the long time was required by the "extreme complexity and diversity of the operations of ECCO and of the fraud schemes perpetrated principally by McCown, but with the help of numerous others."

The grand jury began hearing witnesses May 13, 1975. In its eighteen-month term, the jury did consider several other matters; however, it "met for at least thirteen separate sessions on this particular set of cases, averaging three days each and heard from over 50 witnesses as to their knowledge of 41 separate corporations or enterprises. In addition to receiving thousands of documents, the transcripts of testimony alone amounted to approximately 4,000 pages," Stokes wrote.

The grand jury brought five separate indictments as a result of its investigation, including fraud against the government amounting to approximately $281,000. "As complex as the indictments and the schemes they concern are, they represent only a fraction of the highly questionable transactions and circumstances reviewed by the grand jury," Stokes commented.

Among the charges were that Dr. Earl Evans, consultant brought in by the Ford Foundation, had kicked back consultant fees to ECCO personnel; that Edith Ingram was in a kickback scheme that involved $76,000; that Gerald Poe assisted McCown in the theft of government funds which passed through Poe's aviation company; that Gloria Gardner handled several bank accounts used to misappropriate Ford Foundation and government funds, disbursing the funds to McCown, herself, and Edith Ingram; that Charles Solomon, Atlanta heating and air conditioning contractor, took part in fraudulent theft of consultants' and contractors' fees in connection with McCown and others. McCown died after most of the grand jury investigations were complete, Stokes pointed out. "By that time the . . . evidence was deemed sufficiently convincing by the Grand Jury to authorize the indictment of the others. . . .

"We do not agree in any respect that this case represents persecution of innocent people because of political or reformative activities. Every bit of the proceedings by our office, the FBI, the Internal Revenue Service and the Grand Jury was undertaken because of substantial and convincing evidence of federal criminal violations."

Stokes said he agreed with Arrington that it was a shame these people were on trial, "but the shame is they have traded upon the trust and confidence reposed in them by so many others and used it fraudulently for their own financial advancement."

The defendants used every technique available to them to attack the government's case, focusing on James Leach of the IRS and Robert McKnight, assistant district attorney. They charged that Leach had ties to Hancock's white power structure and that McKnight's efforts were part of a government vendetta. Leach had lived in Hancock County from August 1946 to December 1947, when he was fifteen, and in pre-trial hearings Defense Attorney Reber Boult railed against the IRS for assigning Leach to the case. Defense attorneys also charged that Leach's father wrote a column for the *Sparta Ishmaelite*. His father, a minister living in Florida, did write a brief religious column for the paper, consisting mainly of inspirational Bible verses.

The defense attorneys issued what they called "an overview of the Hancock County story."[2] They said that black control in Hancock County had been subjected to a "concerted attack by elements of the press, business interests, local politicians and the United States government itself." Until 1966, when McCown came, the blacks in Hancock County lived "in a state of neo-slavery." The defense overview continued, "One of the early actions of the new black officials was to raise the property tax valuations of large, long undervalued timber tracts that abound in the county. (Coincidentally, the same Cox interests which own the Atlanta daily papers have a substantial investment in a pulpwood plant in a nearby county.)" The statement about company taxes is incorrect; property values were not raised at the time. The 1977 tax digest did list 8,908 acres as owned by Cox Woodlands of Augusta.

One of the most interesting statements in the overview, in the light of John McCown's close connections with the Nixon administration, was, "The racism of the white power structure of Hancock County found allies in Richard Nixon, who sought to disband OEO, and in Congress, whose distrust of OEO saddled ECCO with the contradictory requirements of maintaining sophisticated accounting and business management systems using local residents who had been deprived of educational, employment and managerial opportunities."

The overview also said, "Beginning in September of 1974 sweeping subpoenas were served on ECCO and most of its affiliated companies. . . . Virtually all records were subpoenaed from the year 1966. Ironically, none of the companies were in existence at that time. When the defendants attempted to quash or modify these vast, sweeping subpoenas, the government filed a distorted, scurrilous response which was given to reporter Nesmith (thus insulating him from libel charges) for a lead story the next day."

A major complaint concerned the effect the subpoenaing of records had on ECCO businesses. "The effect of the highly publicized grand jury investigation of ECCO was crippling," the overview continued. "Credit was withdrawn. Funding was terminated. Staff was cut back for lack of funds. Records were held for months by the grand jury, making it impossible to conduct business in a normal or orderly fashion. Although it was repeatedly promised by the United States Attorney that the working records of the companies would be quickly returned, a court order was ultimately necessary to secure the return of these records some months later. Recently the federal magistrates hearing motions on the case slapped the government's wrist for this and other government misconduct."

The defendants and their attorneys won the support of the NAACP, which joined the defense team, supplying an attorney and other resources. The overview quoted Executive Director Benjamin Hooks as saying,

> The NAACP has, for some 68 years, dedicated itself to eliminating all forms of racial discrimination in this country. During the course of our activities, this discrimination has evolved from the overt to the covert— from the obvious to the subtle and sophisticated. The form has changed but the results are equally offensive. The NAACP feels that the prosecution of the emerged black leadership of Hancock County of Georgia on these questionable charges, through the use of our tax money to support the activities of vindictive public officials, requires our intervention in this matter.
>
> We shall bring all our resources to bear in achieving a just resolve of these criminal charges which I am sure will result in their all being found not guilty.

The October 11, 1977 *New York Times* quoted NAACP spokesmen who said the case was considered of paramount importance in maintaining the morale of Southern blacks involved in community development programs. "For black residents of the country, the implications of the case exceed the cruelty and unjust nature of the indictments. Involved are immense political and economic issues that are crucial to the future of black progress throughout Georgia, and even the South."

Roosevelt Warren and Edith Ingram flew to New York at NAACP expense for meetings with prospective funding sources. Spokesmen would not name the foundations visited nor the sums received, but they were seeking $150,000 to pay court costs. The NAACP was quoted in the *New York Times* of October 11 as saying that by the time the trials were concluded, "few traces will remain of accomplishments that once made Hancock County a regional showcase of black advancement through civil rights activity." The *Times* went on to tell of the fish farm where whites poisoned the fish, "leaving dessicated craters," of the committee-managed hospital now shut down, of the ten submachine guns that Sparta white policemen bought to "keep niggers down."

The article continued: "After that," said Miss Ingram, "whites talked openly of stopping Mr. McCown and the committee's progress, going so far as to predict an investigation of committee finances by the Internal Revenue Service. The IRS later dispatched James Leach, an auditor who is white and who lived in Hancock County as a youth."

Asked later about the charges against the government, Robert McKnight, the assistant United States attorney, said, "The attorneys who represented the defendants, primarily Al Horn, made this a legal battle between the government and the defendants from the word go." A young native of Michigan and graduate of Wayne State law school, McKnight inherited the McCown affair as soon as he arrived in Atlanta. "I came here in the beginning of May 1975 and this case was given to me that week and I took it from there. I came with no set preconceived prejudices about the case. Personally, I abhorred the Mitchell-Kleindienst Department of Justice as much as Al Horn," he said.

"I don't know the internal mental processes that prompted the government initially to get into the affair. I do know what triggered our interest and what triggered the FBI's interest, for example. That's been stated in court to be a culmination of complaints including a tip from people in Atlanta who saw certain spending patterns by McCown and tipped the FBI off. When Jimmy Carter stopped the OEO grant, that caused Sonny Walker, regional director of OEO, to talk to the regional auditor to see what they could do to help McCown. The solution they arrived at was to do an audit and clear him. Well, it did the opposite," declared McKnight. "That got sent to the FBI and it spurred them on. There were the newspaper articles Jim Rankin and Jeff Nesmith did. Maybe it shouldn't be this way, but a certain amount of government investigation gets started by someone in position to start it reading the newspaper and deciding this looks as though it is something we need to look into.

"I can say that when I became convinced personally that McCown was a crook, obviously I was prejudiced against him then. During the first grand jury session I participated in we had some very damaging evidence against him," McKnight said. "I'm prejudiced against what he and some other people did down there. One of the problems I had in letting the case plead out was we didn't get to tell the story of John McCown and Hancock County.

"There was a fight tooth and nail for most of the information that we got and for most of the information they gave up. You had McCown asserting what rights he had not to talk to agents. You had them moving to quash grand jury subpoenas that called for the production of documents."

McKnight said the government had not appealed Judge Moye's decision that the first indictment failed because of the statute of limitations since most of the defendants were named in the second indictment, "except McCown who was dead, Evans who was being tried in Mississippi, and James Henry Jones who was a fairly minor character anyway."

"While we were preparing to return the second indictment we had a number of people coming before the grand jury represented by Al Horn, Reber Boult and a couple of others who were taking the fifth amendment on the advice of counsel. Roosevelt Warren was one of the attorneys advising people to take the fifth. He had already been before the grand jury and had taken the fifth amendment himself. Based on that, we moved successfully to have Al Horn, Reber Boult and their law firm and Roosevelt Warren disqualified from representing witnesses before the grand jury."

McKnight said he was convinced that McCown stole at least

$250,000. He told of two accounts at Citizens Trust Bank in Atlanta, under the name O. R. Moore, the maiden name of McCown's mother. Thousands of dollars had been cleared through the O. R. Moore accounts. Asked directly about these accounts in later interviews, Fraleigh and Horn said they had no information. The accountant, Dr. Neffinger, said he had never heard of the accounts. The principal perpetrator, McCown, was dead at the time of the trials, McKnight said. Dr. Evans had received a stiff sentence in Mississippi. "Two or our key witnesses were Bahamian natives over whom we have no compulsory process. They told us they would come; after a visit of a defense attorney to the Bahamas, they refused. Another key witness repudiated testimony he had given before the grand jury against Roosevelt Warren."

Because the defendants eventually pleaded guilty to minor charges and the grand jury proceedings were secret, little about the years of investigation got into the public record. Some revealing bits appeared in the pretrial hearings and in answers to motions from defense attorneys. Glustrom's attorney asked specific questions about a $4,500 check. (This and the subsequent Evans material concerns the first indictments later held invalid because of the statute of limitations.) The attorney's questions and the government's answers were as follows:

Q. For what purpose was the $4,500 allegedly paid?
A. McCown's use of the money.
Q. For what allegedly improper purpose was the $4,500 used?
A. The trail of the $4,500 check stops with McCown cashing it.
Q. If the $4,500 payment was by check please state: Bank?
A. Citizens Trust Company.
Q. Date paid by bank?
A. October 20, 1971.
Q. Payee of the check?
A. O. R. Moore.
Q. Names of persons who endorsed said check?
A. O. R. Moore, John McCown.[3]

The court records contain another interesting letter in answer to a request from Dr. Earl Evans's attorney. The letter repeated the indictment that Evans had agreed to overcharge for fish sold and consultant services rendered to ECCO, to charge for fingerlings that were never delivered, to have the benefit of moneys in payment for fish far in advance of when they were delivered, and that he had drawn up a false contract under which kickbacks were extracted and had returned kickbacks himself to ECCO.

In answer to questions about specific checks involved, the government said, "Sizeable amounts of cash are missing from the checks listed below in a manner which, in combination with the general method of operation of the defendants, indicates that kickbacks were given to officials of ECCO, Inc."

Date of Check to Earl E. Evans	Amount of Check	Amount Cashed or Missing
6/8/70	$25,000	entire amount
8/6/70	8,000	$2,000
8/10/70	20,000	entire amount
3/29/71	3,000	entire amount
7/25/71	3,035.02	entire amount
9/16/71	5,000	entire amount[4]

In the same letter, the government said that Earl Evans "received the benefit of (although he kicked back part of it) $212,720.23 from his consulting and fish sale contracts with ECCO, Inc. Furthermore, John L. McCown and Edith J. Ingram converted $72,920.10 to their own use under the contract drawn up by Earl E. Evans with Guy Moore."

Although Evans escaped prosecution in Georgia because of Judge Moye's ruling that the statute of limitations had run out, he was convicted in another case in Mississippi. In September 1977 federal marshals arrested Evans at his home in Grady, Arkansas, after his indictment by a federal grand jury at Oxford, Mississippi. The indictment stemmed from an FBI investigation of the OEO-financed Mississippi Delta Catfish Corporation of Greenville, Mississippi, where Evans was director. A two-count indictment charged Evans with interstate transportation of stolen securities, alleging that the checks totaling $143,247 were drawn fraudulently on the bank account of the catfish corporation (*Arkansas Gazette* [Little Rock], Sept. 24, 1977).

A former official of the Arkansas state OEO and a former acting president of Arkansas AM and N College, Evans was hired to oversee the catfish corporation, a nonprofit organization set up to help low-income Delta farmers establish catfish farms. Heralded, like ECCO, as a partial solution to the region's poverty, the project filed for bankruptcy less than two years after it began. When the directors of the corporation learned that OEO would no longer continue funding the project, they called for an inventory and found that two million catfish they had purchased were missing.

Evans's work with ECCO came about through the Ford Foundation, which employed him in 1970 as a consultant for the ECCO catfish farm. This was done in New York City at the request of Bryant George, program officer of the foundation. Evans said he first met McCown in 1968 when he went to Washington to seek federal assistance to help low-income farmers in catfish farming in Arkansas. Evans worked with the Ford Foundation as a consultant for ECCO for a year, receiving about $45,000, which included his expenses.

Magistrate Joel Feldman noted April 11, 1977 that more than fifty pretrial motions had been filed on behalf of the defendants and called their lawyers, Reber Boult, Al Horn, and Bensonetta Tipton, in for a talk.

Defense attorneys were particularly concerned about Marion Fraleigh and her relationship with McCown. They moved that the government not be allowed to present any evidence about her children and their parentage on the grounds that it could "incite, inflame and prejudice the minds of the jurors as to guilt or innocence of the accused." They charged McKnight with saying he would see defendant Marion Fraleigh "nailed to the cross." They were indignant that McKnight had sought to gather evidence about the parentage of her children. The FBI even interviewed her physician.

Gerald Poe testified that an FBI agent and an IRS agent on the case asked if he knew John McCown ran around with a lot of women, inquiring if Poe knew the names of the women and if they handled any of McCown's money for him. Poe said they asked other questions, showing interest in McCown's intimate affairs. (At a December 16, 1977, pretrial hearing, Edith Ingram testified she had been interviewed by IRS auditor Leach several times. "For years 1970 and 1971 all of my bank deposits were added and everything not salary was subtracted and I had to pay close to $3,000 tax on that money. John gave me a notarized statement that said he had given me a certain amount of money to go through my accounts to cover expenses I had paid for him.")

174

Immediately before the trial was to begin in January 1978, Marion Fraleigh's attorney again asked the court to exclude all testimony relating to "her personal and/or intimate relationship with John McCown, and any or all testimony relating to her children." The motion to exclude the evidence said responses from potential jurors indicated jurors were disturbed by interracial dating. "In view of the fact that the defendant is white, that Mr. McCown is black, that Mr. McCown was married to another woman at this time and that the children were born out of wedlock, such prejudice is very real. A large majority of potential jurors have expressed a disapproval of children born out of wedlock and/or to interracial parents, therefore exclusion of such evidence is both necessary and appropriate."

In an affidavit Fraleigh said, "On or about May 2, 1974 John McCown executed two deeds conveying property to me as a gift to our sons, John and Frederick Fraleigh. He stated in the presence of others that he was giving these properties to me for the benefit of our sons because he would never be able to provide for them in the way a traditional father would. He was concerned that, in the event of his death or incapacity, they would not be provided for in his will or trust. He further stated that by conveying this land [some 85 acres] they each have something of their own from him and that they would always have a place they could live."

The defense also pushed hard on charges that electronic surveillance had taken place, a charge McKnight denied. The defense said it could have occurred in connection with McCown's calls to Dr. Martin Luther King, Jr., and Elijah Mohammad, "whose phones the government had tapped."

In grand jury testimony, Glustrom discussed two checks involved in land deals. He said McCown told him a condition precedent to buying a piece of land was payment of $5,000 to a black woman who was a tenant on the property. McCown showed him the house and the woman, Glustrom said, and he [Glustrom] issued a $5,000 check to Edith Ingram to relocate the woman. He also said McCown told him James Henry Jones had done substantial work on this property and was owed some $7,300 for his services. Jones admitted he cashed the check, but not for himself. "To my notion, the check was to get the block plant going. When I saw the check, I didn't question it." Accused of failing to declare the money on his tax returns, Jones said, "If it had been my money I would have declared it. But it went for expenses. I had all those receipts in the trunk of my car, but it rained in my car and messed up the trunk and ruined the records" (*Atlanta Gazette*, May 11, 1977).

The first charges against Glustrom were dropped because of the statute of limitations; the second charges were based on a property deed. Glustrom said he had made out a deed to clear up a title at the suggestion of the IRS agent. Although the government won the decision on a motion to dismiss based on these charges, that part of the case against Glustrom was later dropped. The property was the ECCO theater, which was sold in a confusing series of deals. McCown apparently sold the property for a substantial $10,000 profit without telling Glustrom, and the latter took a $1,500 loss.

In an answer to one of the defendants' motions for a bill of particulars, the government said, "Guy Moore was the grading contractor in the construction of the fish ponds and raceways on the . . . catfish farm. It was out of checks to him that some $72,920.10 was embezzled by the defendants."

One witness told the grand jury that she and other employees were required to perform sexual favors for important visitors from government agencies and foundations. A former McCown lieutenant said, "They would take young girls and make them secretaries. They made prostitutes of them. McCown would select some to entertain visitors. This was tearing away the moral fiber of the community. He kept people stimulated with barbecues and parties, giving them drinks and propaganda."

Jury selection proved to be an elaborate process. Lawrence E. Noble, Jr., associate professor of political science at Atlanta University, made a study of pretrial publicity at the request of the defense counsel. Noble, a board member of the National Jury Project, Inc., is an expert in "thematic analysis of newspaper coverage." He worked on the study with Jay Schulman, a sociologist and founder of the National Jury Project, and with staff members of the Atlanta regional office.

Good journalism as well as bad journalism can build bias in viewers, said Noble. He and his helpers sought to determine if media treatment of McCown had built "prejudgment" of the case in the minds of potential jurors. They studied the *Atlanta Constitution*, the *Atlanta*

Journal, the *Atlanta Daily World*, the *Peoples Crusader*, the *Atlanta Voice*, the *Augusta Chronicle*, the *Macon News*, the *Macon Telegraph*, and the *Sparta Ishmaelite*. Workers found ninety-nine items in the *Constitution* and eighteen in the *Journal*.

"It is my considered opinion that because of pretrial publicity the possibility of defendants receiving a trial from jurors free from pre-judgment in this case is nil. It is clear that defense counsel will need every opportunity to examine potential jurors individually and private-ly," said Noble.

The Friday before the jury selection process began, Edith Ingram pleaded no contest to two misdemeanor charges rather than stand trial on felony charges. She could not have held office as probate judge if convicted of a felony.

Jurors were chosen under the most elaborate precautions, sequestered from each other. Their psyches were probed through a set of questions devised by the defense. Despite Noble's prediction to the contrary, few of them recalled hearing about the Hancock County troubles. Most of the publicity had appeared in 1974, four years earlier. Jury selection began on a cold January day in 1978 in Atlanta's aging federal court-house. Judge Charles Moye put the prescribed questions to the pro-spective jurors in a flat voice, carefully cleared of all emotion. A large battery of defense lawyers seemed physically to overwhelm the some-what diminutive assistant United States attorney. The defendants ap-peared subdued and downcast in the quiet and almost empty high-ceilinged room with its heavy, slightly tattered draperies at the long windows.

Asked if she would mind working for a black boss, a bank clerk said, "Mine is." She did not object to interracial dating, she said. All forty whites said "no" when asked if they believed blacks were more likely to commit crimes than whites, but several whites had trouble with the question on interracial dating. "Whites ought to stay white and blacks ought to stay black," said one. An elderly black man said, "It's all right if they love each other."

The slow jury selection process continued through the week, inter-rupted by a one-day recess when icy weather kept prospective jurors from the courthouse. The trial was expected to go on for weeks, but then suddenly it was over. On Monday, January 30—the second anniversary of McCown's fatal plane crash—the defendants, with the exception of Roosevelt Warren, pleaded guilty to lesser charges in plea bargaining. The government dismissed allegations against Warren. The prosecutors said the pleas were worked out during the weekend, adding that a witness had altered important elements of his testimony.

"The government's evidence would have shown that the person responsible for the vast majority of the wrongdoing was John L. McCown, who is now deceased, and that the [other] defendants were followers who assisted him," a government press release stated. Defense lawyers retorted that their clients were innocent and that the pleas were designed to prevent economic hardship caused by a lengthy trial (*Atlanta Constitution*, Jan. 31, 1978).

Phil Gailey, a reporter for the *Washington Star*, had written many favorable stories about McCown's work during the early days of ECCO when Gailey was a reporter for the *Atlanta Constitution*. At one point, McCown and Fraleigh had summoned him to an Atlanta motel to report an alleged threat to McCown's life by hit men from New York, presumably hired by Sparta whites. Gailey never wrote the story because there was not sufficient evidence and the hit man he was to interview did not show up. Even so, the McCown group remembered Gailey's friendly stories and invited him to cover the trials. It did not quite turn out as they had hoped. Gailey's February 1 story in the *Star*, following the trials, said,

> What is left is the wreckage of a black dream corrupted by McCown. The catfish farm is weed-grown and idle; so are the concrete block and sheet metal plants and all the other ECCO enterprises. The only success story is a 150-unit housing project financed by HUD.
>
> When the indictments began falling, McCown's associates called it the government's obsessive crusade to recapture an archaic hierarchy for Hancock County.
>
> But after plea-bargaining with federal prosecutors, the accused stood in federal court and pleaded guilty: Marion Fraleigh, the only white and woman in McCown's inner circle, to a felony charge of making false statements to OEO auditors; Gerald Poe, operator of an air freight business financed partly by ECCO, and his administrative assistant, Gloria E. Gardner, to a misdemeanor charge of aiding in the conversion of Small Business Administration funds to unauthorized use; John Askew, manager of the public housing project, to a misdemeanor charge of being

an accessory in the Poe-Gardner transactions; and Charles Solomon, a mechanical contractor, to a misdemeanor charge of aiding and abetting in the illegal conversion of OEO funds.

Last year former county commissioner Johnny Warren, a McCown crony, was convicted of lying to a federal grand jury investigating McCown's financial activities.

Even now they all maintain their innocence. They blame their fate on white racism.

Gailey said he was originally favorable to McCown, then later had his doubts. "I thought in spite of his obvious weaknesses he could still manage bringing some things off, maybe make life a little better for these black folks; then his greed took hold.

"My relations with McCown became unpleasant when I explained I would not become emotionally involved in the movement," said Gailey. "I was a reporter and I would walk down the middle of the street and shoot out windows on both sides. I would not be his personal lackey which is what he wanted. The whites in Hancock wouldn't even talk to you. They saw the press as members of the enemy camp and slammed the door on you.

"The Hancock story is a great tragedy. It had all sorts of potentialities to make it a model case. Instead it turned out to be terrible. McCown made racial feelings worse on both sides. Apparently all that money didn't do much for the average black."

The *Macon Telegraph* editorialized on February 4, 1978: "The guilty pleas this week by five associates of the late John McCown concluded a string of legal actions that have proved conclusively how a so-called anti-poverty program defrauded the poor in Hancock County."

Deryl Dantzler of Macon, one of the defense attorneys, wrote the editors in response: "Of the 15 individuals charged during the two-year federal investigation by two grand juries, eight have been acquitted or had charges dismissed. Three jury trials on 16 felony counts resulted in the single perjury conviction. The last group of pleas came after one week of a trial which was expected to last eight to 10 weeks and in entering their pleas these defendants indicated that their primary motivation was to avoid the extreme hardship and expense of the lengthy trial." Dantzler said the editorial showed journalistic irresponsibility (*Macon Telegraph and News*, Feb. 11, 1978).

179

"I and my family were subjected to federal prosecution, subjected to an attempt by some locals to do me in," said Roosevelt Warren. "I know they wanted to get rid of me. I had that said to me many times. . . . The day I was supposed to have closed that loan was the very day my grandfather was buried. I had not even been to the office at Mayfield for over a week."

"I never saw anything I would question," declareds Dr. Neffinger, teacher of business at Atlanta University, who audited the ECCO books. "This doesn't mean it doesn't exist. We looked at the vouchers and payments. Some of those things may have been illegal and under the table, but as far as auditing and putting it together we found nothing. I think in auditing and talking to people we would have had some awareness of wrongdoing, but we didn't.

"We had arguments; we disagreed. The major disagreements were where John would do something and go back and request approval for it. He said he was going to do what he had to do. He built that house down on the river, and as far as we could see it was all strictly legal. The only thing I would question was the concrete block was still receivable on the books of the concrete block factory but that doesn't mean anybody has stolen anything. It is an unpaid bill. The river house was originally intended to be his house; then he realized for some reason or other it wouldn't be any assistance to him and he thought it could make a conference center."

Neffinger said he was working in New York in the summer of 1975 and the prosecutor and Leach called him from Atlanta to ask if he would be willing to come and testify. "I said sure. I guess it became apparent that I was not going to be a good witness. They never called me. I called back when they didn't call and they said they didn't need me."

Judge Moye gave all the defendants probated sentences. Four months later, Edith Ingram sought a reduction in her sentence of five years' probation. The government opposed this, saying to the judge that Ingram had allowed McCown to use her to help wash $15,000 in embezzled funds, that she had received $5,000 in 1969 as part of a scheme to defraud the government, and that she had failed to report her ECCO consultant fees on her federal income tax. Judge Moye refused to reduce her sentence.

In all of the statements about the trials, the clearest and nearest to the truth, if truth could be found in the hundreds of conflicting accounts, was that of Sidney Moore, Glustrom's attorney.

Moore was an official of a state consumer agency, a watchdog for public interests in conflicts with utility companies, when he talked about the case in the fall of 1978. He holds a master's degree in poverty law from the University of Wisconsin and had worked with poverty programs from 1968 to 1974.

When Moore took on Glustrom's defense, he was convinced of his innocence and charges against his client were later dropped. Moore went through the entire origin and history of the Hancock County poverty effort, taking nearly four months to do it. He thus acquired a detailed knowledge of the whole situation.

"You can look at the case in three ways," he said. "Number one, you could say the whole program was a conspiracy to defraud the government of money, as the government charged. Number two, you could say it was a well-intentioned program that was destroyed by the activities and greed of some of those in it. Number three, you could say it was a good program destroyed by the government.

"I prefer number two," he said. "It planted the seed of its own destruction and the government watered it. I do not agree the government was the source of the problem. The government was very generous with the program."

15

The 1978 Elections

*"It is beyond belief that almost twenty times
as many spoiled ballots would appear in a
hotly contested local race as in a statewide run-off without
criminal intervention."
—Judge Charles L. Weltner*

The elections of 1978 were the first to be held following the trials. McCown's lieutenants emerged relatively unscathed by their probationary sentences in federal court. By pleading no contest to misdemeanor charges, Edith Ingram avoided trial for a felony, thus insuring that she could continue holding public office. Johnny Warren, found guilty of perjury earlier, served a few weeks in prison and lost his right to hold elective office but moved into a job created for him at the courthouse. Leroy S. Wiley, clerk of the superior court, was found not guilty of charges against him.

A coalition of conservative blacks and most of the white community again sought to unseat the McCown faction. Following the collapse of ECCO, several of its officials went to newly created jobs such as county planner and building inspector, jobs the almost bankrupt county could ill afford. Even holding elections is an expensive drain on the small budget of a county like Hancock, and in the fall of 1978 five elections were held, two of them caused by irregularities. A special school board election became necessary because the probate judge forgot to put the candidate on the primary ballot. A special primary election was set because the courts ordered it after a study of absentee ballots.

The first election was a Democratic primary. It was followed by a run-off in which the courthouse candidate, Willie Lester, who had served as executive director of the Georgia Council after McCown, defeated Clyde Boone, a Hancock businessman and farmer. Boone, a black man supported by most whites, had won in the regular vote, but when absentee ballots were counted, Lester, a civil rights activist from

182

neighboring Warren County who had lived in Hancock briefly, defeated him.

Opponents charged that the McCown organization, controlling the mailing, went to meet people at their mailboxes as the absentee ballots were delivered and helped them fill out the ballots then and there. Many ballots were returned from one mailing place and in the same handwriting. An opposition candidate said, "Everybody in the courthouse left all their business alone and went out working against us. People were paid by tax money for work they didn't do for weeks. Some of the girls working against us in the 1978 elections were paid with CETA [federal employment program] funds." The absentee ballots had long been a source of contention. Suits were filed in every election beginning in 1970 and still another was filed in 1978. Governor George Busbee again sent Judge Charles L. Weltner, the former congressman and son of Dr. Philip Weltner who had made the exhaustive study of the county in the 1960s, to the Sparta courthouse to hear the charges.

Several hundred voters, summoned by subpoena, spent most of the day answering questions about their absentee ballots. Many had received these ballots on the grounds that they held jobs outside the county. In such cases, the law stipulates that they may not be back in their voting precincts during official polling hours. Dozens of witnesses swore they left Hancock right before 7 A.M. and returned shortly after 7 P.M. on election day. An old woman said she had filled out absentee ballots for herself and her son. Asked where he was, she replied, "Who knows?" She had been doing this for years, she said, because "they" told her it was all right.

Judge Weltner determined that 109 absentee ballots were illegally received. In addition, he found 94 spoiled ballots, most of them from one voting area; personal examination showed that someone had added another marking to each ballot. "It is almost beyond belief," Judge Weltner wrote, "that anyone going to the trouble of seeking an absentee ballot would intentionally spoil that ballot by double-marking. It is beyond belief that 90 percent of the spoiled ballots might occur by pure *coincidence* within one voting sub-area. It is beyond belief that almost twenty times as many spoiled ballots would appear in a hotly contested local race as in a state-wide runoff without criminal intervention."[1]

Since Lester had won by only 137 votes, Judge Weltner decided that the spoiled ballots, in conjunction with the 109 illegal votes, could have determined the result. He ordered another election, which the courthouse candidate won by a large majority. A considerable number of Hancock blacks, particularly older landowning blacks who pay property taxes, strongly oppose the McCown faction that runs the courthouse. Whether rightly or wrongly, they and most of the white community feel that Hancock County elections are not honestly held. Judge Weltner said there was no evidence that the 1978 electoral tampering was attributable to any election official. However, someone with access to absentee ballots spoiled enough of them to throw the election in doubt.

"An honest election will change things," said a white in Sparta. "We hope to have an elections board hold elections here two years from now if we can get the legislation. We have 8,000 persons registered to vote in this county. This gives a chance to slip some in. The voting list needs to be purged." (By November 1978 the figure was 6,302, according to the office of the secretary of state. Even this reduced total is larger than the entire population of the county eighteen years of age and older in the 1970 census. Although the total population was then 74 percent black, whites were a third of the voting-age population, having fewer children.) "When McCown died others just came in and filled his place," the man continued. "I understand they will have overspent the county budget by the end of this year. I still hope that some day that crowd will go."

A black leader said, "Many of our people have become fed up. They have begun to realize nothing is going to happen here as long as this condition prevails. If we can change the atmosphere and leadership we can get something going for our people. Now the courthouse gang has control of the elections." A white businessman said, "Most whites now are thinking in terms of competence in public officials. We would be happy to have blacks who are competent."

"It's worse since McCown has gone," a white woman commented. "He said if he died it would be worse. Now the Warrens are in control. McCown really kept up, with blacks posted on every corner, and he knew where everyone was. He bragged he could tell you where anyone in the county was in ten minutes. I blame the federal government more than I do the blacks."

"We have some black leaders who are closely aligned with white leaders," said Roosevelt Warren. "Those white leaders would like to see a change at the courthouse but in the short period of time black people have had a chance to sit in the courthouse I think they have done a remarkable job.

"I don't like tokenism whether it is white or black. Our elections were whites against blacks. Now they have become whites and some blacks against other blacks. Black candidates don't get white votes. Whites do not splinter. [On the contrary, in 1968 and 1970 many whites voted for James Smith and other black candidates.] Today it was put to me by someone that there should be at least one white commissioner on the county commission board. These same people never indicate to me that the City of Sparta should have a black man sitting on the city council. I have no personal objection to a white or black man sitting on the board of commissioners. My philosophy is that whoever the people choose are going to be the folks that represent county government.

"When John McCown died," Warren continued, "a lot of folks went around saying that the political situation in Hancock County was going to change. The kingpin is no longer here. They assumed that the voting populace of Hancock County was not educated enough nor wise enough nor intelligent enough to be able to make a choice of who they wanted to represent them. I think we have had enough elections since his death to show they are wise enough politically to make their choice. I think there has been a tremendous amount of education on behalf of poor people in this county to the point of realizing they can control their political destiny. Unfortunately, they have very little control over their economic destiny. This is what I feel most concerned about now, what we can do to help the poor people you see walking around. We have a lot of people in this county who want to work and cannot find employment."

"When they get Willie Lester on the commission Marvin Lewis will control everything," a black schoolteacher declared. "Marvin Lewis is the kingpin of the courthouse crowd that includes Leroy Wiley, Edith Ingram and about nine Warrens. James Hunt, who ran ECCO after McCown died, has now moved ECCO from Mayfield to the courthouse. He is chairman of the board of education. [In December 1979 Hunt died in an automobile accident near the site of McCown's plane crash.] Race relations are not any worse. There are so few whites they don't fight back. They don't know what the blacks want them to do, yet the blacks can't make it without them. . . . There's not a road you can

185

travel; they fixed one bridge down at Mayfield and spent a lot of time arguing about changing the name of it because it was named for a white man." [2]

"Many things have changed, and I think irreversibly changed, for the better," said Al Horn. "Black people participate in Hancock County and, despite everything, still can and do control the county. ECCO associates and lieutenants still hold political power as far as running the county government. . . . When John died there was, of course, some jockeying for leadership.

". . . one of the people [George Lott] who felt that he should be in a leadership position is now head of the county commission. The other two members are on the McCown side. He was supported by the white faction. I suppose he figured with a white alliance and a black group that was in alliance with the whites they could control the county, but they were not able to do so."

George Lott, who runs a garage on the Greensboro highway, was still chairman of the commission in 1980. "I'm very religious," Lott avowed. "I believe in what's right. Standards of morals are there even if I don't reach them myself. I don't believe in discrimination under no circumstances. I never dreamed of being a county officer as a boy but I was trained to take advantage of every opportunity. World War II changed the minds of a lot of people, it set the course of my life. I was full of patriotism, wearing that uniform, saluting that flag. I was a soldier, the only black on the bus going from Sparta to Tallahassee, sitting on the very back seat with two whites. I felt uncomfortable that close to the whites and I was pushing against the wall when the driver came back and told me to move. He made me sit on the front step of the bus all the way, wearing that uniform. They did wrong but they thought that was right.

"Then there was the 1954 decision and Dr. King," Lott continued. "I admired Dr. King a lot. He was the man who had the most impact on this world except Jesus, but some spin-offs from his movement didn't turn out good. We started a movement in 1965 and in 1966 Robert Ingram was elected to the school board and James Smith was elected commissioner. John McCown built up confidence and without him the movement would have been at a slower pace. He was very articulate, had talent and would have been accepted by the total community. Then he got hold of a lot of government money. He got drunk with that."

16

Mirror Images

"If it was wrong then [when the whites did it], it is wrong now."
—*Black Minister*

In the days of small-town fairs and carnivals in a more innocent America, one of the attractions was a crazy house filled with strange mirrors reflecting distorted images. Hancock County in the Mc-Cown decade became a crazy house of mirror images, sometimes distorting but always reflecting two centuries of rich history. Conditioned by the stereotypes of the 1960s, outsiders found it almost impossible to comprehend what was going on. To understand, they had to turn things upside down. They had to look at them in the crazy house mirror.

First was McCown himself, the mirror image of the plantation master, updated to the era of private planes and Cadillacs. All of the old injustices remained but were reversed: voting places were selected to discourage white voters, voter registration lists were padded with names of blacks no longer living in the county, armed black men were placed at the polls to intimidate, a white church suffered an armed takeover, a white landmark was burned, and threats to burn the town circulated. There was the appeal to race prejudice in political campaigns (this time reversed) and the exclusion of whites from offices in the courthouse; the public school system had no white teachers; the judicial system was marred by juries that would not convict in criminal cases; public meetings were conducted in such a racist and hostile atmosphere whites would not attend; and in the presence of a countywide surveillance system reminiscent of Castro's Cuba, elections were determined by questionable absentee ballots.

Another strange thing about these violations of rights and principles most Americans take for granted was the reluctance of anyone to do anything about it. State officials, with an eye on Georgia's growing black vote, ran for cover instead of doing their duty. The news media were so accustomed to the other reality in much of the South where

187

blacks were the victims of prejudice and mistreatment, they first accepted McCown's self-serving statements at face value. "McCown could cast a racist light on anything down there," said a reporter who eventually decided he was a crook. "His dramatic manner and actions caught the attention of reporters and produced a bright glare that made it hard to see other things." McCown's handling of the news media bore remarkable similarity to Jim Jones's methods in San Francisco before he went to Guyana. McCown attempted to use reporters and succeeded for a while. When they refused to write exactly what he wanted, he sought to frighten them off by calling them racists and by threatening their employers with multimillion dollar lawsuits.

In a world of television's flickering images, what people think is real is sometimes more important than reality itself. McCown understood this. Those who opposed him did not understand it so well, and it was very late in the McCown era before their story was told. News has its fashions and trends, just as painting, music, and politics do. Even in the South, it was not the fashion in the late 1960s and early 1970s for reporters to appear unfriendly to civil rights activists. A person who probed too deeply into the activities of a John McCown could expect to have his motives questioned. The reporter would certainly be called a racist; he might even be categorized as a Klansman.

The opinionmakers in Georgia, having belatedly come to the cause of the blacks in the state, were hardly in a mood to criticize a black demagogue. The idea of a black racist demagogue was hard to grasp, so a McCown in his era could say and do things that would be impossible for a serious white leader to do or say. Was McCown a mirror image of a Theodore G. Bilbo or a Eugene Talmadge of an earlier time? If so, should the liberals who fought racial injustice of the old kind recognize and fight the new kind?

McCown and his fellow demagogues betrayed those who fought for so many years for racial justice in the South. The people who should have been most indignant at the blight he brought to the black revolution publicly supported him to the end. No black leaders of stature in Georgia expressed the wisdom of a country black minister who summed it all up: "If it was wrong then [when the whites did it], it is wrong now."

A member of the Georgia Council spoke of McCown's ability to go to New York "and play with guilty liberal consciences." A Ford Foundation executive praised McCown for breaking up the old ties between black leaders in Hancock and their white patrons. An Atlanta woman spoke of her enthusiasm for McCown's plans to make Hancock a model black community. They, like many others, had plans for the people of Hancock County. They knew what was good for them and they were going to do good to them. None of them planned to live there or to send their children to schools there or to invest their money there. None of them would suffer if their plans went wrong, but the people of Hancock County would and did.

What was particularly bitter for Hancock whites with a sense of history was the knowledge that their county's comparatively kind treatment of blacks in the past helped bring about their own embarrassment and humiliation by a man they considered an outsider. As the East Germans and the Cubans and the Vietnamese have shown, people vote with their feet. "Hancock was better to the blacks in the old days," said a farmer. "They came in here and didn't leave." Hancock was never considered one of Georgia's tough redneck counties. The county's history was not marred by racial disorders. It was always a leader in the state in the percentage of its blacks who owned and operated their own farms.[1]

Changing the patterns of many generations would have been difficult under the best leadership. McCown's style added to the bitterness and distrust. Supposedly fighting poverty, he accumulated land, expensive automobiles, houses, horses, planes, and women. Even more painful to many people in Hancock County was the fact that nobody seemed to care. If they complained to the Ford Foundation, they received the polite, noncommittal letters bureaucracies are so skilled at turning out. If they asked help from Governor Carter's office, they sometimes received rude replies. The offices of the OEO and the faceless bureaucrats in Washington, D.C., were as remote as the deserts of Saudi Arabia and equally responsive. Politicians saw nothing but trouble in listening to complaints from Hancock County.

McCown's appetite for the lifestyle of the rich was a key factor in the problems he created for himself. His style brought questions and eventually lengthy investigations. Even at the end, McCown's supporters said he had not taken money illegally. He acted unwisely, they said, and he failed to keep proper records, but he did not steal. On the other hand, the assistant United States district attorney was convinced he stole at least $250,000 and described the bank accounts that were used to divert the money. Another federal investigator thought money was hidden away in bank accounts in the Bahamas where McCown had many contacts. Bank accounts there are kept as anonymous as those in Switzerland.

Two years after her husband's death, Annie Mae McCown said she was living on Social Security payments to her minor children. "Everybody believes we have a lot of money," she said. "I hope he comes in a dream and tells me where it is." Mrs. McCown was living in a comfortable brick ranch house in a black Sparta neighborhood when she talked about her financial affairs. A plump, middle-aged woman, she projected an air of sadness and confusion but her face was warm and friendly. Her place had a dispirited air; the lawn was neglected and eroding and the painted trim of the house was flaking.

"He kept things from us," she said. "I learned about the money troubles when he came to me and told me he wasn't going to get a salary. He kept saying he was going to get the money for my son to stay at Clark College but he didn't have it and my son stayed out of school." She explained that the home was FHA-financed and she had to make the payments. "John tried to give everything to his children," she said. "A lot of the things he had he owed money on. He made a salary just like anybody and tried to give us some of the things he didn't have when he was growing up."

McCown died without a will. No property remained in his name in Hancock County at his death. As the time for his trial by the federal government came closer, he began to dispose of his property. In October 1975, according to records at the Hancock County courthouse, he gave his oldest son, Gerald, 100 acres of land and, in addition, a house and lot in a part of Sparta called Guilltown. To his daughter he gave what was known locally as the Edith Clay house. Edith Clay, a black woman, had left the house to McCown to help in the advancement of the Negro race as he saw fit. That same month, McCown transferred the disputed "big house" he was building on the Ogeechee River and the large tract of land that went with it to an agency called Hancock County Comprehensive Health Services.[2] The agency was incorporated

190

March 29, 1974, at a time when the local hospital was failing and McCown was making efforts to keep it open. The last report from the agency filed with Georgia's secretary of state in 1977 listed Roosevelt Warren as registered agent. In June 1980 Warren said the agency was no longer active and the property would revert to McCown's family. By that time, the uncompleted house was vandalized into ruin.

Earlier in 1975, on May 27, McCown transferred to Edith Ingram the house she lives in, a home built and occupied originally by a white Sparta dentist. On May 2, 1974, he transferred to Marion Fraleigh two plots of land, 23 acres and 61 acres, for the use of their twin sons. Fraleigh and her sons left Hancock County in 1979 and moved to Decatur, Georgia, an Atlanta suburb.

Little remains of McCown's empire. The catfish ponds and raceways are overgrown with small trees. Paint is peeling from the brick store in Mayfield that housed ECCO's headquarters, including McCown's office with the long boardroom table, the thirteen high-backed swivel chairs, and the deep carpet. Only the HUD-financed housing projects seem tended, but the houses look strangely out of place in isolated Mayfield. Neat, modern, and suburban looking, the projects have names that sound like real estate developments—Ogeechee Estates, Inc., and Lakeview Village, Inc.

ECCO still existed as a corporation in 1980, although it had not filed reports with the secretary of state in recent years. Roosevelt Warren said in June 1980 that the corporation still owned lands and buildings, the remnants of its earlier holdings. As recently as 1977 the Hancock County tax digest showed buildings valued at $253,499 for tax purposes in ECCO's name and two listings of land, one for 358 acres and another for 676 acres.

Unlike most civil rights leaders, McCown did not associate himself with religion. He used preachers and churches because they were levers to control the community, but he said early, "I didn't come here to convert a lot of souls." He talked about green power and creating jobs. He faced the same problem in building a sound economy that most third-world countries face. No one with capital wants to invest it where it may be insecure. When McCown turned Hancock County upside down, he made it even less attractive to investors than it already was and as a result he destroyed more jobs than he created. No industry, except the ECCO enterprises, came to Hancock County after McCown came. Prospective manufacturers feared their plants and goods might be held hostage in a community subject to the erratic control of one man. The few people in the county who had any capital were already fearful of putting too much of it in local investments. McCown's tactics convinced them their fears were justified. Several wealthy citizens moved away. "It's foolish to fight the whites like that crowd in the courthouse is doing," said a defeated black politician. "The whites have what money is in the county and the county needs industry and jobs."

"Blacks haven't gotten out of the old system of black and white issues," said another black politician. "That's why industry is reluctant to come in. We have created an image of a hell-raising place." One group of blacks, four years after McCown's death, said they had trouble getting jobs in other places because of Hancock County's reputation. They said McCown had taught the young people someone should be handing them something all the time. The welfare mentality McCown emphasized hung on. Hancock became a leader in welfare statistics under McCown's tutelage. With a larger population than Hancock, neighboring Greene County listed 373 dependent children in 155 families receiving welfare aid in March 1980. Hancock had 1,157 in 439 families, more than half of the public-school enrollment.

The empty stores in Sparta's once-thriving little business district say something about the years of constant demonstrations. Businessmen found themselves in the position of paying for their own destruction as McCown used public employees, public vehicles, and foundation funds shielded from taxation to stage the demonstrations. ECCO businesses were not businesses alone, they were political instruments as well. One of the problems the county now faces is the image McCown created. Whites living south of Hancock sometimes instructed their children to detour miles out of the way when driving north to the University of Georgia rather than go through the county. Sparta people were asked by friends elsewhere if it was safe to drive through. Because of these false impressions, land values are lower than similar land in neighboring counties and houses have sold at unbelievably low prices.[3]

McCown spoke often of creating an integrated society. What he did instead was to create a mirror image of the old one. For generations,

Georgia politicians knew it was fatal to be labeled the "nigger" candidate. Registration of thousands of blacks in the 1960s changed that, and it no longer paid to be openly racist. Unfortunately, in Hancock County it still did, but it was a reverse kind of racism. McCown's new plantation was not a happy place for a white man to be. Observing the situation from afar, a long-time civil rights activist in Atlanta commented, "Both in the black and women's movements they are moving away from the idea of fairness toward special treatment and reverse discrimination. The old liberals who complained about the old types of discrimination need to complain about the new."

During the decade in which McCown was supposedly working toward integration and a biracial society, Hancock schools became virtually all black. By 1978, the school system had no white teachers. One token white employee, an administrator, commuted from outside the county. No statistics were available on the number of white students in the system, an administrator said, but he guessed there were "less than fifty." In a homecoming parade that fall, only one white appeared among the hundreds of students marching by.

The courthouse, despite McCown's explanation to the *New York Times* that local blacks were keeping some whites in office, contained only one elected white at the end of the era, and McCown had once tried to get rid of him. "Just a few blacks will vote for whites," said a black schoolteacher who admired McCown and was a flower bearer at his funeral. "The blacks now in power have a great influence on the ignorant mass of our people and they exploit that." A black preacher commented, "Our Negro leaders are like the whites were. They don't want to give up what they've got. When they took over the spirit was to get revenge."

The older, more conservative blacks expressed alarm over trends in county government in 1978 during the election period. "The county is operated by blacks and nothing is happening," said one. "Until you see blacks and whites operating together nothing is going to happen. I believe whites are willing to work with blacks. A lot of them are my friends." Another elderly black said, "At the present time our white citizens are only asking for a fair shake. They pay most of the taxes and have no representation in the government. They want somebody they have confidence in—an honest person." A white woman laid the problems on government interference. "Change had to come," she said, "but if it had come naturally it would have been through the leaders we all respected. McCown came to use the young and the ignorant."

The uneasiness of whites and conservative blacks centered on the courthouse during the elections of 1978. That fall, two claims were made against the county commissioners, attaching the county's bank account for failure to pay just debts. The tax appraiser was being garnisheed for the third time for failure to pay his personal debts, with four money judgments against him. Three claims against the tax commissioner related to his personal debts.

A white businessman discussed the county's heavy debt. "Taxes have not been raised but probably will be. The older blacks are concerned over the situation. The only hope is that they split up and in time a more sensible coalition can be worked out. A lot of whites have simply moved out of the county."

The courthouse clique represents, almost without exception, the old ECCO machine McCown put together. "What we did was create a political base under the guise of economic development," said a disillusioned McCown aide. His old allies still reflect McCown and still speak the outdated rhetoric of the 1960s. McCown's role was that of the dissenter, the protester, the organizer against the establishment. Al Horn said McCown had an antiauthoritarian drive which Horn described as "more than just racial, a class thing almost." McCown opposed those people who wielded power, but when he won it for himself he was far more despotic than they.

On the surface, Hancock blacks and whites get along as well as they get along anywhere. "The majority of the white people in this county will speak and smile and they can be very cordial to you," said Roosevelt Warren. "This is a Southern tradition of open friendliness, but when it reaches the point of accepting you as an equal or accepting you into their homes, then the real person begins to show himself."

"We're not as bad as most places," said a young white man. "I would not be afraid to walk through any neighborhood in this county. Nobody would bother me." Even the most aggressive blacks stress nonviolence and quickly point out that no one was killed in all the years of turmoil in the county. A young woman, moving to Sparta from a Florida city, was amazed that whites had no fear of entering black neighborhoods, something she would not have dared to do at home. Lou Becker, a white educator who worked with McCown, suggested that McCown's restraint kept down violence. Mrs. McCown attributed the restraint to the influence of Dr. Martin Luther King, Jr., "as it was not in John's nature." Roosevelt Warren said the whites were greatly outnumbered or there would have been violence. A white farmer said the same thing, commenting that there were few white males "between twenty and forty years of age." The county's history suggests another reason—its blacks and whites had lived together peaceably too many generations to want to start killing each other.

The attitude of some of the white liberals who attached themselves to McCown was expressed by one who said, "He broke a lot of rules, but they weren't his rules." Carrying this viewpoint to its logical conclusion, McCown finally created enough difficulties for the community and himself to attract the attention of outsiders, some of whom were unreasonable enough to believe that a primary function of government is to maintain an orderly society and to enforce the rules that make it possible to live together.

If McCown failed in both of his goals, developing the economy and a fair biracial society, was there any contribution that he made? "Black people have a sense of pride that they never had before," said Edith Ingram. Others questioned whether the change could not have occurred at less cost. Some blacks who started out with McCown later changed their minds. They generally believe blacks would have gotten what they wanted without McCown. "It would have taken longer, but it would have been better," said one. "It was not what happened but the method that aggravated our situation here. Our people didn't realize they couldn't move the county alone. It would have been better working together." A black leader in Greene County said, "It doesn't matter how bad I want something to happen, it is never worth tearing up my town and county to achieve it. There will be another day and another time when I can get it without destroying the county. Down in Hancock County you folks have torn down the foundation for the future."

The most pessimistic appraisal came from Sonny Walker. "I've learned a lesson," he said. "The lesson is that nothing is really going to be controlled by blacks in this country. I have a very pessimistic view of what the future is for minorities in this country. I don't think

195

we are going to have any more John McCowns getting as far as he went." Walker's pessimism mirrors the disillusionment of many blacks, even blacks like him who have achieved high places. The great masses of blacks have cause to feel even greater disillusionment. Black political leaders have not been able to deliver the modern version of forty acres and a mule.

Hope for the future in Hancock County lies in the past. Behind the headlines of a decade of conflict, life has mostly gone on in its accustomed rhythms, eased by the concern of ordinary people, black and white, for each other. It is this bond on which the community must build. Racial conflict is not the pattern of daily life. Even though the ties grew from an old paternalistic system, their presence has value.

The spark of idealism that some saw burning so brightly in John McCown was eventually extinguished by his own flaws, his pathological greed and thirst for power. The idealists in the Georgia Council, in the Ford Foundation, and in government agencies almost destroyed one of Georgia's most historically noted communities in their efforts to transform it in their own image. Arrogant and ill-informed bureaucrats and foundation officials set about tearing down a community and its leadership without a clear vision of what would replace it. The gaunt chimneys, the ruins of the Clinch house, symbolize the results, the destruction of the existing order without the building of another. In a few short years, they almost succeeded in ripping apart with tax dollars the social fabric carefully woven over two centuries. Hancock County, unlike an individual damaged by the irresponsible acts of a foundation or government agency, cannot expect to seek restitution through the courts for the economic and social destruction done to it by those who sought to do good.

"It was an interesting social experiment," said one Spartan as he surveyed the wreckage. "I just wish it had happened somewhere else."

196

Appendix A

Hancock County Population, 1800–1970

Year	White	Slaves	Free Black	Total	Percent Black
1800	9,605	4,835	16	14,456	33.6
1810	6,849	6,546	25	13,330	48.6
1820	5,847	6,863	24	12,734	54.1
1830	4,603	7,180	37	11,820	61.1
1840	3,697	5,915	47	9,659	61.7
1850	4,210	7,306	62	11,578	63.6
1860	3,871	8,137	36	12,044	67.6
1870	3,645		7,672	11,317	67.8
1880	5,044		11,943	16,989*	70.3
1890	4,739		12,410	17,149	72.4
1900	4,649		13,628	18,277	74.6
1910	4,917		14,268	19,189	74.3
1920	5,136		13,221	18,357	72.0
1930	3,725		9,345	13,070	71.5
1940	3,581		9,183	12,764	71.9
1950	2,984		8,068	11,052	73.0
1960	2,518		7,461	9,979	74.8
1970	2,360		6,659	9,019	73.8

Sources: U.S. Census reports.

*includes 2 Indians

197

Appendix B

Hancock Presidential Returns

Year	Democratic	Whig	Republican	Populist
1836	243	343		
1840	240	481		
1844	330	515		
1848	283	473		
1852	no report			
1856	306	427		
1868	958		85	
1872	633		467	
1876	925		367	
1880	583		383	
1884	642		124	
1888	596		177	
1892	1,436		218	553

Source: W. Dean Burnham, *Presidential Ballots 1836–1892* (Baltimore: Johns Hopkins University Press, 1955).

Notes

Abbreviations

GCHR Georgia Council on Human Relations files, Atlanta University
HCBE Hancock County Board of Education records, Sparta, Georgia

Notes for Chapter 1

1. McCown quoted by Peter Range in "Boss Man," *Esquire*, Jan. 1973, p. 26.
2. *New Republic*, March 6, 1971, pp. 8–9.
3. U.S. Department of State, *Compendium of the Sixth Census* (Washington, D.C.: Thomas Allen, 1841).
4. John Linley, *Architecture of Middle Georgia—The Oconee Area* (Athens: University of Georgia Press, 1972), p. 144. Joan Niles Sears, "The First Hundred Years of Town Planning in Georgia" (Ph.D. dissertation, Emory University, 1977), p. 135, says, "The 'Sparta' designation was given to those courthouse towns which were, ideally, sited in an acropolis location and had entering streets running to the center of the square. The town of Sparta is the earliest of this type in Georgia and served as a prototype."
5. Elizabeth Wiley Smith, *The History of Hancock County Georgia*, vol. 1 (Washington, Ga.: Wilkes Publishing, 1974), p. 65.
6. Tyrone Power quoted in *The Rambler in Georgia* (Savannah: Beehive Press, 1973), p. 113.
7. Ibid., pp. 148–149.
8. Frederick Law Olmsted, *The Cotton Kingdom: A Traveller's Observations on Cotton and Slavery in the American Slave States*, vol. 1 (New York: Mason Brothers, 1861), p. 258, mentions a yellow fever epidemic of 1853 during which Alexander Smets of Savannah wrote to a friend in New York he had fled to Sparta, Hancock County, with his daughters.
9. Vinnie Williams, "Restoration of Rock Mill," *Atlanta Journal and Constitution Magazine*, July 16, 1972, pp. 12–17.
10. Smith, *The History of Hancock County*, I, 41–44.
11. Franklin Square, N.Y.: Graphicopy, 1977.
12. It was apparently much easier for blacks to buy land in Hancock than in surrounding counties. By 1903, blacks owned 1 out of 13 improved acres in Hancock. Neighboring counties with large black populations had the following ratios: Greene, 1 in 31; Putnam, 1 in 30; Baldwin, 1 in 15; Warren, 1 in 80; Washington, 1 in 53. For details see E. M. Banks, *Land Tenure in Georgia* (New York: Columbia University Press, 1905), pp. 64, 69, 89, 120, 138, 140.
13. Russell, *Black Heritage*, p. 113.

14. Ibid., p. 118.
15. W. H. Sparks, *The Memories of Fifty Years* (Philadelphia: E. Claxton, 1882), p. 15.
16. See Appendix A.
17. Figures from United States Census of 1860.

There were fifty families in Hancock in 1860 who had more than 40 slaves each. Hancock exceeded all of its Middle Georgia neighbors (except Columbia), including Wilkes (49) and Morgan (49). Other Middle Georgia counties and their totals were: Greene, 37; Putnam, 45; Warren, 16; Taliaferro, 13; Baldwin (containing Milledgeville, the capital), 18; Columbia, 55; Washington, 27. Burke exceeded all Georgia counties with 86. Others with large numbers of big slaveholders were Chatham (Savannah), 54; Houston, 75; and Liberty, 44.

James C. Bonner in "Profile of a Late Ante-Bellum Community," *American Historical Review* 49 (1944): 663–680, analyzed Hancock's 56 leading planters in the 1860 census returns and determined that they owned more than 55 slaves each, holding among themselves more than half of the land in the county and nearly 40 percent of the slaves. They averaged nearly $70,000 each in the value of real and personal property, an enormous sum in those days. Georgia was the wealthiest state in the union at that time on the basis of per capita wealth in which slaves were counted as property. The distortions in arriving at per capita wealth on the basis of counting whites only and counting blacks as property are obvious and shocking by today's standards.

Some other controversial statistics come from Robert W. Fogel and Stanley L. Engerman, *Time on the Cross: The Economics of American Negro Slavery* (Boston, Toronto: Little, Brown, 1974). Using modern statistical methods and computers, they determined that most owners of fifty or more slaves were very wealthy, with average annual incomes in excess of $7,500, comparable to $240,000 today by their computations (p. 134). They found that slave labor on a good plantation was the first modern assembly line (p. 208). They said the South was rich at the time in comparison with other countries, giving per capita incomes at $140 annually in the North, $100 in the South, $126 in Great Britain, $82 in France, and $41 in Sweden (pp. 249–250).

In his studies of Hancock's planters, Dr. Bonner wrote, "While climate, soil and topography did not endow the community with unusual agricultural possibilities, there are perhaps few places in the cotton belt that have a greater claim to all the romantic notions of the full life under the plantation slavery regime."
18. James C. Bonner, *A History of Georgia Agriculture 1732–1860* (Athens: University of Georgia Press, 1964), pp. 111–114.
19. Ralph Flanders discusses Dickson's relationship with Amanda in *Plantation Slavery in Georgia* (Chapel Hill: University of North Carolina Press, 1933), pp. 271–272. Flanders talked to a friend of Dickson's, B. N. Jewell. There are conflicting accounts, some saying Dickson never had a legal white wife. No one is buried beside Dickson in the Sparta cemetery. John Gaissert, a local historian, wrote in the *Sparta Ishmaelite* July 5, 1979, that as a young man Dickson married Clara Harris, daughter of a prominent Hancock family. She became ill and Dickson trav-

eled with her to many countries to restore her health. She died and was buried in Cuba.

A long article in the *Atlanta Constitution* Dec. 11, 1979, described Dickson's descendants in a series on Atlanta's black aristocracy. Most of the information given by Mrs. Kate McCoy Lee, a descendant of Dickson and of Bishop Lucius Holsey, does not match that in printed sources. Her account confuses Dickson's daughter Julia with his mistress Amanda. Dickson's will is in Hancock County Wills, vol. 1, 454.

20. Willard Range, *A Century of Georgia Agriculture, 1850–1950* (Athens: University of Georgia Press, 1954), pp. 22–23. Range discusses Dickson extensively.

21. David Dickson and James M. Smith, *David Dickson's and James M. Smith's Farming* (Atlanta: Cultivator Publishing, 1910), p. 77.

22. George Gilman Smith, *The Life and Times of George F. Pierce* (Sparta, Ga.: Hancock Publishing, 1888), p. 146.

23. Ibid., p. 437.

24. Ibid., pp. 474–475.

25. Ibid., p. 485.

26. Lucius Henry Holsey, *Autobiography, Sermons, Addresses and Essays of Bishop L. H. Holsey*, 2nd ed. (Atlanta: Franklin Printing and Publishing, 1899), p. 9.

27. Ibid., pp. 17–18.

28. Ibid., p. 12.

29. W. Dean Burnham, *Presidential Ballots 1836–1892* (Baltimore: The Johns Hopkins Press, 1955), pp. 346–347, for Hancock County returns. In 1860, Lincoln received no votes in the county. Bell, the Unionist candidate, received 402. Because of Alexander Stephens's influence, Douglas, the National Democrat, received 148, more than the 128 votes cast for Breckinridge, the Southern Democrat. See Appendix B for results in the county in other presidential elections.

30. Range, *Century of Georgia Agriculture*, pp. 70–71.

31. Richard Malcolm Johnston, *Autobiography of Richard Malcolm Johnston* (Washington, D.C.: Neale, 1900), p. 65.

32. Holsey, *Autobiography*, p. 10.

33. Johnston, *Autobiography*, p. 65.

34. Ibid., p. 180.

35. U.S. censuses reported Hancock's cotton production in bales: 1860, 13,332; 1870, 9,624; 1880, 15,010. Georgia Crop Reporting Service lists later production: 1909, 21,379 bales; 1919, 19,402; 1929, 7,381; 1939, 6,556; 1950, 3,880; 1960, 4,250; 1970, 580; 1977, none recorded.

36. C. W. Norwood, *Sholes' Georgia State Gazetteer and Business Directory for 1879 & 1880* (Atlanta: A. E. Sholes, 1879), pp. 718–719.

37. U.S. Census 1880. Special report on cotton-producing areas.

38. The 1860 U.S. Census listed Hancock real estate at $2,380,855 and personal property (largely slaves) at $7,042,261, for a total of $9,423,116. In 1967, a reevaluation of the tax digest changed the total from $4,713,168 to $16,579,144. The 1967 figures are from the *Sparta Ishmaelite*, Nov. 28, 1968.

39. From United States Department of Commerce in answer to telephone query, 1980.

40. John Donald Wade, *Augustus Baldwin Longstreet: A Study of the Development of Culture in the South* (New York: Macmillan, 1924), p. 167.
41. Colman McCarthy, *"Learn about Georgia, Know These Three,"* *Miami Herald*, Dec. 26, 1976, Sec. E, p. 6.

Notes for Chapter 2

1. William W. Malet, *An Errand to the South in the Summer of 1862* (London: Richard Bentley, 1863), pp. 37 and 47. Malet describes the society and race relations in the Peedee section at the time of the Civil War.
2. *Colorado Springs Gazette Telegraph*, Sept. 23, 25, 26, and 30, 1963.
3. Report issued by Credit Bureau of Colorado Springs Inc., dated Jan. 3, 1969, lists a long record of unpaid bills in Colorado Springs; copy in author's files.
4. Copy of investigator's report in author's files.
5. *Savannah Evening Press*, April 14, 1966. Related items in the *Press*, April 9, 12, 13, 1966, and in the *Savannah Morning News*, April 12, 14, 19, 1966.
6. *New York Times*, Aug. 15, 1965, and Sept. 30, 1965.
7. *Athens* (Ga.) *Banner-Herald* ran a series of stories on the incidents beginning Nov. 26, 1967.
8. Sharon Bailey, "Threat Laid to Action, Inc.," *Athens* (Ga.) *Daily News*, Oct. 22, 1967.

Notes for Chapter 3

1. Pauley to Gardner, Dec. 21, 1965, GCHR.
2. Biographical data from material in GCHR files and from personal interview. Information about her sons from many sources, confirmed by records in federal courthouse, Atlanta (*United States of America* vs. *Roosevelt Warren*, et al., No. CR76–371A.)
3. Minutes, March 9, 1966, HCBE.
4. Art Pine, "U.S. Officials Hail Election of Negroes," *Atlanta Constitution*, Nov. 12, 1966.
5. Minutes, Jan. 3, 1967, HCBE.
6. Atlanta: Regional Economic Development and Business Service Center, Atlanta University, 1965. Photocopy from typescript in GCHR.
7. Executive committee minutes, Aug. 29, 1968, GCHR.
8. *Annual Review*, 1967–68, pp. 3–4, GCHR.
9. *Sparta Ishmaelite*, Sept. 19, 1968, and Nov. 14, 1968.
10. *Sparta Ishmaelite*, Sept. 19, 1968, and Nov. 14, 1968.
11. "Hancock Resigned to Negro Leadership," *Atlanta Journal*, Sept. 22, 1968.
12. *Annual Review*, 1967–68, p. 5; also see executive committee minutes, Aug. 7, 1969, p. 7, both in GCHR.
13. "Boss Man," *Esquire*, Jan. 1973, p. 26.
14. *Creative Loafing* (Atlanta), Aug. 7, 1976.

Notes for Chapter 4

1. *Annual Review*, 1967–1968, p. 5, GCHR.
2. Undated brochure entitled *Georgia Council on Human Relations*, written by Maxine Rock. The officers listed are for 1969–1970.
3. Executive committee minutes, March 13, 1969, GCHR.
4. Minutes, March 16, 1969, and Aug. 19, 1969, HCBE.
5. Copy of handbill in author's files.
6. Minutes, Sept. 5, 1969, HCBE.
7. Ibid., Sept. 8, 1969.
8. Ibid., Sept. 10, 1969.
9. *The People's Voice* is on file in GCHR.
10. Minutes, Sept. 11, 1969, HCBE.
11. Ibid., Sept. 15, 1969.
12. Ibid., Sept. 16, 1969.

Notes for Chapter 5

1. *New York Times*, Aug. 30, 1970.
2. Executive board minutes, May 8, 1969, GCHR.
3. Executive board minutes, July 3, 1969, GCHR. Minutes also include data estimating income at $150,000 to $172,000 and discussing other benefits.
4. *Annual Review*, 1967–1968, p. 4, GCHR.
5. An emergency meeting of the GCHR executive committee was called Aug. 7, 1969, to consider Stubbs's letter. Details come from the minutes of that meeting.
6. Executive committee minutes, Dec. 10, 1969, GCHR.
7. Minutes, Dec. 10, 1969, GCHR.
8. Annual meeting minutes, Sparta, Ga., Jan. 23–24, 1970, GCHR.
9. Ibid.
10. Executive committee minutes, Jan. 24, 1970, GCHR.
11. Executive committee minutes, March 19, 1970, GCHR.
12. Minutes, June 17, 1970, GCHR.
13. The information about the land deals is from the *Atlanta Constitution*, July 3, 1974.

Notes for Chapter 6

1. Executive board minutes, June 17, 1970, GCHR. Date of incorporation from the office of the secretary of state for Georgia. Purposes listed from credit report dated Oct. 20, 1970 (Dun and Bradstreet).
2. *Atlanta Constitution*, July 23, 1970.
3. *Augusta Chronicle*, July 29, 1970.
4. *Atlanta Constitution*, July 23, 1970.
5. Minutes, Feb. 17, 1970, HCBE.

6. Ibid., Aug. 4, 1970.
7. *Atlanta Constitution*, Aug. 21, 1970.
8. Minutes, Aug. 25, 1970, HCBE.
9. *Atlanta Journal*, Aug. 23, 1970.
10. *Atlanta Constitution*, Sept. 3, 1970.
11. Annual meeting minutes, Nov. 20–21, 1970, p. 6, GCHR.
12. Ibid., pp. 7–8. McCown referred to articles in the *Times*, July 28, 1970, and in *Newsweek*, Oct. 19, 1970.
13. Financial statements in GCHR files attached to letter from Robert L. Thompson, St. Louis accountant, addressed to CHR and ECCO directors, Nov. 17, 1970.

Notes for Chapter 7

1. McCown's mother had a photograph of the cast on her living room wall in 1978.
2. This McCown quote appears in the *New Republic*, March 6, 1971, p. 9, and in *Esquire*, Jan. 1973, p. 26.
3. AP story by William L. Chaze, *Atlanta Journal-Constitution*, Oct. 10, 1971.
4. *Constitution*, Sept. 23, 1971. Also *Atlanta Journal*, Sept. 28, 1971.
5. McCown to Carter, Sept. 27, 1971, GCHR. Nothing in the files indicates that the previous request had been written; McCown may have been referring to his earlier visit with Governor Carter.
6. Minutes, Dec. 30, 1970, Jan. 5, 1971, Jan. 14, 1971, HCBE.
7. Ibid., Aug. 20, 1971.
8. Undated handwritten draft, GCHR.
9. Executive committee minutes, Sept. 22, 1971, GCHR.
10. Annual meeting minutes, Jekyll Island, Ga., Oct. 29–31, 1971, p. 4, GCHR. (Mimeographed minutes say 1972, but this is a typographical error.)
11. This and subsequent comments by the accountants appear in a letter to Mrs. Louis D. Becker, then GCHR president. Dr. George Neffinger and Joseph J. Brown raised the questions as they sought to prepare financial statements for GCHR for the period Oct. 1 to Dec. 31, 1971.
12. ECCO financial statement for period ending Sept. 30, 1971, GCHR.

Notes for Chapter 8

1. The letter was widely distributed among Hancock Republicans; copy in author's file.
2. *Atlanta Journal–Constitution*, July 8, 1979; *Constitution* (AP story), June 29, 1979.
3. Minutes, Nov. 14, 1972, HCBE.
4. Official figures from office of Georgia's secretary of state. 1968 returns: Democrats, 2,165; Republicans, 381; American Party, 1,104.

Notes for Chapter 9

1. *Sparta Ishmaelite*, legal advertisements in issues of April 5, May 17, Aug. 16, Sept. 6, Dec. 27, 1973.
2. Carter's letter was released to the press and portions appeared in several news accounts, e.g., *Atlanta Constitution*, April 10, 1974. Copy in author's file.

Notes for Chapter 10

1. *The Eye of the Story* (New York: Random House, 1977), p. 286.
2. *Esquire*, Jan. 1973, p. 170.
3. *Time*, June 17, 1974, p. 40.
4. F. B. Simkins and C. P. Roland, *A History of the South*, 4th ed. (New York: Alfred A. Knopf, 1972), p. 613.

Notes for Chapter 11

1. The series in the *Macon Telegraph* began on June 9 and ran through June 14, 1974. The *Atlanta Constitution* series began June 30 and ran through July 4, 1974.
2. *Esquire*, Jan. 1973, p. 170.
3. Data in letter May 11, 1979, from Sol H. Chafkin of the Ford Foundation answering author's query.
4. *Macon Telegraph*, July 4, 1974; also *Atlanta Journal*, July 3, 1974; *Journal-Constitution*, July 4; *Telegraph* editorial, July 6; *Constitution*, July 5; *Telegraph*, July 25; *Augusta Chronicle*, July 26.
5. Data from conversation with a HUD official.

Notes for Chapter 12

1. Copy in author's files.
2. *Atlanta Constitution*, Oct. 30, 1975. Most of the material is from an interview with George in Washington, D.C., in Dec. 1978.

Notes for Chapter 13

1. This and other details from the National Transportation Safety Board, Factual Aircraft Accident Report MIA-76-A-MØ59.

Notes for Chapter 14

1. The Stokes letter along with other papers relating to the trial can be found in the records at the federal courthouse, Atlanta—*United States of America* vs. *Roosevelt Warren, et al.*, No. CR76-371A.

2. Copy in author's files.
3. *United States* vs. *John Glustrom et al.*, No. CR76-297A.
4. Ibid.

Notes for Chapter 15

1. Judge Charles L. Weltner, order and judgment in civil action file No. 3162, Superior Court of Hancock County, Georgia, Oct. 18, 1978.
2. She refers to a bridge at Fulsome Creek, named for an early settler killed there by Creek Indians in 1777. There is an interesting story about the death of Capt. Benjamin Fulsam (Later Fulsome) in Francis Lee Utley and Marion R. Hemperley, eds., *Placenames of Georgia, Essays of John H. Goff* (Athens: University of Georgia Press, 1975), p. 288.

Notes for Chapter 16

1. E. M. Banks, *Land Tenure in Georgia* (New York: Columbia University Press, 1905), pp. 64, 69, 89, 120, 138, 140.
2. McCown's estate won a suit against Citizens Trust Bank, which the estate charged had failed to insure McCown's life to protect a loan the bank had made on his river property. The estate charged that the bank had agreed to take out the insurance and had deducted a fee for it. The court decided in favor of the McCown estate. Civil suit No. C 22764, Fulton County, Georgia. Dennis C. O'Brien, administrator of the estate of John L. McCown d/b/a *Mayfield Farms and Hancock County Comprehensive Health Services* vs. *Citizens Trust Bank.*
3. Several people interviewed by the author in 1978 said land values were still nearly $100 an acre less than in surrounding counties. A wealthy woman from neighboring Wilkes County remarked to the author on one occasion that the Shivers plantation house, Rock Mill, then for sale at $180,000, was cheap but "could it be moved from Hancock County?" she asked. When Lake Oconee was opened in the late 1970s, ads of persons seeking land normally specified Greene, Putnam, or Morgan rather than Hancock County. During this same period, one plain but large and well located Sparta house sold for under $10,000 and an antebellum house featured in books on Georgia architecture sold for only $18,000. A large Victorian mansion also featured in several publications and located on three acres of land in the center of Sparta was in 1981 still on the market after years of being offered at $35,000.

Bibliography

The *Atlanta Constitution*, the *Atlanta Journal*, the *Augusta Chronicle*, the *Macon Telegraph* and the *Sparta Ishmaelite* covered the McCown era in Hancock County more thoroughly than any other publications. There are numerous references to articles from these newspapers and the *New York Times* in the notes prepared for each chapter. They are not included in the bibliography.

The historical material in Chapter One is based on sources that are listed in the bibliography. The information in subsequent chapters dealing with contemporary times comes principally from personal interviews. Many who were interviewed did not wish to be identified. Hancock County is a small community and the issues involved are still sensitive.

The information about the Georgia Council on Human Relations is based on papers of the Georgia Council deposited in the archives of the Trevor Arnett Library, Atlanta University. This collection was used by permission of the library and the Reverend James L. Hooten, president of the council. Material about the schools came from minutes of the Hancock County Board of Education, interviews, and newspaper accounts.

Although most of the defendants in the trials of McCown's associates took guilty pleas and avoided public trial, there were pretrial hearings and answers to motions by defense attorneys that became a part of the public record. Much information in Chapter Fourteen came from documents in the federal courthouse in Atlanta concerning *United States of America* vs. *Roosevelt Warren, et al.*, No. CR76–371A.

Books and Articles

Andrews, Sidney. *The South Since the Civil War: Fourteen Weeks of Travel and Observation in Georgia and the Carolinas*. Boston: Ticknor & Fields, 1866.

Appleton's Cyclopedia of American Biography. New York: D. Appleton, 1887.

Banks, Enoch Marvin. *The Economics of Land Tenure in Georgia*. New York: Columbia University Press, 1905.

Bartram, William. *Travels through North and South Carolina, Georgia, East and West Florida*. Savannah: Beehive Press, 1973 (facsimile of 1792 London edition).

Bonner, James C. "Advancing Trends in Southern Agriculture, 1840–60." *Agricultural History* 22 (1948):248–259.

———. "Genesis of Agricultural Reform in the Cotton Belt." *Journal of Southern History* 9 (1943):475–500.

———. "A Georgia County's Historical Assets." *Emory University Quarterly* 9 (1953):24–30.

———. *A History of Georgia Agriculture 1732–1860*. Athens, Ga.: University of Georgia Press, 1964.

————. *Milledgeville, Georgia's Ante-Bellum Capital*. Athens, Ga.: University of Georgia Press, 1978.

————. "Profile of a Late Ante-Bellum Community." *American Historical Review* 49 (1944):663–680.

Bryans, Raleigh. "How a Dying Georgia Town Found New Hope." *Atlanta Journal and Constitution*, Oct. 3, 1965.

Buckingham, James Silk. *The Slave States of America*. London, Paris: Fisher, Son, 1842.

Burke, Emily P. *Reminiscences of Georgia*. Oberlin, Ohio: J. M. Fitch, 1850.

Burnham, W. Dean. *Presidential Ballots 1836–1892*. Baltimore: Johns Hopkins University Press, 1955.

Cade, John Brother. *Holsey the Incomparable*. New York: Pageant Press, 1964.

"Catfish Empire." *Newsweek*, Oct. 19, 1970, p. 48.

Chappell, Absalom. *Miscellanies of Georgia*. Pts. I and II. Columbus, Ga.: Gilbert Printing, 1928.

Community Development Concept Plan: Sparta, Georgia. Milledgeville, Ga.: Oconee Area Planning and Development Commission, 1975.

Conway, Alan. *The Reconstruction of Georgia*. Minneapolis: University of Minnesota Press, 1965.

Coulter, E. Merton. *Elijah Clarke's Foreign Intrigues and the "Trans-Oconee Republic."* Bulletin of the University of Georgia, vol. 23, no. 4. Dec. 1922.

————. *Negro Legislators in Georgia During the Reconstruction Period*. Athens, Ga.: Georgia Historical Quarterly reprint, 1968.

————. *Old Petersburg and the Broad River Valley of Georgia*. Athens, Ga.: University of Georgia Press, 1965.

————. *A Short History of Georgia*. Chapel Hill, N.C.: University of North Carolina Press, 1933.

Dickson, David, and Smith, James M. *David Dickson's and James M. Smith's Farming*. Atlanta: Cultivator Publishing, 1910.

Flanders, Ralph Betts. *Plantation Slavery in Georgia*. Chapel Hill, N.C.: University of North Carolina Press, 1933.

Fogel, Robert William, and Engerman, Stanley L. *Time on the Cross: The Economics of American Negro Slavery*. Boston, Toronto: Little, Brown, 1974.

Georgia County Data Book. Athens, Ga.: Bureau of Business Research, University of Georgia, 1963.

Georgia Historical Markers. Valdosta, Ga.: Bay Tree Grove, 1973.

Georgia Statistical Abstract. Athens, Ga.: Division of Research, College of Business Administration, University of Georgia, 1976.

Glick, David S. "Something New in Wallace's Alabama." *New Republic*, Jan. 16, 1971, pp. 11–13.

Gordon, Asa H. *The Georgia Negro, A History*. Ann Arbor, Mich.: Edwards Brothers, 1937.

"Hancock County, Black Takeover of Power." *New Republic*, March 6, 1971, pp. 8–9.

Harwell, Richard. *A Letter from the Georgia Collection.* Athens, Ga.: University of Georgia Libraries, June 1976.

Holsey, Lucius Henry. *Autobiography, Sermons, Addresses and Essays of Bishop L. H. Holsey.* 2nd ed. Atlanta: Franklin Printing and Publishing, 1899.

Johnston, Richard Malcolm. *Autobiography of Richard Malcolm Johnston.* Washington, D.C.: Neale, 1900.

———. *Dukesborough Tales.* Baltimore: Turnbull Brothers, 1871.

———. *Old Mark Langston—A Tale of Duke's Creek.* New York; Harper, 1884.

———. *Old Times in Middle Georgia.* New York: Macmillan, 1897.

Lane, Mills, ed. *The Rambler in Georgia.* Savannah: Beehive Press, 1973.

Leigh, Frances Butler. *Ten Years on a Georgia Plantation Since the War.* London: Richard Bentley & Son, 1883.

Linley, John. *Architecture of Middle Georgia—the Oconee Area.* Athens, Ga.: University of Georgia Press, 1972.

McCarthy, Colman. "Learn About Georgia, Know These Three." (*Washington Post Service.*) *Miami Herald*, Dec. 26, 1976.

Malet, William W. *An Errand to the South in the Summer of 1862.* London: Richard Bentley, 1863.

Mallary, C. D. *Memoirs of Elder Jesse Mercer.* New York: John Gray, 1844.

Milfort, Louis LeClerc. *Memoirs, or a Quick Glance at my Various Travels and my Sojourn in the Creek Nation.* Trans. and ed. Ben C. McCary. Savannah: Beehive Press, 1972.

Moore, Virginia. "Historic Sparta and Hancock County." *Georgia Magazine*, Oct.–Nov. 1965, p. 16.

———. "Proud Old Homes of Sparta." *Georgia Magazine*, Oct.–Nov., 1965, p. 18.

Murray, Paul. *The Whig Party in Georgia, 1825–1853.* The James Sprunt Studies in History and Political Science, vol. 29. Chapel Hill, N.C.: University of North Carolina Press, 1948.

Nelson, Jack, and Bass, Jack. *The Orangeburg Massacre.* New York: World Publishing, 1970.

Nichols, Frederick D. *The Architecture of Georgia.* Savannah: Beehive Press, 1976.

Nielsen, Waldemar A. *The Big Foundations.* A Twentieth Century Fund Study. New York and London: Columbia University Press, 1972.

Northen, William J. *Men of Mark in Georgia.* 7 vols. Atlanta: A. B. Caldwell, 1907–12.

Norwood, C. W. *Sholes' Georgia State Gazetteer and Business Directory for 1879 and 1880.* Atlanta: A. E. Sholes, 1879.

Olmsted, Frederick Law. *The Cotton Kingdom: A Traveller's Observations on Cotton and Slavery in the American Slave States*, vol. 1. New York: Mason Brothers, 1861.

Pennington, John. "A Middle Georgia Heritage." *Atlanta Journal and Constitution Magazine*, Nov. 19, 1972, p. 12.

Phillips, Ulrich B. *Life and Labor in the Old South.* Boston: Little, Brown, 1929.

———. *The Life of Robert Toombs.* New York: Macmillan, 1913.

————. "Origin and Growth of Southern Black Belts." *American Historical Review* 11 (1906): 798–817.

Plan for Progress, Sparta, Georgia (photocopies from typescript). Atlanta: Regional Economic Development and Business Service Center, Atlanta University, 1965.

Range, Willard. *A Century of Georgia Agriculture, 1850–1950*. Athens, Ga.: University of Georgia Press, 1954.

Raper, Arthur F. *Preface to Peasantry*. Chapel Hill, N.C.: University of North Carolina Press, 1936.

Rindfuss, Ronald R. "Changing Patterns of Fertility in the South: A Social-Demographic Examination." *Social Forces* 57 (1978): 621–633.

Russell, Lester F. *Profile of a Black Heritage*. Franklin Square, N.Y.: Graphicopy, 1977.

Scarborough, Ruth. *Opposition to Slavery in Georgia Prior to 1860*. Nashville, Tenn.: George Peabody College for Teachers, 1933.

Sears, Joan Niles. "The First Hundred Years of Town Planning in Georgia." Ph.D. diss., Emory University, 1977.

Sherwood, Adiel. *Georgia Gazeteer, 1827*. Athens, Ga.: University of Georgia Press (reprint), 1939.

Simkins, Francis Butler, and Roland, Charles Pierce. *A History of the South*. 4th ed. New York: Alfred A. Knopf, 1972.

Smith, Elizabeth Wiley. *The History of Hancock County Georgia*. Washington, Ga.: Wilkes Publishing, 1974.

Smith, George Gilman. *The Life and Times of George F. Pierce*. Sparta, Ga.: Hancock Publishing, 1888.

————. *The Story of Georgia and the Georgia People 1732–1860*. Macon, Ga.: George G. Smith, 1900.

Sparks, W. H. *The Memories of Fifty Years*. Philadelphia: E. Claxton, 1882. Macon, Ga.: J. W. Burke, 1882.

Thompson, C. Mildred. *Reconstruction in Georgia: Economic, Social, Political 1865–1872*. New York: Columbia University Press, 1915.

U.S. Congress, House. *Evidence before the Committee on Reconstruction Relative to the Condition of Affairs in Georgia*. Washington, D.C., 1869.

U.S. Department of Commerce, Bureau of the Census. *Negro Population 1790–1915*. Washington, D.C.: Government Printing Office, 1918.

U.S. Department of Commerce, Bureau of the Census. *Historical Statistics of the United States, Colonial Times to 1957*. Washington, D.C., 1960.

U.S. Department of State. *Compendium of the Sixth Census*. Washington, D.C.: Thomas Allen, 1841.

Utley, Francis Lee, and Hemperley, Marion R., eds. *Placenames of Georgia: Essays of John H. Goff*. Athens, Ga.: University of Georgia Press, 1975.

Waddell, James D., ed. *Biographical Sketch of Linton Stephens*. Atlanta: Dodson & Scott, 1877.

Wade, John Donald. *Augustus Baldwin Longstreet: A Study of the Development of Culture in the South*. New York: Macmillan, 1924.

210

Warner, Mary R., chairperson, Committee on the Status of Minority Elected Officials, National Association of Human Rights Workers. *The Dilemma of Black Politics: A Report on Harassment of Black Elected Officials.* Sacramento, Cal., 1977.

Watters, Pat. *Down to Now.* New York: Pantheon Books, 1971.

Welty, Eudora. *The Eye of the Story.* New York: Random House, 1977.

White, George. *Historical Collections of Georgia.* New York: Pudney & Russell, 1854.

———. *Statistics of the State of Georgia.* Savannah, Ga.: W. T. Williams, 1849.

Wiley, Bell I. *Southern Negroes 1861–65.* New Haven: Yale University Press, 1938.

Williams, Vinnie. "Restoration of Rock Mill." *Atlanta Journal and Constitution Magazine*, July 16, 1972, pp. 12–17.

Writers' Program, Georgia, revised and extended by George G. Leckie. *Georgia—A Guide to Its Towns and Countryside.* Atlanta: Tupper & Love, 1954.

Nineteenth-Century Newspapers

Hancock Advertiser, Mt. Zion, Georgia. 1826–30.

The Missionary, Mt. Zion, Georgia. 1819–25.

Southern Recorder, Milledgeville, Georgia. 1820–72.

Sparta Times and Planter, Sparta, Georgia. 1879–81.

Sandersville Central Georgian, Sandersville, Georgia. 1841–1908.

Farmers Gazette, Sparta, Georgia. 1807.

Index